A CITY OF MARBLE

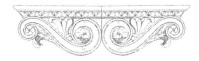

A CITY

Studies in Rhetoric/Communication   *Thomas W. Benson, Series Editor*

Kathleen S. Lamp

THE RHETORIC
OF AUGUSTAN ROME

OF MARBLE

The University of South Carolina Press

© 2013 University of South Carolina

Published by the University of South Carolina Press
Columbia, South Carolina 29208

www.sc.edu/uscpress

Manufactured in the United States of America

22 21 20 19 18 17 16 15 14 13   10 9 8 7 6 5 4 3 2 1

Library of Congress Cataloging-in-Publication Data
Lamp, Kathleen S.
A city of marble : the rhetoric of Augustus and the people in the Roman principate /
Kathleen S. Lamp.
pages. cm. — (Studies in rhetoric/communication)
ISBN 978-1-61117-277-5 (hardbound : alk. paper) — ISBN 978-1-61117-336-9 (ebook)
1. Rhetoric, Ancient. 2. Augustus, Emperor of Rome, 63 B.C.–14 A.D. 3. Latin literature—
History and criticism. I. Title. II. Series: Studies in rhetoric/communication.
PA6085.L36 2013
808'.0471—dc23

2013010905

This book was printed on a recycled paper with 30 percent postconsumer waste content.

To my teachers and my students

Litterae thesaurum est, et artificium nunquam moritur.
Petronius Arbiter, *Satyricon,* 46

CONTENTS

ILLUSTRATIONS

SERIES EDITOR'S PREFACE

The role of rhetoric in Rome after the fall of the republic has been debated for two thousand years. In *City of Marble: The Rhetoric of Augustan Rome*, Kathleen S. Lamp synthesizes scholarship from rhetorical studies and several related fields to create a fresh understanding of rhetorical theory and practice in the principate of Augustus, who ruled Rome from 27 B.C.E. to 14 C.E. Lamp finds that rhetoric in the Augustan age was deeply rooted in earlier rhetorical theories and practices, that it was civic in its themes, that it was widely practiced, and that rhetoric was both verbal and visual, practiced in epideictic oratory, coins, altars, images, wall paintings, public buildings, city planning, and monuments, all working to define the state and the civic role of audiences high and low.

Lamp argues that Augustus was faced with the rhetorical problems not only of how to consolidate his rule in Rome, but also how to create a new system of government and to create rhetoric that defined, legitimized, and popularized it. Enlarging the scope of rhetoric beyond forensic, deliberative, and epideictic speechmaking to include visual and other media, Lamp illustrates, is not simply a projection of twenty-first-century rhetorical perspectives onto Roman rhetoric; rather, Roman rhetoricians themselves included these media in their theories and their practices. A detailed review of Roman theories and beliefs permits Lamp and her reader to engage the multimediated rhetorical practices of Augustan Rome in rhetorical terms—as the Romans themselves would have experienced and understood them.

Beginning with the *Ara Pacis*—the Augustan Altar of Peace—Lamp illustrates the development of the Augustan myth, which rooted the principate in the stories of Aeneas and of Romulus and Remus, establishing sole authority without identifying with the mythically expelled system of Roman kings. She shows how the development of the Augustan myth appealed to and gave a role to the common people of Rome. This was not democracy, but it was broadly popular civic participation, and, while it asserted the authority of the ruler, it implicitly acknowledged the obligation of the ruler to establish and sustain his legitimacy through rhetorical means that were widely shared.

Thomas W. Benson

ACKNOWLEDGMENTS

I would like to thank my teachers: Susan Stevens and James Hoban (Randolph-Macon Woman's College); James Russell and the faculty at the Duke Intercollegiate Center for Classical Studies 2000–2001; Cara Finnegan, Thomas Conley, and Ned O'Gorman (University of Illinois, Urbana-Champaign); and most of all Debra Hawhee (Penn State University), who has been constantly supportive of my research and professional development above and beyond the call of duty. Members of my graduate school cohort and writing group at the University of Illinois supported me in more ways than I can say and for which I am truly grateful.

I would also like to thank my colleagues at Arizona State University in rhetoric and composition, the Department of English, and those who integrate a love of classics and archaeology into their work regardless of home department, especially those who have mentored me as I have settled into my first faculty position. Finally I would like to thank all of my students, particularly those students (and a remarkable colleague), who braved my first graduate seminar on classical rhetoric at ASU and let me try out some of the arguments in this book.

Many early drafts of the chapters were presented at conventions for the Rhetoric Society of America (RSA) and the National Communication Association (NCA). Portions of chapters 2 and 3 appeared in essay form in *Philosophy and Rhetoric* and *Rhetoric Society Quarterly,* respectively. I would like to thank the (anonymous) reviewers, readers, and audience members who provided feedback in these venues. The American Society for the History of Rhetoric (ASHR) continues to strive to provide invaluable opportunities for research and networking at summer institutes, symposia, and panels coupled with NCA and RSA, many of which aided the development of this book. The efforts of Dave Tell, Ekaterina Haskins, Ned O'Gorman, Susan Jarratt, and Michele Kennerly, among many others who devote their time to ASHR, are greatly appreciated.

The Department of English at Arizona State University funded research travel to Italy allowing me to study, move around, and photograph many of the rhetorical artifacts discussed in the following chapters. Daria Lanzuolo at the German Archaeological Institute—Rome (DAI-R), Marina Milella at the Museo dei Fori Imperiali, Lauren Hackworth Petersen and Stephen Petersen (University of Delaware), and Tara Carleton Weaver aided in supplying many of the images for the book. Brent Chappelow provided developmental editing. Richard Leo Enos and an anonymous reviewer for the University of South Carolina Press provided valuable feedback for revision. Remaining errors are mine and mine alone.

Finally, I would like to thank my family, especially my husband, Christopher Freundt, and my parents, Lloyd and Kay Lamp, for the love and support necessary to sustain me through this process.

While this book is the product of my formal education, I hope always to be a student of classical rhetoric.

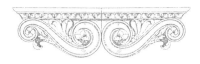

INTRODUCTION

A City of Brick

Perhaps no words that Augustus, the first sole ruler of Rome, who reigned from 27 B.C.E. to 14 C.E., actually spoke are quite as memorable as the ones ancient historians Suetonius and Cassius Dio have attributed to him: "I found Rome built of brick and I leave it to you in marble."[1] For Suetonius, the improvements to Rome were both a matter of practicality and stature: "Since the city was not adorned as the dignity of the empire demanded, and was exposed to flood and fire, [Augustus] . . . so beautified it that he could justly boast that he had found it built of brick and left it in marble."[2] Dio, however, moves beyond Suetonius's reading, arguing Augustus's "city of brick" comment was not merely a reference to the façade of Rome but had more of a metaphorical meaning. Dio explains, "In saying this he was not referring literally to the state of the buildings, but rather to the strength of the Empire."[3]

Metaphor or no, both historians perceive a connection between the physical appearance of the city and Rome's place at the head of the world. Dio's Maecenas explicitly draws attention to this connection in a fabricated speech, positing it as an intentional strategy on the part of Augustus's administration. Maecenas advises Augustus, "Make this capital beautiful, spare no expense in doing so, and enhance its magnificence with festivals of every kind. It is right for us who rule over so many peoples to excel all others in every field of endeavor, and even display of this kind tends to implant respect for us in our allies and to strike terror into our enemies."[4] Here Dio suggests, albeit in hindsight, that Augustus's building program was a conscious "display" of Rome's supremacy meant to elicit a reaction, particularly from those who dwelled outside the city.

Though from Dio's passage it is possible to argue that the physical appearance of the city of Rome was meant to persuade or at least elicit some response, the passage does not lead to the claim that architecture, monuments, and city planning functioned rhetorically in ancient Rome. Quintilian reminds us, "many other things have the power of persuasion, such as money, influence, the authority and rank of the speaker, or even some sight unsupported by language, when for instance the place of words is supplied by the memory of some individual's great deeds, by his lamentable appearance or the beauty of his person."[5] At least for Quintilian, there is a line between rhetoric and persuasion with the physical appearance of the city falling under the latter category. Still, Dio's passage does generate questions about the relationship between the Augustan building program, or more broadly the Augustan cultural campaigns, and rhetoric in the principate—specifically the way in which the cultural campaigns functioned rhetorically to help Augustus gain and maintain power and administer the Roman world.

The idea that aspects of the Augustan cultural campaigns, most notably art and architecture, functioned rhetorically is, perhaps, not a new revelation. After all, George Kennedy acknowledged as much forty years ago when he declared, "In addition to the oratory and criticism which we have considered, other artistic products of the Augustan age contain manifestations of rhetoric."[6] Kennedy goes on to dedicate nearly 3 of his 641 pages to such Augustan artifacts as coins, the Forum of Augustus, and the Ara Pacis Augustae (Altar of Augustan Peace) before moving on to the Augustan poets.[7] Certainly these "artistic products" contribute to Kennedy's conclusion that "as a practitioner of the art of persuasion the greatest rhetorician of antiquity was the man born C. Octavius," later known as the emperor Augustus.[8]

The problem is not, of course, Kennedy's brief survey of Augustan art. After all, art historians such as Paul Zanker have dedicated entire volumes to the "new visual language . . . a whole new method of visual communication" represented by the Augustan cultural campaigns.[9] While Zanker's interest is not rhetorical history specifically, other scholars such as Tonio Holscher and Diane Favro have taken up Augustan art and architecture with at least some attention to the interactions of rhetorical theory and the production of Augustan Rome, if not the implications for such interactions on contemporary understandings of rhetorical history.[10] Rather, the problem is Kennedy's conclusion about the nature of Augustan rhetoric, which is representative of how the principate is viewed in the history of rhetoric. Kennedy concludes, "To win men's minds without opening the door to the dangers of public debate Augustus developed new techniques of verbal and visual persuasion which took over some of the functions and adapted some of the methods of traditional oratory."[11]

Certainly, the classicist Theodore Mommsen's position, that Augustus's principate was "the end to the entire discipline of rhetoric," no longer holds.[12] Still, Kennedy's view—that rhetorical practice continued in the principate, that this practice included "artistic production" but that these practices were inherently antithetical to the spirit of great rhetoric—bridges several lingering disciplinary disputes concerning rhetorical practices in this period, shifting the focus to the *quality* of Augustan rhetoric. First is the so-called "decline theory," that is, whether rhetorical practices suffered adversely in the transition from republic to empire, which leads to broader questions about the practice of rhetoric in non-democratic societies. Second is what counts as a rhetorical "text" and whether rhetorical practice can include "artistic products" that fall outside traditional oratorical genres in classical rhetorical theory and practice.

The "decline theory" stems from the rhetoricians of the first century (chiefly Tacitus's *A Dialogue on Oratory,* though this idea is found in Quintilian, Seneca, Petronius, and "Longinus") and traces a decline in rhetorical practice from the end of the Roman republic through the early empire.[13] This decline, of which a corrupted style is the chief indicator, is, according to Tacitus, due both to poor educational training, namely the practice of declamation, and political conditions. Laurent Pernot stresses that for Tacitus these causes are interrelated because "it is precisely the lack of real political stakes that has forced rhetoric under the emperors back upon declamation." In other words, for Tacitus, "the end of political liberty and the decline of rhetoric go hand in hand."[14]

Standing in sharp contrast to the notion of Tacitus's decline theory is the position that there was a resurgence of rhetoric in the early empire espoused by Dionysius of Halicarnassus. Dionysius champions the return and triumph of the Attic style over the Asiatic, but for him this revival goes far beyond style and is rooted in a return to a rhetoric that is truly a "philosophic art." He praises "the present age and the men who guide its culture—that they were pioneers in the promotion of good taste over bad . . . but equally to be commended is the rapidity with which they have brought about this change and measure of improvement." For Dionysius this change for the better began with "the conquest of the world by Rome."[15] That is, Dionysius praises Augustus, in part, for the return to an Isocratean model of rhetoric that unites rhetoric and philosophy and is rooted in culture.

These two views—the decline theory and the renaissance—have led to various narratives about the quality of the practice of rhetoric in the principate among scholars of rhetoric. Based off of Tacitus, a kind of decline narrative of rhetoric in the Roman empire emerged. According to Pernot, "Traditionally scholars, following Tacitus, have adhered to the decline thesis, as explained by the political situation. This is the source of the prevailing view in modern historiography that holds that rhetoric under the Empire no longer exists or is reduced to declamations, *recitiones,* and empty encomia....Yet such an opinion caricatures the thesis by going further than its original proponents did, for they recognize that even in their own time good orators still existed."[16] The decline narrative, as Pernot puts it, over-reads the decline theory found in the works of the first-century rhetoricians. Even as the field of rhetorical studies moves away from decline theory, a move Pernot argues is historically warranted, it often creeps back in to accounts of rhetoric in the principate as determinations about the quality of rhetorical practice.

Though Dionysius's view concerning the renaissance of rhetoric may be somewhat more appealing, the problem, of course, is that both Tacitus and Dionysius form "a relative construction" of rhetorical history, "which judges the present according to the model of the past."[17] Significantly, there was perhaps more continuity in rhetorical practice than either view suggests. As Pernot reminds us, "once the . . . intellectual shock at the newness of the imperial regime . . . [was in the] past, rhetoric evolved and prospered in a new setting with which contemporaries were comfortable."[18] Building from the idea of a return to a fifth-century Isocratean rhetoric as described in Dionysius, Jeffrey Walker argues:

> The Roman Empire came to resemble a greatly ramified version of the old Hellenistic kingdoms. The "loss of liberty" that is often associated with the republic's end was not so much a loss of liberty per se, nor even a "decline of democracy" (since the Roman republic had really been an oligarchy), but a shift of political hegemony: away from Rome's old, republican nobility, and in the long run away from the city of Rome itself, and towards a cosmopolitan network of elites participating in a system of imperial administration that combined autocracy with oligarchy and left much to the jurisdiction. Within this world, as within the older Hellenistic world, there remained a considerable occasion for pragmatic as well as epideictic rhetoric, and considerable opportunity for the skilled, well-educated (and typically well born) practitioner of discursive art—in local courts and councils; in embassies, petitions, letters, appeals, and lawsuits.[19]

Walker's perspective calls attention to certain problematic assumptions in the decline narrative and at the same time emphasizes what is perhaps the most important aspect of rhetorical education and practice in the principate and early empire—that they continued to be vitally important to civic life.[20]

The second element of Kennedy's position on Augustan rhetoric, though not a new idea, is significant in that he includes "artistic production" among rhetorical artifacts from the principate. Kennedy, equating rhetoric with persuasion, includes monuments and buildings in Augustan rhetorical practices. I would argue this inclusion is historically warranted and not an anachronistic imposition of contemporary rhetorical theory on Roman rhetorical practices. Even a more conservative view that excludes artistic products, such as that of Laurent Pernot, who narrowly defines rhetoric as the "spoken word," predominantly "public discourse," sees an expansion of the domain of rhetoric in the early empire accounted for in Quintilian that encompasses "virtually all forms of discourse."[21] The recognition of the expansion of rhetorical media in the principate is noteworthy, especially given Dionysius's claim that the renaissance of rhetoric in the principate rests on the ability of Augustus and his administration to guide "culture." That culture was heavily influenced by rhetorical theory and, in turn, culture guided civic participation and rhetorical practice.

Given the renewed emphasis on culture in the principate, it is hardly surprising that the epideictic genre expanded and flourished. Once thought to be little more than sycophantic praise in the Roman empire, the genre has been greatly recouped by scholars such as Pernot and Walker. Pernot argues, "the rhetoric of the encomium is the bearer of a morality with strong philosophical undertones" that could contain both "carefully couched proposals as well as subtle exhortation."[22] In other words, traditional epideictic formed a "history of mentalities" that left room to discipline and advise, often crossing into the deliberative genre.[23] Walker, too, challenges the notion that epideictic rhetoric was insignificant, arguing, "under the Roman emperors, what we find is actually a triumph of the Ciceronian ideal—not, however the Ciceronian ideal as propagated by Quintilian and identified with the oratorical practices of the late republic, but the Ciceronian ideal as understood from an Isocratean or sophistic perspective, and as advanced by Cicero himself."[24] Walker, then, sees the flourishing of epideictic rhetoric, in keeping with Dionysius's claims, as a return to fifth-century ideals.

While certainly praise was directed at the emperor, many examples of state-sponsored rhetoric also take the form of epideictic rhetoric. Pernot cautions against dismissing both forms too quickly: "the ancient rhetorical encomium, however, was never just cant, perhaps precisely because of its rhetorical nature. Rhetoric implied, as the ancients saw it, qualities of subtlety, intelligence, culture, and beauty, which went beyond what would have satisfied a purely totalitarian usefulness."[25] Certainly Augustus was quite skilled in the use of epideictic rhetoric, and many state-sponsored projects fall into the realm of the epideictic genre; however, given the philosophical role of epideictic to define a good ruler as well as good citizens, it is unsurprising that the genre shouldered the weight of the transition from republic to empire when, no doubt, there was anxiety about both roles. The genre leaves a great deal of room for subversion, predominantly in what is left unsaid. In other words, because the genre is largely formulaic, in that a speech of praise covers set topics, deviation from form speaks volumes.[26]

With a perspective close to that of Dionysius of Halicarnassus, I argue that Augustus and his administration turned to traditional Roman rhetorical theory and practice, as well as to a revived form of Greek Atticism, of which Dionysius's position is representative, to inform the Augustan cultural campaigns. The cultural campaigns, then, created a large number of rhetorical artifacts that were meant to persuade (and often instruct) the people of Rome in the ways they could think about and participate in a new and unfamiliar type of government. Often these rhetorical artifacts—in the form of buildings, monuments, coins, altars, and even city planning—create a kind of philosophical discourse on ideal citizenship. These rhetorical media were met with popular responses in visual and material forms and establish a kind of bilateral discussion on civic participation in the principate.

Any discussion of the Augustan cultural campaigns, of course, will inevitably lead to discussions of state-manufactured culture and the possibility of culture as oppressive, stifling dissent and even individual expression. There is even a tendency to think of Augustan rhetoric using the contemporary concept of propaganda. Although "propaganda" is a modern concept, fascist rulers, on whose regimes contemporary definitions of propaganda are built, modeled themselves, in part, on Julius Caesar and Augustus, creating a kind of syllogistic logic that makes the concept, however anachronistic and historically inaccurate, at least superficially apt.[27] Contemporary definitions of propaganda are characterized by communication that benefits the propagandist, is "deliberate" and "manipulative," and "part of a systematic plan." Perhaps the most important feature of propaganda is unilateral communication, the antithesis of a "free and open exchange of ideas."[28] While what is or is not propaganda is largely in the eye of the beholder, I examine Augustan culture as visual and material communication, and this examination supports the argument that rhetoric in the Augustan age was bilateral; the Roman people were comfortable expressing themselves and did so.

PROBLEMS WITH SOURCES AND TERMS

There are numerous issues in approaching Augustan rhetorical practices through literary sources, not the least of which is the "relativistic" approach of the first-century rhetoricians. The principate broke the power of the ruling elites, replacing it with a bureaucracy selected from members of the equestrian order, the landed middle class of Rome. Additionally, the principate depended heavily on the approval of the populace of urban plebs. The populace of Rome was much less likely to be represented in, let alone self-represent in, literary sources. No doubt visual and material sources offer a way to gain a better understanding of how the Roman populace saw themselves in relation to the principate. While it is fundamentally impossible to know the subject position of any Roman citizen, I attempt to work within a Roman understanding of rhetorical theory and practice using a variety of sources, including literary sources, inscriptions, and archeological data. It is problematic to read visual and material sources through literary ones. Still, one must contextualize such sources and the knowledge base a viewer might have had as an entry point to then take such sources on their own terms.

Then there is the issue of the scarcity of sources concerning rhetorical theory and practice written during the principate. Kennedy classifies the literary sources on rhetoric as follows: (1) information about the venues in which rhetoric was practiced gathered from classical histories such as Suetonius's *Lives of the Caesars*; (2) the fragmentary works on rhetoric and literary criticism that date to the principate or mentions of these works that are not extant in other texts such as Dionysius of Halicarnassus, Caecilius of Calactae, and "Longinus";[29] (3) biographical information about orators such as C. Asinius Pollio, M. Valerius Messalla Corvinus, Titus Labienus, and C. Cassius Severus and rhetoricians such as Apollodorus of Pergamum and Theodorus which are generally found in classical historical texts; (4) sources on declamation, primarily Seneca the Elder's *The Orator's and Rhetor's Sententiae, Divisions and Colors*; and (5) the poetry of Horace, Virgil, and Ovid and the history of Livy.[30]

While some of these sources address the principate, with the exception of Velleius Paterculus's (ca. 19 B.C.E.–31 C.E.) *Compendium of Roman History,* none of the classical historians from whom we have extent work about the principate actually experienced it.[31] The more substantive works on the principate from classical historians such as Suetonius (ca. 70–130 C.E.), Tacitus (55–117 C.E.), and Cassius Dio (155–229 C.E.) were all written (significantly) after the principate, and each historian sees Augustus through the events that have transpired in the intervening time. This is particularly true of Tacitus, who, classical historian Colin Wells reminds us, "projects back into the past the preoccupations, the interests, and the animosities of his own day."[32] The Augustan literary sources are no less problematic in their use as sources on rhetoric or as examples of rhetorical practice. No doubt Virgil, Ovid, Horace, and Livy all had some rhetorical training and, although their opinions of traditional oratory and the republic itself varied considerably, they were all under the patronage of the emperor with the exception of Livy, who was a friend of the *princeps*.[33]

More substantive works on rhetoric pre- or postdate the principate, including the works of Cicero (106–43 B.C.E.), the *Rhetorica ad Herennium* (early first-century B.C.E.), Quintilian's (ca. 35–100 C.E.) *Institutio Oratoria,* Tacitus's (ca. 56–117 C.E.) *Dialogus de Oratoribus,* and Suetonius's (70–130 C.E.) *De Grammaticis et Rhetoribus.* Of the authors of surviving texts, Cicero is representative of the rhetorical theory and practice available to Augustus and his administration, Dionysius is representative of the Greek Atticism that stressed imitation popular in the principate, and Quintilian is reactive to the changes in theory and practice in the early empire. While the literary sources remain invaluable as a jumping-off point for theorizing and contextualizing rhetorical practice in the principate, it is fundamental to understanding rhetoric to de-center these sources in order to understand how both Augustus's administration and the Roman people defined citizenship in the principate and how those understandings were communicated.

There is surprisingly little work by contemporary rhetoricians that focuses on the principate. A number of scholarly works touch on rhetoric in Rome; however, most focus on the late republic and Cicero or on the Second Sophistic, a period marked by the works of Greek writers spanning roughly from the second to the fourth centuries C.E. This is not to say that visual and material artifacts from the principate have not been the focus of considerable scholarly attention; my point is simply that the scholars who have taken up such artifacts have, with few exceptions, not been scholars of rhetoric.[34] Work that does consider the visual aspects of Roman rhetoric from other disciplines such as classical history, architectural history, or art history, such as Ann Vasaly's *Representations* (which focuses on Ciceronian rhetoric), Diane Favro's *The Urban Image of Augustus,* and Tonio Holscher's *The Language of Images in Roman Art,* have not necessarily been embraced in the field of rhetorical studies to the degree of affecting our larger understanding of rhetoric in the principate.

I seek to add to our understanding of Roman rhetoric by filling in some of the disciplinary gap between the republic and the Second Sophistic. At times this means little more than synthesizing work from other fields from a rhetorical perspective. More often, it means approaching nontraditional rhetorical artifacts as legitimate rhetorical media. I approach Augustan rhetoric with two fundamental assumptions. First, Roman rhetorical practices were visual and material in nature, though these practices are not always reflected in theory. Second, rhetoric and persuasion are not approached as synonymous, though such a definition may be historically warranted; rather, I see rhetoric in the principate as relating to the civic, that is, the duties of the government and the people as defined broadly, often by the epideictic genre, which then impacted other rhetorical practices.

Therefore I approach the rhetorical theory and practice of the Roman principate from a transdisciplinary perspective to show how nontraditional rhetorical artifacts functioned rhetorically in the Roman principate. I begin with artifacts most familiar to the field of rhetorical studies, namely, rhetorical treatises; I then consider those artifacts most obviously using accepted rhetoric techniques in visual form; finally I arrive at those least recognizable but perhaps most significant in the daily lives of the Roman people (coins, altars, wall paintings). This sequence refigures what counts as a rhetorical artifact in classical Rome and inserts a long-excluded rhetorical audience, the urban plebs of Rome, into contemporary understandings of rhetorical history.

To clarify, Augustus, whose given name was Gaius Octavius Thurinus, changed his name to Gaius Julius Caesar Octavianus at the time of his adoption by Julius Caesar in 44 B.C.E., and then was granted the titles of "Augustus," a religious title translating literally as the "sacred" or "august" one, and of *princeps,* a title to denote his civic standing as "the first" among citizens. It is appropriate to refer to the man known as "Augustus" after 27 B.C.E. either as Augustus or the *princeps,* and prior to 27 B.C.E. as Octavian and to his reign as the "principate." This is the nomenclature I have attempted to use to clarify Octavian's early rule (with the Triumvirate) from his sole rule. Though I feel it is historically inaccurate to refer to Augustus as "emperor" or his reign as the "Roman empire," historians do, and this has, no doubt, crept into my vocabulary despite my best attempts to avoid it. After Julius Caesar, all subsequent rulers of Rome took up the name "Caesar," either as part of their name or as an honorific, as is also the case with "Augustus." When I use the name "Caesar," I am referring to Julius Caesar, the uncle and adopted father of Octavian, and I use the term "Augustus" only in reference to the man who was previously known as Octavian. If I refer to later emperors, it is by their name and not their title.

In the interest of encouraging scholars from a variety of backgrounds, particularly young scholars, to consider Roman rhetoric, I have avoided large chunks of untranslated Greek or Latin. Though there is no doubt that one who chooses to work in the field of classical rhetoric must be able to read primary texts, the fact remains that most scholars of rhetoric are no longer classically trained. To exclude the casual reader seems disastrous to the field at worst and callous at best. Latin and Greek texts are presented in this work in translation, and generally the translations are those of expert philologists. For purposes of access to both those of mild curiosity about classical rhetoric and those with proficient classical language skills, I have generally cited Loeb editions (with the Greek/Latin on the left and English on the right) that facilitate access to all interested parties unless a translation by a rhetorician exists. Additionally, I have included Latin or Greek only when it is absolutely necessary to the reading or clarity of the idea. Notes on translations are generally in the notes.

AUGUSTUS'S RHETORICAL SITUATION

The principate, the era marked by the sole rule of Augustus, spans from 31 B.C.E. to 14 C.E., standing as the transitional period between the Roman republic and empire.[1] By the end of 31 B.C.E., the often romanticized chaos that inspired Shakespeare and still captivates modern audiences through television shows such as HBO's *Rome*—the assassination of Julius Caesar, the rise of a young Octavian, the proscription of Cicero by the Second Triumvirate, the vanquishing of the conspirators, several civil wars, and Antonius and Cleopatra's dalliance and defeat—was the stuff of history, even if that history was still being written.

There is a tendency to believe that by 31 B.C.E., and certainly no later than 23 B.C.E., Augustus had gained "real" power and that what followed was little more than window dressing. Octavian's struggle was over by 31 B.C.E., but the would-be Augustus's struggle for power was only just beginning. He was left in precisely the same position that ended in the demise of Julius Caesar: ruling Rome when it was forbidden for a single man to do so. Yet, to define Augustus's rhetorical exigence simply as legitimizing his rule is to classify it too narrowly. More broadly, Augustus had to create a new system of government to replace the failed republic, to define practices of citizenship, and to do so in a way that was not only acceptable to but popular with the people.

While Augustan rhetoric can be viewed as a response to developing exigencies over the period of his rule, the most significant of which occurred upon Augustus gaining sole power in 31 B.C.E., Augustus's rhetorical situation must be clarified in light of the historical, political, social, and mythic history of the city of Rome before the situation of rhetoric in the principate can be examined.

SOCIAL AND POLITICAL CONTEXTS

A complex tangle of conditions contributed to the fall of the Roman republic: the economic practices of the few created a situation characterized by expansionist warfare, the lack of a landed middle-class, the rise of urban poor, a large slave population, a populace without representation, the need for a standing military that in turn became loyal only to their leader and required land as payment for service, not to mention problems with the grain supply and pirates. Though there were probably other ways out of these problems, the continuation of the republic in its existing form was likely not one of them. Divergence between the two parties, the *optimates,* or "constitutional party," and the *populares,* sometimes referred to as the "democratic party," who claimed to hold the people's interest, led to what amounted to (pseudo) class conflicts that were easily and inevitably wielded for political purposes.[2] Conflicts began in earnest shortly after the Punic Wars ended (around 125 B.C.E.) among powerful, seemingly charismatic men who harnessed, more often than not, enormous resources, financial and military; the support of their parties; and, often, rhetorical skill, which eventually led to the civil wars.

It was Octavian, for better or worse, who finally ended the conflict (though he caused much of it as well) after he defeated Antonius at Actium in 31 B.C.E. Syme's foundational work *The Roman Revolution* is dedicated to the principate and characterizes Augustus's rise to sole power in the context of party politics: "However talented and powerful in himself, the Roman statesman cannot stand alone, without allies, without a following. . . . The rule of Augustus was the rule of a party, and in certain aspects his principate was a syndicate."[3] Though Augustus's rule was very much the product of the political parties at Rome, the title of Syme's book indicates that Augustus's rise to power was revolutionary: "in the Revolution the power of the old governing class was broken, its composition transformed. Italy and the nonpolitical orders in society triumphed over Rome and the Roman aristocracy."[4] Still, this "revolution," such as it was, should not be seen as the end of Roman democracy, for to see it that way implies there was democracy in the first place. The Roman republic was not a glorious and free age where all a great statesman needed was the power of his voice.[5] Significantly, the voices of Roman statesman often did more harm than good.[6]

Though the principate is frequently thought of as the death blow to the Roman republic, it is clear that what brought about Augustus's reign started much earlier, and these circumstances both enabled and constrained Augustan rhetoric. The turmoil and bloodshed of the civil and social wars, for example,

enabled what would be Augustus's defining term—peace—a term that was rhetorically powerful only because of what had preceded Augustus's reign. Rome
had endured a great deal in the hundred-plus years between the end of the Punic
Wars and 31 B.C.E. The conflict began between the Roman political parties, the
optimates and *populares,* with the legislation of the Gracchi, eventually culminating in all-out civil war.[7] The first bout of civil war, led by Sulla and Marius,
spanned from 85 to 82 B.C.E. and decimated much of Italy.[8] Abutting the period
of terror of the civil wars were the Social Wars, which lasted from 90 to 88 B.C.E.
and began because of the allies' desire for enfranchisement; and the Slave War,
an uprising of slaves led by Spartacus from 73 to 71 B.C.E. Interspersed in this
domestic chaos were the foreign wars against Mithradates in the East.

    After the first bout of civil wars, the rivalry between the *optimates* and *popu-
lares* continued, though the party lines blurred considerably with Gnaeus Pompey, better known as Pompey the Great. The people were eventually led by Julius
Caesar, a relative of Marius. Two other men prominent in rhetorical history
joined the fray at this time, Catiline, a member of the patrician class who became
a leader of the *populares,* and Cicero, a "new man" who rose to the forefront of
the *optimates.* The former plotted "revolution"; the latter uncovered the plot and
prosecuted the "traitors."[9] In 60 B.C.E., Crassus, Caesar, and Pompey formed the
First Triumvirate, a political power-sharing arrangement that seemed in the best
interest of all (though it did not last long).[10] Caesar assumed sole power as a
dictator in 46 B.C.E. and welcomed his enemies, including Cicero, back to Rome
(rather than proscribing them) only to be assassinated himself on March 15, 44
B.C.E., by a faction of the senatorial party led by Cassius and Marcus and Deci-
mus Brutus.[11] Though the Senate's reign of power continued, the real contest was
over who would succeed Caesar. The most prominent contender was Antonius.[12]

    Eventually Antonius, Octavian, and Lepidus formed the Second Triumvi-
rate and immediately proscribed their enemies, which led to the death of many,
including Cicero. The Triumvirate successfully defeated the "conspirators" at
Philippi in 42 B.C.E.[13] The proscriptions were a terrifying and bloody time. Classical historian Colin Wells has estimated that at least 130 senators were exiled
and an unknown number of equestrians were exiled or killed and their property seized.[14] Still there was no stability to be found. With Lepidus in exile, what
was left of the agreement between Antonius and Octavian dissolved in 32 B.C.E.
and civil war broke out. Octavian finally defeated Antonius and Cleopatra at the
battle of Actium in 31 B.C.E., after which both committed suicide.

    The significance of the turmoil for the Roman citizens in the late republic
was fundamental for their acceptance of the principate. The violence of civil
and social wars, slave revolts, proscriptions, and land seizures took a toll on
many famous Romans—Cicero, most notably, but Virgil had property confis-
cated as did Horace's family.[15] The populace was, no doubt, as Tacitus claims, "so

desperate for peace that "they preferred the safety of the present to the danger-ous past."[16] Augustus both promised and delivered peace (at least on the home front), but "peace" was also a valuable rhetorical strategy; as Cicero had demon-strated before his death, to reference the bloodshed of the past, however covertly, was to emphasize the prosperity of the present.[17]

To whatever degree Augustan rhetoric was enabled by the relative peace that followed the battle of Actium in 31 B.C.E., it was constrained, at least to the same extent, as Dio explains, in that the "Romans hated the actual name of monarch so vehemently that they did not refer to their emperors either as dictators or kings."[18] Of course this left Augustus in a rather tight spot, as Kennedy argues; "although not a distinguished public speaker, [Augustus] . . . had a profound understanding of the rhetoric of empire. A variety of titles and religious forms were used to mask the reality of his power; art, architecture, inscription, and urban planning conveyed the aura of a new golden age."[19] However, seeing the challenge before Octavian in 31 B.C.E. as one readily met by deception overlooks the very real dependence of Augustus's reign on its acceptance by and popularity with the Roman people, and, as such, dismisses both the significance of Augus-tan rhetoric and the will of the populace.

That popularity was gained on multiple fronts and often simply required meeting the material needs of the people, which was then publicized and used to Augustus's rhetorical advantage. It also meant considering and addressing popu-lar sentiment as to why the republic had failed, which generally amounted to a belief in a "failure to adhere to a traditional value system that places the common good, the *res publica*, ahead of private interests." As such, "the Augustan solution, therefore, was a conscious return to and rearticulating of these basic values and principles."[20] Finally, given that Rome was very much in need of new oversight, Augustus's administration sought "to have as many people as possible partici-pate in the life of the state."[21] Classicist Karl Galinsky is quick to point out this was not "democratization" as such, but it was also a long way from the tyranny often associated with the age.[22] While attempts to gain acceptance for the princi-pate were "rhetorical" in that they represented a type of persuasive communica-tion between the people and the government about the workings of the state, more often than not this communication was a negotiation of a definition of a "good" government and citizen, debatably the goal of rhetorical practice since at least the fifth century B.C.E.

THE OLD MYTHS: ROMAN FOUNDING MYTHS AND THE JULIAN LINE

History, society, and politics might seem to be the most significant contexts for understanding Augustan rhetoric, but the mythic history of the city provides a powerful context for understanding Augustan rhetoric. For Romans, the distinction between myth and history was not particularly clear-cut. For example, Quintilian describes three types of narratives: "fictitious," "realistic," and "historical,"[23] the last of "which contains the narration of actual events."[24] Though mythic history to contemporary audiences would seem to fall outside historical narrative, Quintilian clearly places such narratives in this category, mentioning Romulus and the She-wolf as an example.[25] Myth, nonetheless, played a significant role in constraining the available means of governing the city as well as how Augustus could promote his reign, and ultimately provided a significant, if not the most significant, rhetorical strategy for justifying the principate.

Three different Roman myths affected the political beliefs of the citizens of Rome and in turn constrained the ways in which Augustus could present his rule to the public: the Aeneas myth, the myth of Romulus and Remus, and the tale of the expulsion of the kings from Rome. The first two myths were the traditional founding stories of Rome, both of which Augustus referenced in his state-sponsored rhetoric; the latter served as an impediment in the minds of the people to accepting Augustus's rule. No doubt the Aeneas myth, as composed by Virgil, trumped the others after the principate, forming the basis of the new political myth of Augustus.

Aeneas

Aeneas is mentioned in various Greek and Roman sources with the basic story as follows:[26]Aeneas, the son of Anchises and Aphrodite (Venus), who is mentioned in Homer's *Iliad* as a Trojan leader, flees Troy with his father and his son Ascanius, abandoning his wife but not his household gods in the process. Aeneas then goes on his own epic journey fated by the gods Jupiter and Venus, becoming briefly waylaid by Juno at Carthage with the mythic queen Dido. Eventually, at the urging of Mercury, Aeneas continues and, depending on the version, founds Rome or another Italian city (either Lavinium, named after his new wife, or Alba), leaving the actual founding of Rome to his descendents.[27] Prior to Aeneas's arrival in Italy, Lavinia was betrothed to (or at least admired by) another king, Turnus, who waged war against Aeneas and is eventually killed by the hero.

Virgil's *Aeneid,* likely begun between 30 and 28 B.C.E. with the encouragement of Augustus and distributed after Virgil's death in 19 B.C.E., became important, if not foundational, to Augustan rhetoric in several ways.[28] First, in order to allow for complimentary comparison between Aeneas and Augustus, Virgil makes Aeneas a more sympathetic character, which permits the likening of the two men's deeds, such as "fighting sacrilege."[29] This transformation included converting Aeneas from a hero whose characteristic trait was his prowess as a warrior into a man defined by his piety.[30] Second, the *Aeneid* establishes

Augustus's rule as fated since the time of the Trojan War; as classicist H. P. Stahl argues, in Virgil's *Aeneid,* "The ultimate purpose of [Aeneas's] arrival, according to divine revelation, is the worldwide rule his descendent Augustus will one day peacefully [exercise]," making Augustus's "earthly achievements . . . [the] fulfillment of a divine mission."[31] Third, though related, the *Aeneid* connects the Julian line to Aeneas and thus Venus. From the time of the Triumvirate, this lineage was frequently used by Augustus as the basis for arguments concerning the destiny of the Julian line to rule Rome in virtually every media.[32] Virgil's *Aeneid* seamlessly joins Aeneas, Romulus and Remus, and the Julian line, thereby making Augustus's rule destined from the founding of the city of Rome.[33]

The impact of Virgil's *Aeneid* on Augustan Rome was profound; it established "Aeneas as a national hero at Rome," supplanting all earlier narratives and impeding future innovation.[34] The Aeneas myth became the basis of the new Augustan political myth, with Aeneas serving as a point of amplification for Augustus and as an exemplar for imitation for the Roman people.

Romulus and Remus

The myth of Romulus and Remus also addresses the founding of the city of Rome and was reconciled with the Aeneas myth as early as the third century by making Aeneas the founder of another Italian city and Romulus, a descendent of Aeneas, the founder of Rome.[35] The Romulus myth establishes the founding of the city of Rome in 753 B.C.E. and the "foundation of Roman institutions," including the start of the "regal period" where Rome was ruled by a king (*rex*) along with a Senate.[36]

The myth begins in Alba Longa, the city founded by Aeneas (or his son), after the former king of Alba Longa, Numitor, has been overthrown by his brother Amulius. A prophecy declared that Numitor's male heir, a grandson, would kill Amulius and return his grandfather to the throne. To prevent this, Amulius had Numitor's daughter made a Vestal Virgin; however, Amulius's actions did not prevent Rhea Silvia's (or Ilia in some versions) rape by Mars. She gave birth to twins, Romulus and Remus, whom Amulius ordered exposed or drowned, but instead they ended up afloat on the Tiber. When they came ashore, the twins were cared for by a she-wolf and a woodpecker—both animals associated with Mars—before being raised by a shepherd and his wife. Eventually the travels of Romulus and Remus brought them back to Alba Longa, where they fulfilled the prophecy before founding the city of Rome, where they offered asylum to (male) criminals. These men needed wives and found them by inviting the women of a neighboring Sabine tribe to a festival with the plan to carry off the women of that tribe for themselves. In most versions of the myth, Remus was killed by his brother Romulus, who was chosen as king, over a disagreement arising from the walling of the city. Romulus continued to serve as the first king of Rome, siring the line of Roman kings, before disappearing in a thunderstorm on the Campus Martius to become (associated with) the god Quirinius.[37]

The use of the Romulus myth already provided orators with a powerful rhetorical repository by the end of the republic. For example, Cicero compared himself to Romulus in first *Catilinarian* "to make it appear that Rome had passed through a crisis so grave that its salvation was a new beginning and its unchanged aspect was a testament to Cicero, its savior and 'refounder.'"[38] At the same time, Cicero portrayed himself as humble, "present[ing] all that had happened as an expression of the will of the gods."[39] Augustus apparently took note, using similar comparisons between himself and Romulus both to pardon his earlier deeds by comparing them to Romulus's and to suggest a "rebirth" for the city of Rome. The allusions between Augustus and Romulus were apparently quite clear, at least to later historians such as Dio, who suggests that Octavian actually preferred the title "Romulus" to "Augustus," though the Senate opted for the latter.[40]

The Expulsion of the King

The dislike of monarchy by the Roman people, to which Dio calls attention, had its roots in the mythic history of the city and formed a powerful constraint for Augustan rhetoric. The system of kingship established by Romulus ended in 510 B.C.E. and is often referred to as the "expulsion of the kings" or the "expulsion of the Tarquins," which ended the "regal period" in Rome.[41] The expulsion of the Tarquins began with the rape of Lucretia, a virtuous and chaste Roman woman and the wife of Tarquinius Collatinus, by Sextus, the son of the last king of Rome, Lucius Tarquinius Superbus.[42] As a result of the rape, Lucretia killed herself, prompting revenge by her relatives, particularly Lucius Iunius Brutus, who then expelled the Tarquins from Rome and began the Roman republic.[43]

The mythic history of the expulsion of the Tarquins also signifies a distaste for Eastern systems of rule that, in part, predisposed Romans against any type of sole ruler, as well as dynastic succession. This predisposition crops up repeatedly in the Roman literary sources. For example, Tacitus begins his *Annals*:

> When Rome was first a city, its rulers were kings. Then Lucius Junius Brutus created the consulate and free Republican institutions in general. Dictatorships were assumed in emergencies. A Council of Ten did not last more than two years; and then there was a short-lived arrangement by senior army officers—the commanders of contingents provided by the tribes—possessed consular authority. Subsequently Cinna and Sulla set up autocracies, but they too were brief. Soon Pompey and Crassus acquired predominant positions,

but rapidly lost them to Caesar. Next, the military strength which Lepidus and Antonius built up was absorbed by Augustus. He found the whole state exhausted by internal dissensions, and established over it a personal regime known as the principate.[44]

Tacitus's account of the events leading up to the principate points to how easily the mythic history of the city blends into the more recent history, but also that, at least for Tacitus, the principate represented a return to the autocratic government that existed in Rome prior to the republic.

Though Cassius Dio expresses few of the reservations regarding a monarchy found in Tacitus, he also contextualizes Augustus's reign in terms of the rule of the kings, and he too indicates that Augustus had to negotiate the mythic history of the expulsion of the Tarquins in establishing his rule.[45] Dio speaks of Augustus's rule as established in 27 B.C.E.: "Through this process the power both of the people and of the Senate was wholly transferred into the hands of Augustus, and it was from this time that a monarchy, strictly speaking, was established. It is true that the Romans hated the actual name of monarch so vehemently that they did not refer to their emperors either as dictators or kings or anything similar. But since the final decision in the governing process is referred to them, it is impossible that they should be anything other than kings."[46] For Dio, it is evident that Augustus's rule was a monarchy, but it is the Roman political ideology, stemming in part from the mythic history of the expulsion of the Tarquins, that prevents Augustus from ruling as a king, requiring him to conceal the nature of his power.

Although Augustus avoided any aspect of his rule that would bring up associations with the corrupt kings of Rome, no doubt in part because he had the all-too-recent assassination of the "tyrant" Julius Caesar as a reminder of where such carelessness could lead, the *princeps* did seem to invite comparison with another king of Rome—Servius Tullius. Servius was murdered by Superbus, who conspired with Servius's daughter Tullia. Servius, who was said to be descended from slaves, was credited with many reforms, including the enfranchisement of freedmen, the establishment of the *compitalia,* the census, the first Roman coinage, a paid army, and the "Servian Wall."[47] Augustus's reforms of many of the Servian establishments, particularly the *compitalia,* the cult of the crossroads associated with the Lares, often invited comparison between the two men and, thus, the amplification of Augustus's deeds.

Roman Mythic History and Political Use

These three myths are of considerable importance in understanding the nature of Augustus's rhetorical power in the principate. Augustus frequently used a variety of rhetorical techniques to draw comparisons between himself, Aeneas, Romulus, and Servius Tullius. In addition, the myth of the expulsions of the Tarquins created a situation where Augustus could not rule as a monarch, at least not in name, though the recent history of the city made this constraint easier to overcome. One significant strategy in overcoming this constraint was to shift the responsibility of Augustus's rule to the gods through the construction of the Augustan political myth as expounded in Virgil's *Aeneid.* The importance of this political myth—that Augustus was destined to fulfill a divine mission to (re)found a city that would rule the world that began with Aeneas's journey to Italy, continued through Romulus's founding of Rome, and finally culminated with the golden age of Augustus where "peace" and stability abound—cannot be overstated. This myth informs virtually every rhetorical action taken by Augustus after 27 B.C.E., and if there is an Augustan ideology, surely it is evident in this political myth.

RHETORIC'S SITUATION: ORATORY IN THE PRINCIPATE

The contexts that enabled and constrained Augustan rhetoric also had a very real and lasting impact on rhetorical practice at Rome. While scholars tend to think of democracy and rhetoric as interdependent (and certainly this seems to be the opinion of Tacitus), rhetoric, at least Greek rhetoric, had a rocky start at Rome. Suetonius, in his brief comments on the practice and teaching of rhetoric in *De Grammaticis and Rhetoribus,* sees rhetoric as something that shaped Rome, but points out that the practice of (Greek) rhetoric was banned in Rome initially and only later accepted.[48] He writes, "By degrees rhetoric itself came to seem useful and honourable, and many devoted themselves to it as a defence and for glory."[49] Though oratory obviously occurred early in the republic, the Greek tradition of rhetoric was initially viewed as both foreign and potentially as a dangerous tool of social mobility, shedding light on the "democratic" practices of the Roman republic.[50]

The idea that oratory was an equalizer of class in Rome, no doubt, comes from believing what Cicero had to tell us about the republic, which is supported by Tacitus, who idolized Cicero.[51] Contrary to the suggestion that, if "ambitious Republicans" lacked "wealth, an aristocratic heritage, and military sagacity, they could travel one further avenue to success: rhetoric," Syme argues that oratory was only one very small piece of political success in Rome and that new men like Cicero—that is men who were the first to achieve senatorial rank in their family—were exceedingly rare.[52] Cicero is even more atypical in that, though Tacitus claims "the boldest spirits had fallen in battle or in the proscription," Cicero was the only "man of consular rank actually killed" in the proscription.[53] Because

Cicero was an anomaly, a tool of a party, and though rhetoric may have been his only resource (he was rich, but not vastly wealthy and had no military prowess to speak of), we must use him, and thus Tacitus, with caution as a source for the significance of oratory as an equalizer of class in the republic.

Still, taking into account the perspectives of the authors, sources such as Dio, Suetonius, and Tacitus do relate a good bit about changes in oratorical venues in the principate. These sources convey information about the venues for the traditional division of genres in most rhetorical treatises: "forensic" or "judicial" as practiced in the courts; "deliberative" as practiced in the legislative bodies such as the Senate and the popular assembly; and to a lesser extent, "epideictic" as practiced on ceremonial occasions such as when the consuls assumed office or at state funerals. Often the first two genres are labeled the "practical" genres of rhetoric, though it is particularly misleading to do so. In addition to these venues of oratory, schools of declamation were increasingly the places of rhetorical education and for rhetors to showcase their abilities. Augustus's principate certainly saw changes in, though not the eradication of, all of these venues.

Forensic Rhetoric: The Courts

The courts offered perhaps the surest way for an orator to gain renown; yet Cicero represents the majority of examples of judicial speeches from the republic. Often it seems that in Rome an orator was able to make his name in the courts by defending clients, which could then translate to a political advantage leading to more important oratorical opportunities. During the principate, the courts were restructured by Augustus. Though perpetually a scene of class struggle, by the time of the principate the courts had become corrupt and were greatly in need of reform, particularly where matters of the provinces were concerned.

In efficiency and justice the courts were much improved under Augustus, though this perhaps did not translate to a higher quality of judicial oratory or happier orators. Augustus's first major reform transferred control of the courts, like virtually all other administrative positions, to the equestrian order.[54] The reforms to the courts also apparently included strict time limits and a dress code. While Tacitus's character Messalla agrees that the reforms made the courts "more practical," he laments the restrictiveness of both time limits and uncomfortable dress.[55]

Though the new structure of the courts may have improved justice, stifling the practice of forensic oratory in the process, there is no doubt that this is only half the story. Tacitus points to two other audience-based factors that constrained forensic oratory. First, his Marcus Aper suggests that audiences had become rhetorically savvy, with many having had "systematic training in the rudiments of the art" of rhetoric, expecting more from an orator than in the past, particularly a "flowery ornamental style of speaking; they will no more put up with sober, unadorned old fashionedness in a court of law."[56] That is, audiences expected entertainment perhaps more than judicial process when watching trials.

The second problem according to Tacitus was that the principate created a double-bind in that an orator could be caught between defending a friend and offending the emperor.[57] This precarious position, though, was at least partially self-imposed out of a desire for political advancement. After all, Marcus Aper in discussing Maturnus's decision to leave oratory to take up historical writing frames his decision chiefly in terms of personal gain.[58] Similar, though perhaps more dire, constraints were in place during the party politics of the republic, particularly as it dissolved into factionalism—a tightrope Cicero had to walk on occasion.[59] Though Tacitus's Maternus suggests that the "old-fashioned outspokenness" is no longer present in oratory, Suetonius says Augustus did not mind (at least some) criticism.[60] It is certainly important to consider the constraints on the orator and their effects on judicial oratory in the principate: judicial oratory in the principate was probably less fun, but the courts were likely greatly more efficient and, significantly, more just.[61]

Deliberative Rhetoric: The Senate and Popular Assembly

Though the courts were reformed, probably for the better, the venues of deliberative oratory, particularly the Senate, did see a reduction of power. Still it is important to consider who was participating in the deliberative bodies in the republic and what types of participation replaced those institutions in the principate. The principate marked many changes in the political institutions of the republic, most significantly the consolidation of official power into the figure of the *princeps* and senatorial reform, which stripped that body of many powers concerning finance and foreign policy.

Augustus placed in his office the power of several traditional Roman offices: "the functions of the Senate, the magistrates, and the laws."[62] The concentration of power in the figure of the *princeps* may have led to a lack of civic participation in the traditional offices of the republic. As early as 12 b.c.e. there was difficulty filling the office of the tribunes because of the "disappearance of its powers."[63] As Dio recounts, "Since nobody was any longer willing to stand for the tribuneship, the posts should be filled through the appointment by lot of some of the former quaestors who had not yet reached the age of forty."[64] The turn to the traditional offices of the republic to legitimize the power of the *princeps* did not seem to fool anyone, other than possibly Velleius. Dio saw the move as nothing but a screen for monarchy.[65] Still, it was necessary to exercise great care with the senatorial reforms.

As Dio makes clear, the Senate was a necessary institution for the Roman people. Dio's Maecenas, in his speech to Augustus on the benefits of a sole ruler, advises Augustus that "it is important to emphasize the fact that the Senate is sovereign in all matters."[66] Dio describes the transformation of the Senate through Augustus's reign at various points in his history. Of the political bodies of 27 B.C.E., Dio says, "The Senate as a whole continued to sit in judgment on its own, as it had done before, and on certain occasions conducted negotiations with delegations and heralds from both peoples and kings. Besides this the people and the plebs continued to meet for elections, but nothing was done that did not meet with Augustus's approval."[67]

Dio recounts the purging of the Senate in 18 B.C.E., in which Augustus himself chose six hundred men to remain in the Senate, which had grown "too large" (though one problem was that many senators did not meet the financial requirements designated by Augustus, which were meant to delineate the social classes more clearly).[68] Dio, as well as Suetonius, casts these reforms in the interest of bringing the Senate back up to par.[69] Eventually, Dio claims that political participation in the Senate dwindled, indicating a low turnout in 9 B.C.E. prompting Augustus to issue fines for those senators who did not attend.[70] Still, Dio claims that debate continued, most likely concerning the affairs in the city of Rome. Dio describes this debate as "to some extent democratic" even if resolutions were delayed in waiting for the requisite number of senators.[71]

Still, both Dio and Suetonius express optimism over the form of government as established by Augustus. In fact, Dio argues, in the speech Maecenas makes to Augustus on the benefits of a sole ruler, that allowing the smartest people to govern, while making sure each contributes what he is able to the state, is in fact more democratic than a republic.[72] While one can debate the merits of Dio's political philosophy, the point remains that the principate gave many who had not had prior access to political power a chance to participate in the civic affairs of Rome. This leads Dio to take the stance that, if not "more democratic" than the end of the republic, the principate allowed more direct participation by more people in running Rome. Suetonius too says, "To enable more men to take part in the administration of the State, [Augustus] devised new offices: the charge of public buildings, of the roads, of the aqueducts, of the channel of the Tiber, of the distribution of grain to the people."[73] That is, while traditional venues of oratory such as the courts and Senate may have been limited and the "democratic" process of the republic was altered, the citizens of the principate, many of whom would not have had the opportunity to do so in the republic, had the ability to participate in their government, at least in some form, and one of the main rhetorical enterprises of Augustus's reign was to suggest possible means of civic participation.

Epideictic Rhetoric: Ceremonial Venues

Likely all can agree that the so-called "practical" genres of rhetoric saw great changes in the principate.[74] There is also consensus that epideictic rhetoric flourished, though what one considers "epideictic" is open to some debate.[75] Problematically, often epideictic rhetoric is dismissed as "mere" praise, even sycophantic praise, that is, "empty" and devoid of value, dismissing important social, philosophical, and deliberative aspects.[76] Both Jeffrey Walker and Laurent Pernot have done much to dissuade the notion that epideictic rhetoric is insignificant. For Pernot, traditional epideictic forms a "history of mentalities" that left room to discipline and advise.[77] Walker argues that, "under the Roman emperors, what we find is actually a triumph of the Ciceronian ideal," the flourishing of epideictic rhetoric and a return to fifth-century ideals.[78]

A description of the rhetorical tactics common in the epideictic genre as manifest on the Ara Pacis Augustae follows, but it useful here to briefly establish the role of the epideictic genre in Rome. Quintilian captures the importance of the genre in imperial Rome as well as its practical importance: "This class appears to have been entirely divorced by Aristotle, and following him by Theophrastus, from the practical side of oratory (which they call *pragmatike*) and to have been reserved solely for the delectation of audiences, which indeed is shown to be its peculiar function by its own name, which implies display [*ab ostentatione*]. Roman usage on the other hand has given it a place in the practical tasks of life. For funeral orations are often imposed as a duty on persons holding public office, or entrusted to magistrates by decree of the Senate."[79] While Quintilian stresses the importance of the epideictic genre in the form of eulogy in political life, he takes exception with Aristotle, classifying Roman epideictic as quite practical.

No doubt, eulogy and the *gratiarum actio,* the speech of praise made by the consuls for their (s)election, are the two best-known forms of epideictic rhetoric in Rome,[80] but Pernot, following later developments of the genre as outlined by Menander, explains, "peace, economic prosperity, urbanization, secure travel, multiplication of festivals, heightened role of municipal elites and imperial bureaucrats, reverence towards the emperor—all these developments presented new objects and new occasions for rhetorical praise, making it more necessary than it had ever been before."[81] The epideictic genre could define the qualities of good leaders and citizens, especially as those roles underwent huge historic changes, and it could question how individuals, cities, and countries met those standards in significant ways to which rhetorically savvy audiences were attuned.

It is likely that deliberative and judicial rhetoric continued to flourish in the provinces to a much greater extent than in Rome, and Pernot's mention of "municipal elites and imperial bureaucrats" stresses the importance of differentiating rhetorical practices in Rome from those in the provinces and brings in a fourth type of rhetoric. This fourth type that, no doubt, flourished under the empire can be broadly defined as imperial rhetoric, which included the affairs of "local courts and councils; in embassies, petitions, letters, appeals, and lawsuits."[82] We have, however, very little evidence for such rhetorical practices, though it is clear such practices existed. Still, it is important to consider imperial rhetoric as a significant outlet for the skills of those who were rhetorically trained in addition to schools of declamation and the traditional judicial and deliberative venues—the courts, the senate, and popular assembly.

THE ROMAN PRINCIPATE was both vastly different and not so different from what preceded it. As Pernot puts it, "The Empire did not provoke a radical mutation, but a series of transformations, of changes of emphasis and innovation that make up a different landscape, even though the elements may not all be new.[83] Perhaps the largest and most immediate rhetorical challenge faced by the principate was to define what the people could expect from their leader and what Augustus expected from the citizens, all the while training those citizens to run the new bureaucracy. Defining these roles had often been the purview of the epideictic genre, as it would be again in the principate. It is, however, limiting to think of Augustan rhetoric as "merely" epideictic—all pretty words and empty praise. The roles of the *princeps* and the people were far from set in the principate and would continue to evolve over the decades of Augustus's reign. The histories of Rome—mythic, political, and social—would continue to inform the negotiation of these roles and remain significant to understanding them.

2

SEEING RHETORICAL THEORY

Certainly the transition from republic to principate led to changes in the practice of rhetoric in Rome, which, for at least to some scholars, indicate a broadening in the practice of rhetoric.[1] For example, for Laurent Pernot, who defines rhetoric rather narrowly as "persuasive speech," the early empire is a time when rhetoric expands beyond the traditional genres to include many other literary genres.[2] While Pernot is thinking of things like poetry, literary criticism, history, and philosophy, genres other scholars might argue had been considered rhetoric all along, for Pernot there is something specific about "eloquence" and rhetorical education, "particularly . . . forms of expression drawn from the preparatory exercises, on speeches inserted into narrative, arguments, stylistic effects, and the resources of memory techniques and delivery" that seeps across genres in the early empire.[3]

Rhetorical theory and practice in the late republic and early empire demonstrate a certain broadening of rhetoric in classical thought. This broadening, I would argue, funnels more traditional rhetorical practices not only into many literary genres, but also into a variety of media like monuments, coins, and city planning.[4] Such changes in rhetorical theory and practice are evidence toward the inclusion of such nontraditional rhetorical media within the standard of classical rhetorical theory without anachronistically imposing contemporary practice on the past.

RHETORICAL THEORY IN ROME
Definitions of Rhetoric

One means of understanding how rhetoric was theorized in the early empire comes from probing classical definitions of rhetoric. Recently, some scholars, seeking to understand the role of the visual in Greek rhetoric, have closely examined Aristotle's definition: "Let rhetoric be [defined as] an ability, in each [particular] case to see the available means of persuasion."[5] Though this is potentially a fruitful place to start, at least for making the case that the visual was understood by the Greeks to be a rhetorical element, the definition is less applicable to Roman rhetorical practices. After all, Aristotle gives this definition after a long passage on the power of words. The acceptance of nontraditional rhetorical media in classical rhetorical theory based on this definition depends on the persistence of Aristotle's psychological model of the "mind's eye" in Roman thought. It is slight reach to suggest that the "mind's eye" concept is carried forward into Roman thought.

Quintilian, on the other hand, gives a definition of rhetoric useful for conceptualizing the role of the visual in Roman rhetorical theory when he refutes "the common definition of rhetoric as the power of persuading."[6] He notes that a number of rhetoricians such as Isocrates, Plato's Gorgias, and at times even Cicero[7] have described persuasion as the aim of rhetoric.[8] Quintilian's main objection to definitions that focus on rhetoric as persuasion is as follows:

> But many other things have the power of persuasion, such as money, influence, the authority and rank of the speaker, or even some sight unsupported by language, when for instance the place of words is supplied by the memory of some individual's great deeds, by his lamentable appearance or the beauty of his person. Thus when Antonius in the course of his defence of Manius Aquillius tore open his client's robe and revealed the honorable scars which he had acquired while facing his country's foes, he relied no longer on the power of speech, but appealed directly to the eyes of the Roman people. And it is believed that they were so profoundly moved by the sight as to acquit the accused. Again there is the speech of Cato, to mention no other records, which informs us that Servius Galba escaped condemnation solely by the pity he aroused not only by producing his own young children before the assembly, but by carrying round in his arms the son of Sulpius Gallus. So also according to general opinion Phryne was not saved by the eloquence of Hyperides, admirable as it was, but by the sight of her exquisite body, which she

further revealed by drawing aside her tunic. And if all these have the power
to persuade, the end of oratory, which we are discussing cannot adequately
be defined as persuasion.[9]

In addition to noting in the course of recounting and refuting these several
instances of persuasion as rhetoric, Quintilian clearly describes the power that
the sense of sight has to move the emotions of an audience. He suggests that the
visual does not require the mediation of words—that is, that things like scars can
serve as symbols to move an audience in the same way speech can or even in a
way speech alone cannot. In suggesting that not everyone would separate the
nonverbal means of persuasion—"money," "influence," "authority and rank of
the speaker," "sights unsupported by language" such as the "memory of some individual's great deeds," "appearance," and "beauty"—from the realm of rhetoric,
Quintilian demonstrates that at least some would have considered these elements
as rhetorical under a commonly circulating notion of rhetoric as persuasion.[10]

This popular definition of rhetoric as persuasion has great value in explor-
ing the role of the visual in Roman rhetorical theory and practice in general. It
also is helpful in specifically addressing visual and material rhetoric used in the
principate. Still, it is plainly evident that Quintilian does not view these practices
as rhetorical; rather, he looks on what modern scholars might call "material" or
"visual" rhetoric with disdain, lumping both in the category of "harlots, flat-
ters and seducers."[11] Historically, rhetoric has been called worse; nonetheless, the
definition of rhetoric as persuasion in Roman thought leaves much wanting as
a starting point to understanding the rhetorical underpinnings of the Augustan
cultural campaigns.

Categorization of the Arts

Though Quintilian's consideration of definitions demonstrates that some might
have considered the visual to be part of rhetoric in Roman thought, a more likely
starting point for arguing that nontraditional rhetorical media ought to be seen
as a feature of Roman rhetorical theory is found in Quintilian's categorization
of the arts. He classifies the arts based on their ends. He describes arts that "are
based on examination" such as "astronomy" to be "theoretical arts," arts based
in "action" such as "dance" to be "practical arts," and arts based on "producing
a certain result" through "the completion of a visible task" such as "painting" to
be "productive." Quintilian admits rhetoric can be all three of these things in
various forms. For example, rhetoric can be theoretical in one's "private study"
(what contemporary scholars of rhetoric might call "rhetorical criticism"), practical when one delivers a speech, and productive when one writes a speech or
produces a "historical narrative." Still, Quintilian sees rhetoric as predominantly

a practical and therefore a performance-based art.[12] However, Quintilian's account of rhetoric as at times falling under all three categories of arts suggests that his concept of rhetoric was extremely broad and contextually bound.

Perhaps the most significant change in the practice of rhetoric in the principate, one Quintilian and Tacitus react against, is from practical to productive art. At the beginning of Tacitus's *Dialogue on Oratory* we find his character Maternus turning his back on oratory to compile a volume on Cato and mentioning that his next project will be a tragedy.[13] Maturnus's turn to the productive arts is representative of the period. Tacitus, whose own career as an orator/historian resembles that of his character Julius Secundus, suggests that poetry (and history) might be an area that admits of more freedom,[14] and the works of Dio, Suetonius, and even Tacitus himself demonstrate the same notion. Dio does not reference rhetoric specifically, but his own rhetorical training is evident in a variety of ways, most clearly in the fictitious speeches he attributes to the likes of Augustus, Antonius, Maecenas, Agrippa, Livia, and Tiberius. "Tiberius's" eulogy of Augustus shows Dio had a working knowledge of the conventions of epideictic oratory; at the same time, the eulogy clearly differentiates Dio's history of Augustus's reign from his character Tiberius's eulogy. The latter is close in substance to Augustus's own (panegyric) account given in the *Res gestae*. Dio was clearly rhetorically savvy and chose to write a history. Suetonius, who served as imperial secretary to Hadrian and had a career as an advocate and writer under Trajan, writes panegyric modeled in part on Augustus's own *Res gestae* and Pliny's panegyric of Trajan and, in doing so, displays his rhetorical training.[15] In other words, Dio, Suetonius, and Tacitus were all rhetorically trained and chose to practice productive arts well into the Roman empire.

Though it is impossible to draw direct connections between Augustus and his specific input on most individual rhetorical artifacts, he was also, as expected for a man of his class, educated in rhetoric and practiced oratory throughout his reign. Suetonius says Augustus was trained by Apollodorus of Pergamum, had a clear and concise style, appeared in court to defend his friends, and preferred to write his speeches out rather than memorize them.[16] Dio notes that Augustus gave eulogies for most of his family members and chosen successors who died, including Marcellus, Agrippa, and Octavia.[17] Dio also mentions that Augustus sat in on court deliberations, but he makes it sound as if Augustus did not participate, though Dio does describe several cases where the emperor pleaded cases for friends.[18] These activities show that Augustus, like Suetonius, Dio, Tacitus, and most men of the upper classes, received an education in rhetoric, that he made use of his rhetorical training in the traditional venues for oratory in the administration of the empire, and that he perhaps also funneled his training in productive ways.

This "funneling," then, results in a palpable "expansion" of rhetoric. Conservatively, one area where Pernot notes this expansion is in literary criticism, where he uses two markers to define when criticism can be considered rhetoric—the use of rhetorical concepts and criticism of (or an outside interest in) oratorical texts.[19] These two markers, particularly the first, might apply broadly to many arts, verbal and visual, in the early empire. Pernot does not see this broadening of rhetoric as intentional, but rather as result of an "element of the culture and mental makeup of the time."[20] Simply put, rhetorical education still reigned supreme, but political and social advancement no longer depended on the courthouse or the senate floor. Rhetoric flourished, but not only in the form of oratory.

The Mind's Eye: The Aristotelian Psychological Model

One significant way the visual may have played a role in the realm of rhetoric is via what I refer to as the "psychological model" of Aristotle. Scholars such as Ned O'Gorman and Sarah Newman have argued that for Aristotle, perception, knowledge, thought, memory, imagination, deliberation, and, therefore, the art of rhetoric were all based on the sense of sight.[21] O'Gorman argues, based on his examinations of *phantasia* (a rhetorical technique used by orators to create emotion in audiences by depicting a vivid scene) in *De anima* and the *Rhetoric*, that "rhetoric is for Aristotle an art that may shape opinion and direct the affections through the creation of image."[22] O'Gorman first shows that, for Aristotle, "all human deliberation depends on *phantasia*."[23] He argues that "the relationship between phantasmatic and pragmatic rhetorics depends on the degree to which public deliberation is like private deliberation."[24] Therefore, the role of the visual is not limited to the personal (psychological) or even the epideictic genre but can also play a role in deliberative rhetoric.

This psychological model is significant on several fronts. First, it suggests that Aristotle's definition of rhetoric includes visual means of persuasion in addition to words. Second, it suggests that, at least in Aristotle's line of thinking, the difference between words and images is not so great. O'Gorman shows that Aristotle's views on the relationship between the visual and the verbal influenced Roman thought generally and that evidence of that influence specifically appears in the terminology in Quintilian's discussion of *phantasia* and *enargeia*. Nonetheless, even though Quintilian does use the term *phantasia* similarly to Aristotle, it is still hard to determine precisely how much of Aristotle's thinking on the relationship makes it into Roman thought.

Visualization

Any discussion of "the mind's eye" inevitably leads to the role of techniques in "bringing before the eyes," usually *enargeia* or *phantasia*, though other terms such as *ekphrasis, hypotypsis, diatyposis, evidentia, repraesentatio, illustratio, dem-onstratio, descriptio,* and *sub oculos subiectio* function similarly because they all deal with the construction of a "visual image" through "concrete detail."[25] These terms often have to do with either creating emotion in the rhetor in order to convey that emotion to the audience or with creating an image through words in the minds of the audience in order to move them in some way.

Two of the most frequently discussed terms in Roman rhetorical theory are *enargeia* and *phantasia.* Quintilian defines *enargeia* as a "vivid illustration" or "representation" that goes beyond "clearness" and instead "consists in giving an actual word-picture of a scene," which forms a "mental picture" for the audience and makes the audience a "spectator."[26] Quintilian composes an example of *enargeia* to demonstrate the emotional effect it can create.[27] Quintilian briefly mentions another figure that appeals to the visual, *phantasia,* "or imagination, which assists us to form mental pictures of things."[28] Quintilian points out that "the prime essential for stirring the emotions of others is . . . first to feel those emotions oneself."[29] He says, "It is the man who is really sensitive to such impressions who will have the greatest power over emotions."[30] The purpose of conveying such emotion is clearly to move the audience, but as Longinus explains, *phantasia* is a particularly powerful rhetorical tactic that "far exceeds the limits of persuasion" and "draw[s our attention] from the reasoning to the enthralling effect of the imagination."[31]

The discussion of *enargeia* and *phantasia* in Roman rhetorical treatises is important for understanding the relationship between rhetoric and the visual for several reasons. First, the language used seems to suggest, as O'Gorman has argued, that Aristotle's psychological model persisted in Roman thought, at least in certain respects. Second, these discussions serve as a theoretical starting point for connecting the common rhetorical practice of creating an environment to suit the rhetor's needs with Roman rhetorical theory as espoused in treatises and handbooks. That is, *enargeia* and *phantasia* can help to bridge what seems to be a sizable gap between Roman rhetorical theory and practice. As Ann Vasaly argues, "an orator trained and practiced in using these techniques" of "bringing before the eyes" "to exploit the associations of places and monuments not visible to his audience would obviously be well equipped to draw on the characteristics of the place where he gave his speech as well, in order to amuse, convince, or arouse his listeners."[32] Finally, as Aristotle's definition of rhetoric also reveals, the difference between words and images was not so great in Roman thought.[33]

The Canon of Memory

Though definitions of rhetoric, ways of categorizing the arts, and rhetorical methods of bringing imagery before the eyes offer starting points for considering the role of the visual and material in the rhetoric of the principate, there is perhaps no more fruitful area of Roman rhetorical theory for theorizing the relationship between the Augustan cultural campaigns and rhetoric than memory. Traditionally one of the five parts of the art of rhetoric, systems of memory contained a strong visual and spatial element, influencing invention and likely the ways Romans understood and constructed their environments.

Cicero and Quintilian, as is well known, both describe a system for improving memory based on visualization, space, and movement. This system was meant to help orators remember their speeches: they would first memorize the rooms of a house or the buildings of a public space, memorize the various objects in those spaces, and then finally connect symbols, which were associated with the various aspects of the speech, to form a kind of memory device through visualization, movement, and association. Cicero's Antonius elaborates on this system of memory when he says, "The memory of things is the proper business of the orator; thus we may be enabled to impress on ourselves by the creation of imaginary figures, aptly arranged, to represent particular heads, so that we may recollect thoughts by images, and their order by place."[34] Crassus again emphasizes this system as utilizing space and movement through that space: "Certain places must be fixed upon, and that of things which they desire to keep in memory, symbols must be conceived in the mind, and ranged, as it were, in those places; thus the order of things, and the symbols of the things would denote the things themselves; so that we should use the places as waxen tablets, and the symbols as letters."[35] Though examples of this system often suggest using the rooms of a house, Quintilian says that "public buildings, a long journey, the ramparts of a city, or even pictures" work as well.[36] This system of memory, sometimes referred to as the "mnemonic system," has encouraged scholars to connect nontraditional rhetorical media with Roman rhetorical theory.

Emphasizing both the visual nature of the human mind and the specific impact that visual and vivid language have on the memory, Cicero's Antonius elaborates on the mnemonic system. He argues:

> Of all the senses that of seeing is the most acute; and that accordingly, those things are most easily retained in our minds which we have received from hearing or the understanding, if they are also recommended to the imagination by means of the mental eye; so that a kind of form, resemblance, and representation might denote invisible objects, and as such as are in their nature withdrawn from the cognizance of the sight, in such a manner, that what we are scarcely capable of comprehending by thought we may retain as it were by the aid of visual faculty. By these imaginary forms and objects, as by all those that come under our corporeal vision, our memory is admonished and excited; but some place for them must be imagined; as bodily shape cannot be conceived without a place for it.[37]

It is the connection between the visual and the mental process in Roman think-ing that allows Cicero's Antonius to focus on specifically visual ways for the ora-tor to improve his own memory. The method Antonius describes stimulates memory through a process of visualization, and he emphasizes the impact of images on the mind. Antonius suggests that ideas, words, and thoughts are best retained when associated with a visualized place; therefore, in using the imagi-nation to add a visual and spatial dynamic to the parts of the speech, speech is retained by the mind.

Quintilian focuses on another visual means of improving memory—writ-ing. Quintilian's discussion of the use of writing necessarily begins by disput-ing the long-standing Platonic assumption that writing harms memory. He describes the practice of reading a text repeatedly to commit it to memory: "For he will have certain tracks to guide him in his pursuit of memory, and the mind's eye will be fixed not merely on the pages on which the words were written, but on the individual lines, and at times he will speak as though he were reading aloud."[38] Here Quintilian claims that writing is also a visual means of stimulat-ing the mind's eye, a process that is similar to that of associating symbols with objects. He goes on to endorse the technique of improving memory through reading to oneself rather than being read to on the grounds that "the perception of the eye is quicker than that of the ear."[39] Again, like Cicero's Antonius, Quintil-ian is suggesting that which is seen is taken up and retained more quickly than that which is heard. Quintilian emphasizes the visual nature of writing; by read-ing over a speech repeatedly, an orator will be able to picture the words on the page while delivering the speech. For Quintilian, the specifically visual nature of the written word functions as a memory device when seen repeatedly.

Both Cicero and Quintilian are discussing means by which the orator can improve his own memory for the sake of retaining knowledge for the purpose of making arguments and giving speeches, but the classical notion of memory sug-gests an important link between the visual, rhetoric, and (public) memory. Both Cicero and Quintilian argue that repeated exposure to visual media, be it writing or public spaces, shapes memory, and memories require a place—a key feature of Roman rhetoric. Presumably, if people were routinely exposed to the same spaces, images, words and symbols, those things would impress themselves in the people's memories. Moreover, the technique of associating symbols with objects has potential implications for building campaigns and turning the process of memory outward, thereby creating a public memory.[40] Quintilian alludes to the formation of such public memory, and he insinuates that memory itself can function persuasively when he argues that one thing that functions persuasively "unsupported by language" is the "memory of some individual's great deeds."[41]

Potentially, repeated exposure to spaces that already have symbols imposed on them in the form of words and images could function much the same way as the system of memory by heads (associating the parts of a speech with objects in a space that Quintilian and Cicero describe) to form public memory, which could then act persuasively with or without the mediation of an orator.

ROME: A CITY OF MARBLE

At the same time that Cicero and Quintilian draw many connections between the visual and rhetoric, the most provocative of which fall under the canon of memory, oratorical practice in Rome suggests that orators likewise routinely considered their visual and material environments in constructing and performing the oratorical act. Orators in Rome routinely gestured to their surroundings, including buildings, statues, and monuments, to harness the memory or emotion of a certain structure; they used the built environment as a setting or stage for the oratorical act, going as far as to manipulate the setting for rhetorical purposes; and they used the built environment as a means of invention, thus suggesting the potential of the built environment to shape or even control the oratorical act. The connection between the visual and rhetoric does not end at theory. Instead, these connections are manifested in oratorical practice in ways not accounted for by theory alone.

The building process in Rome created a certain legitimacy and embodied public memory, and these structures were used in oratorical practice. Not only did rhetorical theory shape Augustan structures and create rhetorically savvy viewers, but also Augustan cultural campaigns functioned rhetorically without the mediation of an orator.

Building Programs in Rome

There was a certain innate legitimacy associated with the construction of Roman buildings, which, perhaps not surprisingly, extended to the rhetorical use of buildings in oratory. First, in the Roman republic there were limited occasions for erecting public buildings. Generally the privilege to build monuments was reserved for triumphing generals or magistrates with *imperium* in the case of temples.[42] The former required the approval of the Senate; the latter could occasionally bypass that process. For the most part, however, there had to be some consensus on the building project, and the sponsor had to have a degree of popularity because the right to build was essentially a state-sanctioned endorsement of the individual that would result in greater "personal celebrity and prestige" and was often a source of "blatant self-promotion."[43] In addition to these public enterprises, there were private buildings as well, including family houses and funeral monuments.

In classical sources there is a connection between building projects and public notoriety or popularity: Cicero, in a letter to his friend Atticus, comments on

Lepidus Aemilius Paullus's restoration of the Basilica Aemilia. Cicero says, "It goes without saying that a monument like that will win for him more popularity and glory than anything."[44] In addition, Cicero expresses the desire to buy property, which will literally keep him in the public view.[45] Vitruvius, too, "directly associates the use, size, decoration, and form of a house with the status of the resident."[46] So then buildings, both public and private, were used to gain popularity and notoriety in Rome.

Buildings and other public works, the naming of the structures, and inscriptions naming the benefactor served as a kind of history, if not public memory. For example, Suetonius says in introducing Augustus's family, of which little was known: "There are many indications that the Octavian family was in the days of old a distinguished one at Velitrae; for not only was a street in the most frequented part of town long ago called Octavian, but an altar was shown there besides, consecrated to an Octavius."[47] Besides public works being rather generally associated with social standing, buildings could also be tied to specific events. For example, Suetonius associates the Temple of Mars with Augustus's victory at the battle of Philippi. He says of Augustus, "He had made a vow to build a temple of Mars in the war of Philippi, which he undertook to avenge his father; accordingly he decreed that in it the senate should consider wars and claims for triumphs."[48] So then, the Temple of Mars was linked to the memory of Augustus's battle at Philippi, both by the event it was meant to commemorate as well as by use.

The Visual in Oratorical Practice

Certainly public building projects in Rome have a long history independent of rhetoric and were often meant to do little more than gain notoriety or popularity for the sponsors; however, there is overlap between the two traditions. As is well attested, the harnessing of memory or meaning in a structure was common practice by rhetors, particularly through the use of gesturing. Gregory Aldrete specifically addresses the role of gestures in the principate, arguing that "buildings and spaces themselves that formed the background or setting" and that "were often loaded with symbolic meaning or powerful associations" became part of the speech through the orator's gestures.[49] Specifically referencing Augustan structures, Aldrete mentions that the Curia Julia and the *clipeus virtutis* (shield of virtues) would have provided two such visual reference points available to speakers in the Senate.[50]

Ann Vasaly discusses the same phenomenon: orators, specifically Cicero, often gestured to structures to recall the meaning imbued in edifices for rhetorical purposes. However, Vasaly's work shows that orators often did more than just gesture. Vasaly argues that Cicero, for example, chose to stage his first *Catilinarian* in the temple of Jupiter Stator. The setting allowed the orator to harness the emotional impact of the myth of the temple's construction through an extended parallel argument comparing Cicero to Rome's mythic founder Romulus and Catiline to the Sabines, an outside threat to the city of Rome. Later, when he could not find dramatic enough setting for his third *Catilinarian*, Cicero constructed one himself.[51]

Building on the work of Aldrete and Vasaly, I would suggest that nontraditional rhetorical media, specifically in the form of buildings and monuments, played an important role for orators, functioning as a repository of public memory that they could gesture to in both the late republic and the principate. Significantly, it is possible to extend Vasaly's account and to argue that such structures were useful not only for emotional impact, as in the case of Cicero's first *Catilinarian*, but also as a starting point, literally a locus, for creating a parallel argument. This has important implications for understanding the rhetorical significance of the Augustan cultural campaigns, which, in addition to having possibly been influenced by rhetorical theory and practice, may have also in turn influenced rhetorical invention. Augustan structures carried a certain legitimacy, both because of the process required by Roman law in order to build and because of their nature as visual and material media that affected audiences in an immediate way that words alone could not. These monuments gave Romans a shared rhetorical vocabulary from which they could efficaciously draw and which would be immediately intelligible to their interlocutors.

Not surprisingly, none of the oratorical practices described by Aldrete and Vasaly are mentioned in rhetorical theory, which is not to say they were not rhetorical; however, Vasaly has suggested that "the Greek-derived structure of Latin rhetorical treatises would have made it difficult to provide an adequate theoretical description of technique."[52] Or more simply, Roman rhetorical theory did not keep pace with practice. Either way, it is clear that understanding the relationship between the visual and rhetorical practices in Greek rhetorical theory is inadequate for understanding the same relationship in Rome.

Memory and the Roman People

While the works of Aldrete and Vasaly shows that orators used the visual and material for emotional impact, several other important connections can be made between systems of memory and the urban environment in Rome. First, systems of memory, though traditionally used by an orator as a memory device to retain a speech, were turned outward in the late republic and principate. This suggests that audiences possessed the knowledge to construct narratives from their environment and, in considering the Augustan cultural campaigns, that Rome, as a city of marble, was rhetorically constructed.

Citing one more brief example, Vasaly argues that Cicero turned the system of memory outward to help his audience remember his speech when he described objects stolen by the provincial governor Verres. She describes the strategy as follows: "Cicero may well have understood that the mnemonic techniques by which he impressed ideas on his own mind could be employed to impress concepts on the minds of his listeners."[53] In other words, in addition to helping orators remember their speeches, the mnemonic system could also serve as an organizational means made apparent to the audience for the sake of improving retention of an orator's argument. Tacitus reminds us that even those Romans who were not exposed to a rhetorical education were becoming more rhetorically savvy, suggesting that it is possible Roman audiences were familiar with the mnemonic system.[54]

This familiarity likely influenced the way Romans experienced the visual and their built environment. Vasaly claims, "ancient, nonliterate society may well have possessed powers of pictorial visualization much greater and more intense than our own."[55] While this visual culture may have made rhetorical techniques like *enargeia* or *phantasia* as well as the oratorical practices of gesturing to and/ or manipulating the surroundings particularly effective, a familiarity with the mnemonic system may also have shaped the way Romans experienced the Augustan cultural campaigns. Favro argues that "as an aid in the memorization of long speeches, teachers of rhetoric instructed orators to fashion environments (loci) in their minds and to stock them with memorable objects (*imagines*) representing various concepts. . . . Familiar with this mnemonic system, learned Romans were predisposed to look for an underlying, coherent narrative in built environments."[56]

Favro, who discusses the architectural and spatial features of the Augustan building program, argues that systems of memory influenced both those who might view urban environments as well as those who constructed them. She makes a case that, because teachers of rhetoric recommended "*imagines,*" that is, the objects with which one associated the heads of speech, "that were unusual in scale, color, or form," it is not coincidental that the Augustan building program sought to create such places.[57] Ultimately, Favro provocatively links techniques of memory found in Roman rhetorical theory to Augustus's building program, suggesting the city was designed to evoke a specifically Augustan narrative of its history and that the people of Rome could decipher such a narrative.[58]

The works of Aldrete, Vasaly, and Favro make important connections among rhetorical theories, particularly the mnemonic systems, oratory as practiced by Roman rhetoricians, and building projects. They suggest four basic premises that underlie arguments to the effect that nontraditional rhetorical media figured as rhetoric in Rome. First, rhetors were in the practice of not only using but also manipulating their environments in order to utilize either the memory of a place or object. This allowed rhetors the use of an emotion associated with a structure or the possibility of assigning a (new) meaning to that structure as part of the rhetorical act. Second, the same structure or object could function as a repository for memory, meaning, or emotion that shaped the process of invention for the rhetor. Third, Roman audiences' familiarity with the mnemonic system predisposed them to look for visual narratives in the built environment. Fourth, theoretically, mnemonic systems influenced the construction of the Augustan building program with the end goal of producing a rhetorically significant cityscape. These four basic premises form what I believe to be the most convincing way to begin to argue that the Augustan cultural campaigns, consisting predominantly of visual and material media, did function rhetorically in the principate and were consciously used by Augustus's administration not merely for the sake of delighting or moving audiences but also for the purpose of instructing them as to how to conceive of the principate and how to participate as citizens in the new Roman empire.

THE THEORETICAL CURRENT that moves through rhetorical treatises, to oratorical practice, and eventually into the construction of the Augustan cityscape makes it possible to theorize the city of marble as a rhetorical text. Broadening the definition of what counts as a rhetorical artifact in the late republic and early empire answers the call for a "rhetorical archaeology" that seeks out new primary texts in the classical period.[59] Such "texts," in the form of visual and material artifacts, have a great deal to tell scholars of rhetoric about how the people of Rome—that is, the plebeians, freedmen, slaves, and other urban dwellers who did not compose oratory experienced and participated in the Roman state.

In Rome a very small percentage of the populace was literate, and political offices were reserved for a select few men from a very select few families. And though Tacitus reports that the people were becoming more rhetorically savvy—and by this he seems to mean that they started to demand an ornate or polished style—rhetorical education in the early empire was still accessible to men of a certain class only.[60] When it comes to production of texts, at least in the principate, visual and material artifacts offer a much more inclusive source for understanding the communication between the state and the people.

Understanding Roman rhetorical theory and practice as something inherently visual and material opens the door for examining a wider range of legitimate rhetorical artifacts in the principate—the products of the Augustan cultural campaigns as well as media created by the people of Rome in response to the principate. Examining such artifacts fills an important void in both the history of rhetoric and in thinking about the relationship between the *princeps* and the people in this period. If scholars of rhetoric are interested in the relationship between the government and the people and in the question of how decisions were made in the early Roman empire, scholarship must focus on the rhetorical materials that were most accessible to the people—visual and material artifacts.

Examining visual and material artifacts from a rhetorical perspective allows for a more nuanced understanding of rhetorical practices in Rome and of the kind of exchange that took place between Augustus's administration and the Roman people. One reason (of several) scholars suggest that Augustus's reign was so overbearing—thus allowing it to get by without recourse to rhetorical means of influence or rhetorical audiences—is the uniformity of everything Augustan. As Paul Zanker says, "It is astonishing how every kind of visual communication came to reflect the new order, how every theme and slogan became interwoven."[61] By recognizing Augustus's city of marble and the larger cultural campaigns as a rhetorical text, however, scholars are in a unique position to uncover the interplay of dominant and popular rhetorics and to show how rhetorical techniques like imitation were used and how the end result of Augustus's reign systematizes public memory. In other words, what at first appears uniform is actually a subtle give and take, even an exchange, between a rhetorical program on the part of Augustus's administration and the people that continues to systemize responses, including those of scholars. This understanding of Augustus's reign challenges both the assumption that Augustus had no need of rhetoric and that there were no rhetorical audiences in the principate while also opening the door to many new primary texts.

3

THE AUGUSTAN POLITICAL MYTH

Augustus is remembered as a number of things—as a boy of nineteen who was named as Julius Caesar's successor; as a general who marched on Rome not once, but twice; as a youth who inspired disdain from Cicero; as a victor over Antonius and Cleopatra; as a patron of the arts whose sponsorship led to the "Golden Age" of Roman poetry and literature; and finally as a beloved ruler, religious leader, and "father of his country" who "found [Rome] . . . built of brick and left it in marble."[1] Though Augustus, then called Octavius, was introduced to public life at age twelve when he delivered a funeral oration for his grandmother, and though he continued to practice public oratory throughout his life, the one thing Augustus is not remembered as is a great orator.[2] Still, George Kennedy labels Augustus "the greatest rhetorician of antiquity" and describes the Ara Pacis Augustae as a significant form of Augustan rhetoric.[3] And there is no more apt starting point for an exploration of Augustan rhetoric than the Ara Pacis.

The Ara Pacis, commissioned in 13 B.C.E. by the Senate and Roman people upon Augustus's return from a successful campaign in Spain and Gaul, took the place of the usual triumphal procession.[4] In his *Res Gestae,* a self-authored list of Augustus's accomplishments, which stood near the Ara Pacis, Augustus places a great deal of importance on the altar referred to here as "an altar of Pax Augusta": "When I returned from Spain and Gaul, in the consulship of Tiberius Nero and Publius Quintilius, after successful operations in those provinces, the senate voted in honour of my return the consecration of an altar to Pax Augusta in the Campus Martius, and on this altar it ordered the magistrates and priests and Vestal virgins to make annual sacrifice."[5] As Augustus indicates, the Ara

Pacis was a celebration of his own military success, but it also functioned to garner support for the Julian line and for Augustus's successor. This second function follows an established and widespread state-sponsored campaign to create a political myth connecting the Julian line and hereditary succession with the prosperity of Rome.[6]

The Ara Pacis is the most complete illustration of the Augustan political myth in verbal or visual form, making it a significant, if not the most significant, rhetorical artifact of the principate. One possible reading of the Ara Pacis is as a narrative construction of the political myth, emphasizing the ways in which classical rhetorical techniques are at work in the iconography of the altar. Such a reading forms a bridge between theory and practice, moving toward an understanding of rhetoric in Rome as an integrated verbal, visual, and material practice.

In reading the Ara Pacis, other similar messages from verbal media of the same period should be included. The goal is not to suggest that verbal and visual communication work in the same way, but rather to supply the critical cultural knowledge necessary to "read" the altar, while also showing the similarity of messages across state-sponsored media in the principate. This methodology is, of course, problematic in assuming that an "ordinary" Roman had access to, let alone an understanding of, the literary sources referenced here. It is inadequate to argue that the themes in literary sources were widely circulating, though they were; ultimately it is impossible to know the subject position of any Roman. Still, literary sources offer the least ambiguous point of entry for contemporary scholars in understanding Augustan visual rhetoric.

A reading of the Ara Pacis can also serve as a starting point for understanding how the Augustan cultural campaigns, particularly the building program, formed an official account of Augustus's reign that gave the viewer a great deal of agency. The Ara Pacis clearly establishes the political myth of Augustus in state-sponsored form and perhaps served as an inventional *locus* of sorts for the construction of popular discourse, verbal and visual. The altar was a key piece of Augustan visual rhetoric because popular media drew from official iconography, thereby reiterating state-sponsored messages, shaping the public memory of the principate, and ultimately reifying Augustus's account of events.

THE ARA PACIS AUGUSTAE

History

The Ara Pacis would have originally been situated in the *Campus Martius* near the *Via Flaminia* and Augustus's mausoleum in a park-like setting, which featured a large sundial with an obelisk at the center. The Ara Pacis, constructed of white Luna marble from northern Italy, consists of the altar proper and an enclosure wall, which is carved inside and out (see fig. 1). Two of the friezes on

1. Ara Pacis Augustae, 13-9 B.C.E. From the front. Roma, Museo dell' Ara Pacis.
Photo: Kopperman, Neg. D-DAI-Rom 66.103.

the outside of the enclosure wall show long religious processions. The southern frieze features images of attendants, Augustus, priests of the four state cults,
Agrippa (who was Augustus's son-in-law, close friend, general, and designated
successor but died during the construction of the altar), and the imperial family. The frieze on the northern wall features the senators and their families. It is
unclear whether the friezes depict the same religious procession in two parts or
two separate events, an actual event, or an idealized procession.

The outer wall also has four individual mythological scenes. The first on the
west wall features Aeneas with his son and the mythic white sow making a sacrifice to his household gods (see fig. 2). The other panel features Mars presumably
at the *Lupercal,* the wolf's cave where Romulus and Remus were nursed (see fig.
3). Both of the scenes refer to the mythical founding of Rome and the lineage of
the Roman people, as well as the Julian line. The east friezes, those most visible
from the road and therefore debatably the most important, feature two female
goddesses. The first is *Roma* seated between *Honos* and *Virtus* (see fig. 5). The
other much-debated scene depicts a female figure that I will refer to as *Tellus* (see
fig. 6). This goddess's iconography is extremely complicated and vague, allowing for multiple readings.[7] The six friezes described above are set over a vegetal
motif with various animals. The narrative begins on the west wall in mythic time
with the founding myths of the city. It then progresses to the present at the point

in time when the altar was dedicated, and then shifts into the mythic present/ future, showing the abundance brought to the people of Rome by Augustus with the gods' favor.

The Ara Pacis, while the high point of Augustan art, was not particularly inventive. Many scholars have discussed the style and antecedents of the Ara Pacis in sculpture, such as the Shrine of Janus Geminus, the Athenian Altar of Pity, and the Sanctuary of Athena in Pergamon.[8] It is worth noting that, though some privileged Romans and possibly even the sculptors who made the Ara Pacis might have seen the monuments that art historians have argued influenced its production, they were not accessible to most Romans. Only the Republican Shrine of Janus Geminus would likely have been seen by the average Roman. Finally, though the style of the friezes on the Ara Pacis is potentially of interest for scholars of rhetoric particularly because, as art historian Tonio Holscher has argued, there seems to be a connection between style in classical rhetorical treatises and style in classical art, the use of certain styles with particular subject matter had solidified by the principate.[9]

Though the sculptors of the Ara Pacis have never been identified, it is clear that they were not only the best sculptors in Rome, but the best sculptors in the Roman empire. Art historian Donald Strong argues that Agrippa was largely responsible for finding artists on his trips east as well as for overseeing the construction of the altar.[10] Therefore, though a concept similar to manifest destiny is depicted in the subject matter on the altar, the aesthetic quality of the altar offers an argument in and of itself. Rome now had access to the best artists in the world, capable of producing the most beautiful work, suggesting Rome's role as ruler of the world and everything in it. Augustus's involvement in the design of the monument is ultimately unknown, though it is likely he had a hand in many, if not all, of the major projects of the period.

Though the quality of the art work on the Ara Pacis was exceptional for the period, the themes and style of the altar were not.[11] It is true the Augustan building program did little that had not been done before; however, the mass, scale, and sheer repetition in virtually every medium, verbal and visual, of Augustus's cultural program was startlingly new, at least in the Roman world.[12] While it is in many ways representative of art of the period and the general themes of the Augustan cultural programs generally, the Ara Pacis is the most complete example of the Augustan political myth in state-sponsored media. This myth was disseminated over and over again in literature and poetry, in abbreviated form on coins and sculpture, and was imitated in popular media. By focusing on the altar, it is possible to begin to discern how the political myth was constructed. The altar, then, offers one way to begin to understand the circulation of state-sponsored or official iconography and the construction of the memory of Augustus's reign.

The Founding Myths

The narration of the Augustan political myth begins with the two mythic scenes on the west wall, which recount the founding of Rome. While the Roman people would likely have known both the myth of Romulus and Remus as suggested by the Mars scene and the myth of Aeneas, a new version of the Aeneas myth, written by Virgil, was circulating after 19 B.C.E. and was meant to draw as many similarities between the hero and Augustus as possible.[13] In addition to introducing the mythic history of the city of Rome, the Aeneas and Mars scenes also introduce the mythic lineage of the Julian line from which Augustus was descended. In utilizing these myths, Augustus uses the past to legitimize the present by depicting himself as the fulfillment of a divine plan, but Augustus also shows that he is ultimately constrained by the republic, the custom of his ancestors, and the collective beliefs of the Roman people.

The two scenes of Mars and Aeneas function to introduce Augustus's mythic genealogy while also serving as the traditional starting point for a panegyric speech. The author of the *Rhetorica ad Herennium* writes that an orator should consider the "external circumstances" of the subject including "the ancestors of whom he is sprung [and] if he is of illustrious decent."[14] Quintilian similarly suggests a speech of praise should include the ancestry of the subject.[15] Though the altar can be read as an encomium of Augustus, it is also important to note that the mythic scenes celebrate not only Augustus but also the Roman people, who play a large part in the success of the principate.[16] As classical historian Walter Eder notes, "Augustus wished to create a mythology of the state more than a mythos of a ruler."[17]

While the Roman people may not have literally believed the founding myths, the myths did invoke a sense of pride, and the people "were able to feel emotionally excited about the traditional stories of the gods."[18] Cicero, and possibly by extension other elites, found the religious practices of the masses "superstitious" but also took great pride in participating in state religion, in part because of the honor involved.[19] Cicero's stance suggests not only the belief of the masses in the gods and the effectiveness of using mythic iconography as the basis of argument targeting mass audiences, especially of urban plebs, but also that the appeal of religious iconography extended beyond the plebs to the Roman elite, though for different reasons.[20]

Though stylistic conventions had largely solidified by the time of the principate, art historian Tonio Holscher calls attention to the Aeneas scene as typifying the conventions of the period. He notes that the backdrop uses the Hellenistic style, meant to convey emotion or drama, while Aeneas is shown in the classical style to give him dignity.[21] The use of the classical style in depicting Aeneas also allows for greater comparison with Augustus because, as Holscher notes, mythic subjects were usually depicted in the Hellenistic style while the ethos necessary for Roman statesmen demanded the classical style.[22] The artistic convention of using the Hellenistic style again emphasizes the emotion such scenes could convey to the audience while depicting Aeneas in the classical style highlights the comparison between Augustus and Aeneas.

The narrative of the Ara Pacis, then, begins on a note of common ground with almost all of the Roman people, which would have invoked feelings of pride, heritage, and patriotism. If the altar is read in this manner, the two mythic scenes function analogously to the exordium, which according to Cicero "brings the mind of the auditor into a proper condition to receive the rest of the speech" and which Quintilian says is for "making the audience well-disposed, attentive and ready to receive instruction."[23] Cicero defines five types of audiences and two approaches for the exordium, the "introduction" and "insinuation." He defines the latter as "an address by dissimulation and indirection [which] unobtrusively steals into the mind of the auditor," reserving this type of introduction for the "difficult case" when the audience is "violently opposed."[24] Augustus's Ara Pacis, therefore, begins on a note to draw in those opposed to Augustus's rule as well as on a note of interest for all, including the less politically inclined. This rhetorical technique suggests that Augustus faced a mixed audience of hostile elites and more neutral nonpolitical equestrians and plebeians who did not fully accept his rule or the idea of dynastic succession.

The Aeneas scene, like all images on the altar, contains a variety of elements that would allow various readings, depending on the audience (see fig. 2). The scene depicts Aeneas, surviving hero of the Trojan War, sacrificing to his household gods. Accompanying Aeneas is his son Julus-Ascanius, founder of the Julian line, as well as two attendants, one with fruit, the other with a sow. The sow conjures up two possible myths: that of the sow sacrificed as thanks to his household gods for escaping Troy and that of the sow with the thirty piglets that served as the omen to signal Aeneas where to settle.[25] The prophecy of the sow is delivered to Aeneas in Virgil's *Aeneid:* "When in your distress, by the waters of a secluded stream, you find a sow lying under the oaks on the shore, just delivered of a litter of thirty young, a white mother reclining on the ground, and white young at her teats—there shall be the city's site, there a sure rest from your toils. And fear not the gnawing of tables that await you; the Fates will find a way, and Apollo be present at your call."[26] In recalling the sow as a sign from the gods, the viewer would likely recall the gods' favor in the founding of Rome and the Julian family's connection with Venus. In addition, there is an explicit reference to the piety of Aeneas, which will be continued by his son and eventually by Augustus.

The household gods depicted in the Aeneas scene would have had a wealth of meaning for the people of Rome. Aeneas made the sacrifice to his household gods when he came to the city of Rome, which was a homecoming of sorts.

2. Ara Pacis Augustae, Aeneas scene. Roma, Museo dell' Ara Pacis.
Photograph, Kathleen Lamp.

Augustus's return from campaign was a similar homecoming, inviting identification between the two men.[27] This comparison between Augustus and Aeneas falls under the definition of "amplification" as explained by Aristotle. Aristotle gives many examples of amplification, including "making comparison with famous people; for the subject is amplified and made honorable if he is better than [other] worthy ones."[28] Quintilian, too, discusses techniques of amplification: "one thing may be magnified by allusion to another: the valour of Scipio is magnified by extolling the fame of Hannibal as a general."[29] Scipio's defeat of Hannibal is made more impressive because the rhetor builds up Hannibal's achievements. On the Ara Pacis both techniques are used. Augustus is compared directly to his famous ancestor, but the deeds of Aeneas are also magnified to heighten Augustus's accomplishment of similar feats.

The Aeneas scene, compared with the depiction of Augustus, invites a direct identification of Augustus with his mythic ancestor. Here Aeneas is depicted as he is in Virgil's *Aeneid,* not as a young man fleeing Troy with his son and father in tow, but as the older, mature, and pious Aeneas.[30] Both men are pictured with their togas drawn over their heads, another sign of reverence, in the act of sacrifice (compare figs. 2 and 4).[31] In addition, both men are shown in relation to family members, meant to conjure the idea of familial lines or familial succession specifically related to the Julian line.[32]

In comparing the two men, a Roman viewer might be invited to consider other similarities as drawn out in the *Aeneid* and to see both men as "executor of a divine mission; administrator of the nation's interests; facing irresponsible, godless, and criminal factionalism—these are features shared by the founder of the Julian race . . . and by his descendant."[33] Perhaps the most important theme in the Aeneas scene is the notion of fate or manifest destiny. Virgil's *Aeneid* describes the concept of fate that extends from Aeneas's arrival in Rome to Augustus's role in expanding the empire: "Turn hither now your two-eyes gaze, and behold this nation, the Romans that are yours. Here is Caesar and all the seed of Iulus destined to pass under heaven's spacious sphere. And this in truth is he whom you so often hear promised you, Augustus Caesar, son of a god, who will again establish a golden age in Latium amid fields once ruled by Saturn; he will advance his empire beyond the Garamants and Indians to a land which lies beyond our stars, beyond the path of year and sun, where sky-bearing Atlas wheels on his shoulders the blazing star-studded sphere."[34] This passage, the basis of the narrative on the Ara Pacis, establishes the Augustan political myth and the idea that Augustus's rule and the conquests of the Roman empire were fated from the moment Aeneas set out from Troy to found Rome.

The Ara Pacis invites comparison not only between Augustus and Aeneas but between Augustus and Romulus. The Mars scene suggests the heritage of the Roman people in the form of the myth of Romulus and Remus.[35] The scene depicts Mars at the *Lupercal,* the wolf's cave, where Romulus and Remus were suckled after being abandoned by their uncle Amulius, who was attempting to avoid the prophecy that one of the boys would overthrow him. Hannestad notes that in the processional scene on the South wall under Augustus's right hand is not an altar, as usually interpreted, but instead a *lituus,* or an augury tool. If this is the case, the iconography would again identify Augustus with Romulus as the *lituus* was the insignia of rulers, including Romulus.[36] In addition, Romulus was used by Augustus as a herald of a new age in other iconography, particularly on coins, as "the animating force that informs" the new age.[37]

While the Mars scene serves as the pedigree to the Roman people and as an invitation to identify Augustus with Romulus, the image also serves to illustrate the military strength necessary for Augustan peace. Perhaps surprisingly on an altar dedicated in place of a triumphal procession, there are only two references to war, one considerably vaguer than the other. The presence of Mars on the altar supports the concept that Augustus has regained the gods' favor and thus Rome has had success in battle leading to prosperity. The combination of Mars and Romulus also suggests the violence involved in the founding of the city. Commenting on its founding by Romulus, which resulted in his brother

3. Ara Pacis Augustae, Mars scene. Roma, Museo dell' Ara Pacis.
Photograph, Kathleen Lamp.

Remus's death, Harris and Platzner observe, "The city was thus named *Rome—* conceived in the policy of aggressive expansion enforced by violence and all part of a divine plan for the establishment of Rome."[38] Just as violence was required in the founding of the city by Romulus, Augustus had acted in a violent and bloodthirsty manner in the past.[39]

The scene also suggests a parallel between the divine plan for Romulus and the necessity for Rome to regain its position at the center of the world under Augustus. Ovid makes mention of these deeds in the context of Augustus's fated mission near the end of the *Metamorphoses*: "He as successor to the name shall bear alone the burden placed on him, and, as the most valliant avenger of his father's murder, he shall have us as ally for his wars. Under his command the conquered walls of leaguered Mutina shall sue for peace; Pharsalia shall feel his power; Emanthia Philippi shall reek again with blood; and he of the great name shall overcome on Sicilian waters . . . . Nay, whatsoever habitable land the earth contains shall be his, and the sea also shall come beneath his sway!"[40] Ovid goes on to mention Philippi, Actium, and Augustus's other campaigns against "barbarian lands," all as actions necessary to fulfill his fate. The civil wars, the proscriptions which accompanied the Triumvirate, and the settlement of soldiers on seized land all associated with the campaigns mentioned by Ovid must have remained controversial aspects of Augustus's reign. After all, Tacitus says of the period after Actium "there certainly had been peace but it was a blood-stained peace."[41] On the Ara Pacis, unlike in Ovid's *Metamorphoses*, the viewer would have to supply this knowledge and fill in the premise that these events were part of Augustus's fate and therefore beyond his control. The Ara Pacis does not depict Augustus's warlord-like acts, but the narrative could justify them through mythic history and a powerful comparison to Romulus.

The mythic scenes could serve to launch the narrative on the Ara Pacis by recalling the founding myth in the minds of the Roman people. Rhetorically, this would be an extremely convincing way to gain common ground with a Roman audience, as the founding myth held shared cultural value. The scenes also permit Augustus to invite comparisons among himself, Aeneas, and Romulus by Roman audiences. In addition, the founding myths portray the pedigrees of Augustus and the Julian line, a standard beginning in epideictic rhetoric. The myths allow Augustus to introduce the themes of fate, piety, and violence legitimized in the mythic and collective history of the Roman people. The narrative on the Ara Pacis begins in mythic time and suggests the ancestors of Augustus founded the city with the gods' favor.

A Missing Scene

Just as Roman viewers would have been able to fill out the Mars and Aeneas scenes with their knowledge of myth, they would also have to fill in Augustus's argument on the Ara Pacis through enthymematic reasoning. While Augustus depicts his rule in the most positive light only, the narrative often justifies the less pleasant events the Roman people have suffered through during Augustus's rise to power. Just as the viewer can connect the violence of the civil wars and Augustus's foreign campaigns to Romulus's deeds in founding the city, the viewer is invited to think of the city before Augustus's reign.

Although the narrative on the altar moves directly from mythic time to the depiction of the religious procession in Augustan Rome, the scene of Augustus's and the senators' piety invites the viewer to think of the neglect of the gods prior to Augustus's religious reforms. While Ogilvie makes a case that the Roman people never abandoned their religious beliefs, he describes the late republic as a place where "many temples had fallen into decay and many priesthoods were left unfilled."[42] Moreover, Ogilvie suggests that the people likely associated the hardship they experienced during the late republic and the civil wars as related to their "neglect of religion."[43] Horace captures this sentiment well: "Though guiltless, you will continue to pay for the sins of your forefathers, until you repair the crumbling temples and shrines of the gods, and the statues that are begrimed with black smoke. It is because you hold yourselves inferior to the gods that you rule. For every beginning seek their approval; to them attribute its outcome. Because they have been neglected, the gods have inflicted many a woe on sorrowing Westland."[44] The Ara Pacis invites the Roman people to blame themselves for their hardships while depicting Augustus as responsible for the return of the gods' favor.

The altar implies this enthymematic argument by showing the four priests of the state cult, including *flamen Dialis,* or the priest of Jupiter, a position a Roman viewer would likely have known had stood vacant for seventy-five years because of its difficult and unpleasant requirements before Augustus found someone to fill it.[45] The depiction of the *flamen Dialis* along with the illustration of Augustus's own piety, shown as comparable to that of Aeneas's, encourage viewers to question if they had neglected the gods while at the same time drawing them into Augustus's religious reforms, which in turn served to garner support for his rule, his family, and his successor. The similarities between Aeneas and Augustus depicted on the Ara Pacis not only glorify Augustus but also emphasize both as models of piety worthy of imitation for the Roman people who have neglected their gods. The importance of imitation in rhetorical education is stressed by Quintilian; that is, the imitation not just of exemplary texts but also of individuals, as the most important method of learning, which is accomplished best by praising famous men and their best traits. For Quintilian, a paradigm, a speech, or even a person could form the exemplar for imitation.[46]

On the Ara Pacis, Augustus's deeds can easily be compared to Aeneas's own through amplification, but in addition, Augustus also imitates the piety of his ancestor and invites the Roman people to imitate both men's behavior. Augustus, throughout his rule, used the strategy of imitation so frequently as to suggest the use was conscious. Suetonius recounts that Augustus, who wanted the people to return to traditional Roman dress, would himself wear this clothing and berate those who did not.[47] Dio recounts a similar instance: Augustus, when speaking to a group of equestrians who had failed to marry and procreate in accordance with the Julian law, held his own adopted sons, thus modeling the behavior he wished the men to emulate.[48] As Paul Zanker notes, "Augustus offered himself as the greatest *exemplum* and tried in his private life and public appearance to be a constant advertisement for the *mores maiorum* [the custom of the Roman ancestors]."[49] The Ara Pacis, then, through imitation instructs the people of Rome as to how they should behave in order to maintain the gods' favor. It is perhaps not surprising that the Roman people began to imitate the piety of Augustus in popular art.

The Procession: Augustus, the Imperial Family, the Senate, and State Religion. The altar's north and south walls feature the procession of the four state priests, Augustus, the imperial family, and the senators and their families. While the narrative of the altar starts in mythic time, the processional scenes move to Augustan Rome. Augustus is depicted with his toga pulled over his head but also wearing a laurel crown, mixing the symbols of piety and triumph (see fig. 4).[50]

4. Ara Pacis Augustae, Augustus. Detail from south frieze.
Roma, Museo dell' Ara Pacis.
Photograph, Sansiani, Neg. D-DAI-Rom 57.883.

This indirect reference to war suggests that Augustus's campaigns were fated and supported through his piety. In addition, the death of Lepidus in 12 B.C.E. left the office of *pontifex maximus,* chief priest, open for Augustus, making Augustus's piety appropriate to his new office.

Augustus, as *pontifex maximus,* took on the responsibility of mediating the people's relationship with the gods because, as Ogilvie notes, the role of determining the gods' will and seeking their approval was the responsibility of state religion.[51] Similarly, art historian David Castriota notes that the role of the king in ancient non-Roman art was "to secure or mediate these divine blessings."[52] Castriota goes on to say that the Greeks "specifically appropriated the concept of the major deity as progenitor and protector of the royal dynasty and the king as earthly counterpart or executive."[53] It seems that, while the notion of theocracy was decidedly un-Roman, the depiction of Augustus on the Ara Pacis dabbles with such imagery, albeit adapted to the constraints of Roman tradition.

The depiction of the senators and their families on the north frieze of the Ara Pacis *Augustae* can be explained in a number of ways. The iconography strives to show that Augustus has not altered the constitutional structure of the Roman republic. As classicist Christian Meier argues, "Augustus could only defeat the Republic thoroughly and definitively by restoring it," and so in the Ara Pacis, the senators function to legitimize Augustus's rule.[54]

The depiction of the Senate might also bring to mind the second *lectio senatus,* which Augustus initiated in 18 B.C.E. Augustus's intent was to purge the Senate and leave it with three hundred members; however, the senators' resistance left Augustus wearing armor under his toga, and in the end, he relented, settling on leaving six hundred members instead.[55] Eder argues that this concession restored the Senate to a place of prominence, and while the Senate lost some of its former power, Augustus did pass several laws, including one that gave the Senate's decision the power of law.[56] The depiction of the Senate on the Ara Pacis shows both that Augustus continued to rule in a constitutional manner and that Augustus was honored by the Senate and the Roman people by the construction of the altar and ruled at their request.

Children are depicted prominently on the north and south friezes of the Ara Pacis. The children in the senatorial frieze suggest two possible arguments. First, they establish that the qualification for the Senate has traditionally been familial, since "the whole structure of Roman aristocratic society was dynastic" in the republic.[57] A Roman audience might also connect familial succession to the idea that *auctoritas,* roughly translated as "authority," could be handed down in republican families.[58] With these depictions, the altar roots the concept of succession in republican custom.

Second, the children on the altar suggest the moral reforms legislated by Augustus such as the *lex Iulia de maritandis ordinibus* and the *lex Iulia de adulteriis coercendis* of 18 B.C.E., which offered incentives for procreation, promoted marriage, punished adultery, and were meant to keep the population of nobles higher than the numbers of freed slaves.[59] Thus, the Ara Pacis was not targeting just plebian or illiterate audiences, a claim that largely dismisses the importance of visual communication, to whom these laws would have had few ramifications but instead suggests that different messages on the Ara Pacis were focused at specific audiences. In the case of the children, the altar targets the upper classes, specifically equestrian men, particularly those who subscribed to Stoicism or Epicureanism, systems of belief that discouraged marriage and procreation and were thus in direct conflict with Augustan moral reforms.

Dio puts a speech in the mouth of Augustus that both supports this reading and makes connections between the founding myths and the Julian Laws. Dio claims that in 9 C.E. Augustus made a speech to the equestrians on the importance of marrying and having children. Though this speech is most likely a work of fiction by Dio, it nevertheless suggests both the importance of the issue to Augustus and the way that the founding myth served as an inventional resource: "Try to imagine, then, the anger which the great Romulus, the founder of our race, would rightly feel, if he were to recall the circumstances in which he himself was born and could compare with your situation, in which you refuse to beget children even in lawful wedlock. Would it not enrage the Romans who were his followers, if they knew that after they had gone so far as to carry off foreign girls, you by contrast have no feeling even for those of your own race, and that after they had engendered children by the women of an enemy country, you refuse to beget them even by women who are your fellow-citizens?"[60] On the Ara Pacis, we see the couching of a political necessity, that of maintaining the ruling class, against the social reality that threatened the longevity of the Roman elite.

Augustus's own "obsession with the matter of succession" began, according to Diana Kleiner, during his prolonged ill health "in the second half of the 20s B.C."[61] While succession certainly is a theme expressed on the Ara Pacis, it becomes more apparent if we consider the altar *in situ.* Other monuments surrounding the Ara Pacis in the *Campus Martius* included the Augustan sundial with an obelisk at the center as well as the mausoleum and the *ustrinum,* the location for the funeral pyre. Hannestad says the area contained "a great many portents concerning the child Octavian associated with the sun, maintaining that a direct line led from the birth of the *princeps,* via victory and world domination, to Pax, with promises of a future deification symbolized by the mausoleum and the ustrinum."[62] The same themes of succession and world domination, which arise out of the narrative, are reinforced by the setting of the Ara Pacis.

The processional scenes render the purpose of the Ara Pacis Augustae most starkly; the altar has established the right of succession and inherited *auctoritas* by inclusion of the senatorial families on the south frieze. A parallel argument is made on the north frieze concerning succession. Whereas Romulus serves to announce the Golden Age, Augustus is shown as enacting the qualities necessary to bring about the Golden Age. A clear theme on the altar is that sustained prosperity depends on the continued rule of the "male progeny" of the Julian line.[63] Thus, the successor of Augustus is depicted on the Ara Pacis. At the time of the consecration this would have been Agrippa; however, he died later that year. Other possible heirs are shown on the altar as well, including Drusus, who tugs on the robe of Agrippa, and Tiberius, both of whom were the sons of Augustus's wife Livia by her first husband. Also pictured is Germanicus, the son of Augustus's niece, and possibly Gaius and Lucius, Augustus's nephews.[64]

The depiction of heirs likely stems from Augustus's own difficulties gaining power after the death of Caesar, despite Caesar's recognition of him as rightful heir. Whereas Augustus had to fight literally and figuratively for the support of the Roman people, the narrative of the Ara Pacis potentially eases this transition for Augustus's successor in what could have been a volatile period after his death. Augustus "tried to obtain for his heir a repetition of the *consensus universorum* that had marked him as the sole possessor of power."[65] Walter Eder stresses that, because Augustus gained recognition from the Senate and people for the good works of his successor, "it would have been hard for them to deny recognition after the death of Augustus to a person whom they had frequently acknowledged in their decrees to be worthy of especial honor and recognition."[66] With the death of Agrippa during construction of the altar, there was no clear successor; however, the Ara Pacis makes the possible heirs visible and connects them to the role of mediating the relationship between the people and the gods while basing the concept of succession on senatorial families of the republic.

Tellus and Roma: Prosperity and Abundance under Augustus

The narrative told on the Ara Pacis Augustae begins in the mythic past, proceeds to the Augustan present, and moves again into the mythic present/future. The two mythic scenes on the east wall would have been the most visible from the Via Flaminia, a highly traveled road, suggesting these two friezes were considered the most important and debatably the most influential on the altar.[67] Both scenes

5. Ara Pacis Augustae, Roma scene. Roma, Museo dell' Ara Pacis.
Photograph, Kathleen Lamp.

depict personified goddesses. The female figure shown on the north side represents *Roma,* and the one on the south is often referred to as *Tellus,* a mother-earth deity. *Roma* is shown seated on a pile of arms, the spoils of Augustus's campaigns (see fig. 5). Next to her should be personifications of *Honos* and *Virtus,* two Roman military virtues; however, the reconstruction is somewhat incomplete.[68]

Roma represents the only clear reference to war on the altar and conjures the concept of "manifest destiny." If we trace the concept through the narrative on the Ara Pacis, Rome was founded and populated by Aeneas and Romulus with the favor of the gods Mars and Venus and also Jupiter. Through Aeneas, the Julian line was founded, and Augustus was fated not only to rule Rome but to create a vast empire, bringing Rome to glory. Here we see it is not just Augustus's fate to rule Rome but Rome's destiny to rule the world.[69] The *Roma* scene offers the conclusion to the narrative on the Ara Pacis and to the *Aeneid.* Anchises says to his son Aeneas, "You, Roman, be sure to rule the world (be these your arts), to crown peace with justice, to spare the vanquished and to crush the proud."[70] The Ara Pacis displays Augustus's possession of the same Roman strengths as Aeneas. In addition to displaying that which would make Rome great, the *Roma* scene again offers some justification for Augustus's more bloodthirsty acts.

In the *Aeneid,* Virgil suggests that fate and piety override the will of *Aeneas,* particularly when he has to leave Dido, the mythic queen of Carthage. When Mercury encouraged Aeneas to continue on his journey at Jupiter's request, he says, "If the glory of such a fortune does not stir you, *and for your own fame's sake you do not shoulder the burden,* have regard for growing Ascanius, the promise of Iulus your heir, to whom the kingdom of Italy and the Roman land are due."[71] Augustus has fulfilled his fated destiny in making Rome triumphant over the world; however, his behavior, though at times lacking, is justified just as Aeneas's was by the more important mission demanded by the gods.

While the notion of manifest destiny might have held some pride for the Roman people, the *Tellus* scene offers the concrete benefits of Augustan peace (see fig. 6). The goddess's iconography is often disputed among scholars who alternately identify her as *Pax, Tellus, Italia,* or even Venus.[72] Although her identity remains disputed, the message is clear: Augustus has created great prosperity.[73] Horace describes the abundance of the Golden Age reminiscent of the *Tellus* scene in his *Carmen Saeculare:* "May Mother Earth, fruitful in crops and cattle / Crown Ceres' forehead with a wreath of wheat-ears / And dews and rains and breezes / God's good agents / Nourish whatever grows."[74] The goddess is shown seated holding twins, and on either side of her are personifications of breezes on land and sea. Also depicted are various animals and grain. All of the imagery conveys ideas of fertility, prosperity, and plenty.

Tacitus rather cynically suggests that "Augustus won over the soldier with gifts, the populace with cheap corn, and all men with the sweets of repose."[75] Less

6. Ara Pacis Augustae, Tellus scene. Roma, Museo dell' Ara Pacis.
Photograph, Kathleen Lamp.

cynically, Velleius Paterculus, who experienced the principate firsthand, praises Augustus for the state of prosperity his reign has created: "There is nothing that man can desire from the gods, nothing that the gods can grant to a man, nothing that wish can conceive or good fortune bring to pass, which Augustus on his return to the city did not bestow upon the Republic, the Roman people, and the world."[76] While the material benefits derived from Augustus's reign might not be considered rhetoric but more nearly bribery or as Tacitus suggests a type of coercion, on the Ara Pacis we see the material benefits of Augustus's reign used rhetorically. That is, it is not enough that Augustus has created an empire or that Rome rules the world; the Ara Pacis reminds the people that the comforts they enjoy are due to his rule and the gods' favor and that the Golden Age has arrived.

There is no doubt that, after the great hardship of the social and civil wars, the people were desperate for the stability of peace. Though perhaps exaggerating, Tacitus says of Augustus, "Then he gradually pushed ahead and absorbed the functions of the Senate, the officials, and even the law. Opposition did not exist. War or judicial murder had disposed of all men of spirit. Upper-class survivors found that slavish obedience was the only way to succeed, both politically and financially."[77] Classicist Christian Meier, lacking some of the venom Tacitus had for both Augustus and those who allowed the republic to slip away, comments, "The renewed civil war after Caesar's assassination, with its widespread suffering and stress, probably caused such an increase in the yearning for peace, security, and safety of property that a potential monarch could exploit it to his advantage and gain a following—if, that is, he could credibly present himself as the only person capable of realizing peace."[78] Exploitative or not, here the Ara Pacis claims not only that Augustus was fated by the gods to bring peace but also that only succession by a member of the Julian line could maintain the prosperity depicted in the *Tellus* scene.

The collective past that begins the altar's narrative was likely a highly effective starting point with most Roman people. These scenes establish that Aeneas and Romulus founded Rome with the favor of the gods and at their command. In addition, the scenes tie Augustus's lineage back to Aeneas and therefore to Venus while also connecting the Roman people back to Romulus. These scenes introduce the idea that Augustus's rule, Rome's place at the head of the empire, and the coming of the Golden Age were all fated. The altar then moves into the present, and Augustus is depicted similarly to Aeneas. Augustus has fulfilled his fate and through piety has restored Rome to its rightful place in the world and regained the gods' favor. In addition, the north and south friezes establish the concept of succession as a republican tradition. The processional scenes also invite the Roman people to think of the hardship they endured during the civil wars when the priesthoods where left empty and the temples abandoned. The final mythic scenes of *Tellus* and *Roma* end the narrative reminding the Roman people of Rome's supremacy and their own prosperity. The narrative as well as the surroundings, including the mausoleum, strongly suggests that the abundance brought to the people can be maintained only through continued rule of the Julian line. The Ara Pacis Augustae delivers a persuasive message about the importance of recognizing the Julian successor of Augustus.

WHILE THE EPIDEICTIC GENRE is often thought of as creating concensus, in the case of the Ara Pacis, the visual media allows for a more individualized reading, which is in keeping with Roman thinking on the genre making the visual media particularly appropriate.[79] The "display" found in the epideictic genre is twofold. First, it positions the orator and the audience in the oratorical act. Quintilian uses the word *ostentationis* to refer to the quality of display inherent in the epideictic genre, which suggests the idea that all an orator had to do was display, exhibit, or reveal an instance worthy of praise or blame to the audience, who could then use shared social knowledge to judge (the depiction of) that instance.[80] Of course, it was up to the orator to make use of that social knowledge while also using the genre to cultivate judgment. Second, the notion of "display," according to Quintilian, depends on the goal of epideictic oratory, which is to delight an audience, suggesting a freer use of ornament than in other branches of oratory.[81] The impact on these dual meanings of "display" translates quite literally on the Ara Pacis. This ornateness—the aesthetics of language—translated readily into visual beauty. That is, style in language, as Holscher argues, is not unlike style in sculpture. Also, the relationship of the audience to the orator becomes even more pronounced inasmuch as the Ara Pacis displays an ideal model of citizenship, which the people are then able to accept or reject, reforming the ideal model all the while cultivating civic judgment.

The Ara Pacis Augustae was a state-sponsored rhetorical text that sought to justify Augustus's reign and dynastic succession through the construction of a political myth targeted to a wide variety of Roman audiences while conforming to a number of constraints, including Romans' disdain for a sole ruler and dynastic succession. It was the most complete version of the Augustan political myth to be found in visual rhetoric.

This reading of the Ara Pacis suggests that classical rhetorical theories can be found operating in visual form on the Ara Pacis in a variety of ways. First, the mythic scenes function as an exordium for an audience hostile to the rhetor as well as the traditional starting point for a speech of praise. Second, the Ara Pacis demonstrates the rhetorical strategy of amplification by inviting comparison between Augustus and Aeneas as well as between Augustus and Romulus and the rhetorical strategy of imitation by showing Aeneas as the exemplum for Augustus's piety as well as Augustus as a model for the people. While amplification had a long tradition in the epideictic genre, the use of exemplars to teach style, virtue, and civic judgment was gaining new favor as Greek Atticism grew in popularity.

In addition, enthymeme is at work throughout the friezes of the Ara Pacis: first, the altar requires the viewer to construct a narrative argument from various scenes, and second, a crucial part of that narrative, the period of turmoil at the end of republic, is missing entirely and must be supplied by the audience. The function of enthymematic argument, broadly conceived, has two major implications for Roman viewing practices. First, the construction of arguments found on the Ara Pacis relies largely on the viewer. Specific readings of the iconography target certain audiences, ranging from urban plebs to Roman elites. Though the same messages abound in other media, the way these themes are shown on the Ara Pacis gives the Roman viewer a significant amount of agency in the process of constructing a narrative.[82] Second, but related, is the role of the Ara Pacis in systematizing the political myth of the Julian line. Certainly other rhetorical artifacts of the period, such as the *Aeneid,* construct a similar myth while Augustus's own *Res Gestae* offers a more "factual" account of the same events. Again, however, the Ara Pacis works differently from verbal artifacts, allowing the audience greater control over the construction of the myth. For example, while a viewer who lived through the civil wars might insert the missing scene, as I have suggested, a viewer who did not live through the civil wars might not. In other words, as a long-standing rhetorical monument, the Ara Pacis was open to various readings over time, depending on the social knowledge a viewer brought to the altar, making it a dynamic and rhetorically powerful text.

Finally, there is an important relationship between memory and the Ara Pacis. The Ara Pacis evokes the memory of the Roman people rhetorically to construct a narrative and recall the events of Augustus's reign. John Bodnar, in *Remaking America,* argues that "Public memory emerges from the intersection of official and vernacular cultural expression."[83] I would argue that the Ara Pacis precisely fits Bodnar's characterization of "official rhetoric," and while the altar cannot be read as a construction of public memory alone, it is a major official or state-sponsored text.[84] The iconography of the altar was repeated in a variety of popular media. The Ara Pacis served as a type of repository, or commonplace, for popular rhetorics wishing to depict aspects of Augustus's reign or their producers' participation in it. Taken together with the Ara Pacis, then, vernacular or popular media reiterate and reify the political myth on the altar, forming a public memory in the principate.

Ultimately it is hard to gauge how Romans reacted to the Ara Pacis, as the sources that have survived are virtually devoid of comment on the monument, short of telling us it existed and what it was meant to commemorate. In addition, the Ara Pacis was one relatively small, though impressive, part of a massive campaign in support of Augustus and his household. Augustus, the much (though not universally) beloved father of his country, died a natural death, after which he was deified. Tiberius was recognized as Augustus's successor without major conflict, though Tacitus mentions that an armed guard was necessary or at least thought to be necessary at Augustus's funeral.[85] While the success of the principate was rooted in military strength and the prosperity and stability of the people of Rome, Augustan rhetoric, as represented by the Ara Pacis, played an important role in easing ideological change and promoting support for the Julian line. Though it would be overreaching to suggest that the Ara Pacis, and by extension Augustan rhetoric, was responsible for the success of the principate, the Augustan narrative was at least in some respects persuasive to the people of Rome and reveals a great deal about the rhetorical practices of the period that remain largely misunderstood.

4

LET US NOW PRAISE GREAT MEN

The technique of imitation, as is well known, has a long history in rhetorical education. As early as the fifth century B.C.E., Isocrates stresses the importance of imitation in order to develop moral character and critical judgment. For example, he advises the ruler Nicocles to "Imitate the actions of those whose reputations you envy," but also to be an exemplar by "urg[ing] the young to virtue, not only by teaching but also by demonstrating to them how good men should behave."[1] Isocrates, however, insists that the memorializing of such an exemplar should fall to the orator and warns against using statues for such a purpose, precisely because they are poor models for imitation.[2] Isocrates explains his reasoning to Nicocles in the *Evagoras*:

> Nicocles, I think statues of bodies are fine memorials, but that images of deeds and of character are worth much more, and one can observe these only in skillfully produced speeches. I prefer these, first because I know noble men are not so much esteemed for their physical beauty as honored for their deeds and intellect. Second statues necessarily remain among those who set them up, but speeches can be conveyed throughout Greece, published in gatherings of men of good sense, and can be welcomed by those whose respect is worth more than that of all others. In addition to these things, there is the fact that no one would be able to make their own body resemble a statue or painting, but it is easy for those who wish to take the trouble and are willing to be the best to imitate the character and thoughts of others that are represented in speeches.[3]

Isocrates's preference of memorializing with speech rather than statues stems from several lines of reasoning.

No doubt Isocrates, who grew quite rich from student fees, is cordoning off a marketable and prized body of knowledge for those who can produce (and can instruct the production of) speeches such as the *Evagoras*.[4] Perhaps as well, Isocrates's occasional preference for oligarchy shows itself here, reserving models of imitation (and access to the knowledge required to rule) to those "men of good sense . . . whose respect is worth more than that of all others," no doubt a select (literate) few.[5] The problem of circulation of an exemplar is perhaps more interesting to contemporary scholars.

Still, the most interesting objection made by Isocrates to using statues as memorials is their limited use as models of imitation—that they would be ill suited for bodily imitation and do not aptly convey "character and thoughts," which should properly be the qualities imitated. This anxiety reveals an underlying concern about the formation and endurance of legacy in public memory. In other words, Isocrates does not trust the memory of a ruler's "character and thoughts" to the people but only to the writings of an orator, where they can be properly memorialized. Whether this is a result of his low opinion of the masses or the necessary rehabilitation of Evagoras's legacy, a common problem faced by the orator in composing epideictic rhetoric, is difficult to say.[6] Despite such concerns, using statues as exemplars for imitation to improve the virtue of the Roman people is precisely the goal undertaken in the Forum Augustum, a tradition with a long history in Roman private life, and one, I would argue, that is very much in keeping with Isocratean ideals, at least in practice.

7. Aureus of L. Livineius Regulus, 42 B.C.E. Obv. portrait head of Octavian; rev. Aeneas with Anchises. The British Museum, London. Reg. 1864,1128.23. *Photograph © the Trustees of the British Museum.*

Along with amplification, imitation was a significant rhetorical technique employed by Augustus's administration. Aeneas was perhaps the most frequent figure posited as an exemplar other than Augustus himself. The hero makes multiple appearances in Augustan art, as on the Ara Pacis, where he is depicted as the father of (Julius) Ascanius, Augustus's mythic ancestor, and as an exemplar of piety, filial and religious. Aeneas is present in Augustan imagery much earlier as well, though perhaps with less emphasis on piety. In 42 B.C.E., the young Octavian, not yet having taken the title "Augustus," uses an abbreviated version of the flight of Aeneas. The coin depicts Aeneas and his father on the reverse of an Aureas opposite Octavian's portrait head, emphasizing the filial piety shown by Aeneas carrying his father Anchises on his back from the destruction of Troy (see fig. 7). While the demonstration of filial piety by Aeneas on the Aureas invites a comparison to Octavian's filial piety—after all, Octavian had just defeated the conspirators who assassinated his adopted father—the same image was used by Julius Caesar to denote his lineage tracing back to Aeneas and, thus, Venus.

Later images created by Augustus's administration focus not only on filial piety but also on religious piety and on Aeneas's status as favored by the gods.[7] Images such as the one on the Ara Pacis, commissioned by the Senate and Roman people and dedicated in 9 B.C.E., depict the hero completing his epic journey with the help of the gods while keeping his household gods nearby, gods that are not coincidentally also Augustus's household gods (see fig. 2). These depictions of Aeneas, which create identification between the hero and Augustus, then, become offerings of both Augustus and Aeneas as exemplars of piety for imitation to the Roman populace.[8]

Imitation was a rhetorical strategy in the Forum of Augustus, which included a later example of the flight of Aeneas, with the relatively simple technique of amplification common in the epideictic genre evolving into a much more complex form of imitation and emulation. This practice of imitation, on which rhetoricians such as Cicero, Dionysius, and Quintilian based the education of the orator, represents a shift in emphasis in rhetorical education in the principate. This shift, in many respects a return to an Isocratean model, influenced the Augustan cultural campaigns, including the statue group of Aeneas and the *summi viri,* often referred to as the "Hall of Fame," in the Forum of Augustus. These statues form a visual epideictic text meant to aid the development of civic judgment and character that had formed a basis of the epideictic genre and Greek *paideia* since the fifth century B.C.E. The Roman precedents of the so-called "hall of fame," namely funeral *imagines* (wax funeral masks kept in the family atrium) and sculpture gardens of wealthy Romans, which eventually featured Greek philosophers, suggest a long tradition of material practice of the epideictic genre at Rome—a species usually given short shrift in Roman rhetorical theory and practice before the empire. Viewing the Forum of Augustus as a

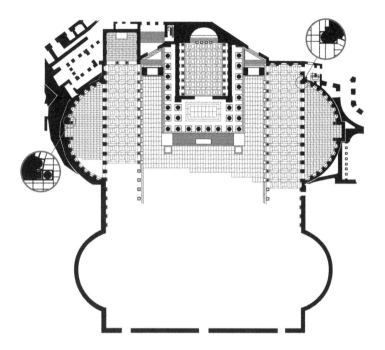

8. Rome, Forum of Augustus. Plan showing recently excavated double exedrae.
Museo dei Fori Imperiali, Rome.
Illustration, Archive of the Museum of the Imperial Forums, Sovraintendenza di Roma Capitale.

manifestation of epideictic rhetorical practice is more historically accurate than connecting the practice of imitation to literary imitation or histories that focus on individual figures.[9]

THE FORUM AUGUSTUM: AN OVERVIEW

The Forum of Augustus, completed in 2 B.C.E., continued to develop the Augustan political myth by joining the mythic founders of Rome with Roman leaders of the more recent past.[10] The forum housed the temple of Mars Ultor, Mars the Avenger, which was promised during the Battle of Philippi in 42 B.C.E. when Augustus (and Antonius) defeated the conspirators who killed Julius Caesar, the same occasion which prompted the minting of the coin discussed above.[11] More than twenty years after the battle, Augustus's negotiation of the return

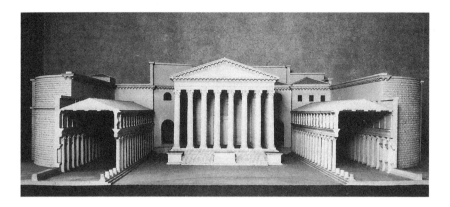

9. Forum of Augustus, model showing Temple of Mars Ultor and the colonnades that housed the *summi viri*. Museo dei Fori Imperiali, Rome.
Photograph, Archive of the Museum of the Imperial Forums, Sovraintendenza di Roma Capitale.

10. Forum of Augustus, archaeological remains of the Temple of Mars Ultor.
Photograph, Schwanke, Neg. D-DAI-Rom 84.2920.

of the Roman standards lost by Crassus to the Parthians, a diplomatic victory for which he also credited Mars Ultor, likely prompted the construction of the temple. The standards were eventually housed in the Temple of Mars.[12]

As on the Ara Pacis, the Forum of Augustus recalled the two founding myths of Rome and the ancestry of the Roman people and the Julian line. Statues of Mars, the father of Romulus and Remus, and Venus, the mother of Aeneas, were featured in two locations in the Temple of Mars Ultor, which stood against the back (northeast) wall of the Forum (see fig. 8). The temple housed cult statues of Mars, Venus, and possibly the divine Julius, behind which stood the standards returned from the Parthians as well as Julius Caesar's sword.[13] Mars and Venus appeared again in the pediment of the temple centered between Mons Palatine and Romulus to their right and Fortuna, Roma, and Tiber Pater to their left.[14] "Augustus" was inscribed on the entablature just below the statue of Mars.[15] Though this inscription is not unlike other dedicatory inscriptions in some respects, it also served to situate Augustus among the deities of the pediment.

While both Fortuna and Roma were depicted in the pediment group fulfilling a role not unlike Roma and Tellus on the Ara Pacis, Mars and Venus themselves symbolize the mythic history of Rome, the prosperity brought by the Julian

11. Forum of Augustus, archaeological remains of the northwest exedra, which housed the Aeneas group.
Photograph, Schwanke, Neg. D-DAI-Rom 84.2852.

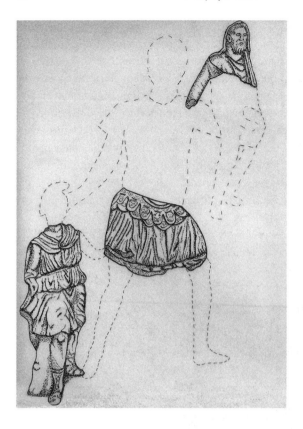

12. Re-creation of the Aeneas group from the Forum of Augustus,
    based on replicas of the group found in two Spanish
    provinces. Museo dei Fori Imperiali, Rome.
    Illustration, Tara Carleton Weaver.

line, and the duality of war and peace. In other words, here the gods encapsulate
the entire Augustan political myth. While the cult statue of Mars depicted the
god as an older, bearded, "father figure," which was appropriate as the ancestor of the Roman people, the pediment figure portrayed a younger, semi-nude,
armed god of war with a globe under his foot, denoting the military and imperial
dominance of Rome, not unlike the Roma figure on the Ara Pacis.[16] In the Forum
of Augustus, Venus is responsible for the softer side of Roman domination—
fertility, peace, prosperity, and abundance—just as the "Tellus" figure functions
on the Ara Pacis.[17]

    In front of the temple, in the center of the forum, stood a statue of Augustus
in a quidriga, a horse-drawn chariot, with inscriptions recounting his military

successes and the granting of his recent title, *pater patriae*.[18] Again, the dualities of war and peace, *virtus* and *pietas,* military and civic, are balanced with the depiction of Augustus as a triumphing military leader and his title *pater patriae,* which stressed his role in the civic life of Rome. It is important to note that Augustus was represented apart from the deities of the Temple of Mars and the historical figures of the *summi viri* and apparently was present only at the bequest of the Senate.[19]

Certainly Augustus's presence in the center of the forum could create many of the same points of amplification found on the Ara Pacis. Additionally, the forum cultivated a point of amplification with Alexander the Great. It is possible that in the square room of the forum directly to the north of the apse of the Temple of Mars stood a colossal statue of Alexander and that two paintings of the leader by Apelles figured prominently in the forum.[20] The comparison with Alexander is not particularly surprising given Augustus's frequent identification with the ruler; still, it does mark a fulfillment of the Augustan political myth: rather than the promise of peace and prosperity and the restoration of Rome as ruler of the world found on the Ara Pacis, the comparison with Alexander (and his empire) invites the people to see the Augustan political myth as completed, at least by Augustus.

The statues in the Forum of Augustus also drew out the same points of amplification from the Augustan political myth as depicted on the Ara Pacis. To the right and to the left of the Temple of Mars stood two exedrae. The northwest exedra housed a marble statue group depicting the flight of Aeneas, the Kings of Alba Longa, and Augustus's ancestors, including the Julian and Octavian lines.[21] In the northeast exedra stood a statue of Romulus and statues of great men from Roman history.[22] While the Ara Pacis suggested both Augustus and Aeneas as exemplars of virtue, the forum explicitly addressed the importance of imitating great men by presenting the *summi viri* down each portico.[23] Columned porticoes ran parallel to the Temple of Mars. Each portico and exedrae contained niches along the back wall, which housed the "great men," well-known figures from Roman history. Additionally, more recent bronze statues of triumphing generals were placed between the columns of the porticos.[24]

Topping the portico containing the "hall of fame" ran a second portico comprised of caryatids, draped female figures serving as columns, with a shield and a male face between each, which may have symbolized the peoples conquered by Rome.[25] Velleius describes inscriptions of the names of the Roman provinces in the forum, invoking a similar idea.[26] The caryatids rather obviously recall the Porch of the Maidens from Erechtheion on the Athenian acropolis, and this comparison between the whole of the Forum Augustum and the Athenian acropolis was likely intentional. According to Karl Galinsky, "The Augustan forum was the equivalent of the Acropolis to express, through architecture and its decoration, the grandeur and the meaning of empire."[27]

While the architectural precedents for the forum were (intentionally) wide ranging, the forum was visually striking on another level.[28] The conquests of (Julius Caesar and) Augustus had given Rome access to artists, artisans, and materials beyond the means of the republic. The quality of the sculpture on the Ara Pacis functioned as a material rhetoric claiming the supremacy of the Roman empire. In the Forum of Augustus, a similar message was present, this time in the vast selection of marbles from all over the empire. While the coloring of marbles such as *giallo antico* (yellow from Numidia), *africano* (black with red/purple from Ionia), *pavonazzetto* (white with purple veins from Phrygia), *bardiglio* (light gray with blue-gray stripes from Carrara), and *cipollino* (green from Greece) must have been visually stunning, the marbles also represented the material resources of the Roman empire—the fruits of the fulfillment of the Augustan political myth.[29]

A VENUE OF ORATORY: THE USES OF THE FORUM AUGUSTUM

The Forum of Augustus was not just meant as something beautiful to look at or as a reliquary of Roman history but was built out of necessity. There are two detailed accounts of the designated uses of the forum. Cassius Dio's account focuses on the forum as a center of Rome's military decisions and accomplishments:

> In the preparation for the dedication of the new Forum and the temple of Mars, it was voted that Augustus and his descendants should go there as often as they wished, while those who were leaving the age-group of boys being enrolled among the youths of military age should on that occasion invariably present themselves there; that those who were being posted to commands abroad should ceremonially start from it; that the Senate should pass its decrees there in respect of the granting of triumphs; and that the victors, after celebrating these, should dedicate to this god Mars their scepter and their crown; that those and all others who received triumphal honors should have their statues in bronze erected in this Forum; that if ever a military standard captured by the enemy were recovered, they should be placed in the temple; that the festival should be celebrated beside the steps of the temple by cavalry commanders of each year; that a nail should be driven into the wall of the temple by the censors at the end of their term of office.[30]

From Dio's account, it is easy to see how scholars might arrive at the conclusion that "the temple and forum constituted the military center of ancient

Rome, where the memories of past victories were continually refreshed by the addition of new trophies and mementos."[31] The rhetorical significance of the Forum Augustum—setting past injustices right, represented by the occasions that led to the dedication of the Temple of Mars Ultor—were continually (re) associated with the forum through use: deliberations about war and the display of military standards.[32] Still, the rhetorical function of the forum was far greater and did not end with enshrined public memory or deliberations of war.

Suetonius suggests that the forum was a venue for a number of traditional rhetorical practices:

> His reason for building the forum was to increase in the number of the people and of the cases at law, which seemed to call for a third forum, since two were no longer adequate. Therefore it was opened to the public with some haste, before the temple of Mars was finished, and it was provided that the public prosecutions be held there apart from the rest, as well as the selection of jurors by lot. He had made a vow to build the temple of Mars in the war of Philippi, which he undertook to avenge his father; accordingly he decreed that in it the senate should consider wars and claims for triumphs, from it those who were on their way to the provinces with military commands should be escorted, and to it victors on their return should bear tokens of their triumphs.[33]

In other words, the forum was not only the military center of Rome; it was a place where deliberative and judicial rhetoric concerning matters of the Roman empire were decided. Additionally, virtually everyone involved with the administration of the empire—the *princeps,* the senate, juries, orators, provincial governors, generals, and even young men assuming their adult role as citizens—had to pass through the Forum of Augustus. Eventually the major rhetorical practices of empire, the reception of foreign embassies, and hearings regarding the provinces occurred in the forum as well.[34] The Forum of Augustus was not only a stunning piece of visual rhetoric; it was a venue of rhetorical practice, as well as training ground for that practice.

IMITATION IN ROMAN RHETORICAL THEORY AND PRACTICE

The Lack of Roman Panegyric

Of the three genres of rhetoric, generally Roman rhetorical practice is thought of as taking up forensic and deliberative oratory. George Kennedy notes of the republic that "epideictic oratory of the Greek sort was largely nonexistent in Rome. The only native epideictic form was the eulogy (*laudatio funebris*) for members of noble families."[35] The empire, then, marks a flourishing of

epideictic rhetoric, which according to Jeffery Walker underlies all rhetorical practice, and a triumph of the Ciceronian ideal . . . as understood from an
Isocratean or sophistic perspective, and as advanced by Cicero himself."[36] The
"Isocratean *logôn technê*" based on the philosophical-literary *paideia*," absent in
the Roman republic, according to Walker, reemerges in the empire.[37]

In this Isocratean model, the epideictic genre serves as popular manifestation of a rhetorical education meant not only to praise a person while offering
a model of imitation, but also to reaffirm the cultural standards of right and
wrong, and to produce civic responsibility.[38] For example, Isocrates's *Evagoras*
praises the dead king, provides a model for the current ruler, Nicocles, and serves
as instruction to the people as how to perform their duties as citizens. Similarly
in *Nicocles,* Isocrates, writing in the voice of the ruler, claims, "I consider finest,
most appropriate to a king, and especially suited to me, those discourses which
advise me on my conduct in general and on political matters, and among these,
those which teach dynasts how they should treat their people, and the citizens
how they should regard their leaders."[39] In a sense, while the epideictic genre
requires the orator to have a "knowledge of all of the virtues" and of "the judgment of mankind," it is at the same time culture-forming inasmuch as it presents, literally "displays," a model of civic participation that may be accepted (and
emulated) or rejected by the audience.[40]

Imitation as an educational technique had perhaps changed little from fifth-
century Athens as found in the Sophistic tradition, though it (re)emerged with
new emphasis in the principate. Stanley Bonner, using Horace's education as an
example, emphasizes the father's role in early childhood education, which was,
in part, to point out men who were appropriate models for imitation.[41] Though
this had to do with the modeling of certain behavior, qualities, or virtues, Pernot
suggests that much of the power of republican rhetoric, unlike Greek rhetoric,
came not from skill but from *auctoritas,* or the authority of the speaker;[42] the
models selected by a boy's father, no doubt, also demonstrated *auctoritas,* which
young boys from elite families could, then, learn to construct for themselves.[43]
Pernot argues that the original objection to teaching rhetoric in Rome was that
such an education might rival the authority of traditional *auctoritas* possessed
by the elite, thereby promoting the *populares.*[44] While certainly this fear was
never fully realized, the early empire did allow for more social mobility. Considering this new mobility, one wonders about the possible models of *auctoritas,*
particularly if they did not exist in the home.

While a boy's father and/or a slave or freedmen might provide early education, "from Augustus onwards, the tutorial system was encouraged at the very
highest level, in the form of state appointments of teachers for the children of
the imperial family." While Augustus used his family to model the type of education he wished for others, the "accession of tutors . . . would appear to have

been something of a luxury. Moreover, as this kind of tuition was provided by scholars . . . it was an intellectual and cultural education, and it would presuppose a basis of elementary knowledge, which might also be imparted within the home."[45] While rhetoric remained the predominant subject for young men in the principate, it was secondary education, though as in early education, imitation played a prominent role.[46]

The Isocratean model as represented in Cicero, centers on developing the "judgment" and "intellectual grace," of the orator.[47] Rhetorical education, then, is inherently broader than the technical knowledge found in rhetorical handbooks such as Cicero's own *De Inventione* or the *Rhetorica ad Herrenium.* Instead, rhetorical education, acquired through "study and imitation," depends on the formation of "the acuteness of the logicians, the wisdom of the philosophers, the language almost of poetry, the memory of lawyers, the voice of tragedians, [and] the gesture almost of the best actors."[48] The product of such an education is the ideal orator, according to Cicero, and this ideal is not merely one who can win cases but a *vir bonus* who unites "wisdom with eloquence."[49] On his shoulders rests the welfare of society and "by the judgment and wisdom of the perfect orator, not only his own honor, but that of many other individuals, and the welfare of the whole state are principally upheld."[50]

The significance of imitation is clear in both Cicero and Quintilian.[51] Cicero's Antonius instructs that a duty of the teacher is "to point out to the student who he should imitate, and in such a manner that he may most carefully copy the chief excellencies of him who he takes for his model. Let practice then follow, by which he may represent in his imitation the exact resemblance of him who he has chosen as a pattern" for the sake of developing style as well as judgment.[52] Quintilian, too, repeatedly stresses "imitation" as a substantive part of the rhetorical education that aids in "character development," "acquisition of judgment," and development of "excellence in morals as well as in eloquence." Similar to the role of the father, one of the teacher's chief responsibilities is to make sure the student understands which characteristics of an orator or text are worthy of imitation and why.[53]

While significant in Roman rhetorical theory, imitation was perhaps even more important among Greek rhetoricians associated with Atticism and eventually the Second Sophistic.[54] Certainly this is the case with Dionysius of Halicarnassus, and his perspective again represents a return to the Isocratean principles of the fifth century. For Dionysius, "students of political thought must examine" those who are "the most important ancient orators and historians," their "manner of life and style of writing" and their "characteristics."[55] The following books of his *Ancient Orators* each function as a guide to students to know what about that orator is worthy of imitation.[56] Pernot claims Dionysius's "*Critical Essays* are the first body of criticism we have stressing imitation of the classical authors, an attitude that will prove fundamental throughout the Imperial Age. . . . Subscribing to an Isokratean ideal of rhetoric as 'political philosophy,' that is a moral discipline befitting the citizen, he wished to propose models that will aid his readers in developing their eloquence and in particular their style."[57] It is this view of imitation, on which, according to Pernot, the "*paideia* rested" that was made popular in the principate.[58]

While imitation of exemplars was clearly alive and well in rhetorical education, the empire brought new occasions for epideictic rhetoric, which provided exemplars. One could argue, however, that these new public ceremonial occasions were built on long-standing practices of elite Roman families and often made private practices public. These practices, with an emphasis on the visual and material, coincided with epideictic oratory, particularly eulogy, which taken together with the resurgence of mimesis and the Greek *paideia* came together in the Forum of Augustus.

VISUAL CULTURE AND IMITATION

Though imitation as found in rhetorical education and the epideictic genre influenced the construction of the Forum of Augustus, a number of other practices often bound with the epideictic genre, including *imagines*, wax death masks of notable members of a family kept in the household atrium; the continued popularity of the Greek *paideia*; and, related, Epicurean philosophy also had a significant impact. Though *imagines* and Epicureanism seemingly have little to do with the epideictic genre as typically thought of, in Rome they form components of civic and thus rhetorical education and ultimately shape the practice of panegyric in the Roman empire.

Funeral Masks and Roman Eulogy

It was usual practice for a eulogy to be delivered at a Roman funeral. Accompanying this tradition, elite Roman families with ancestors of high rank would have wax funeral masks made of their ancestors, which were worn in funeral processions and then displayed in the household atrium.[59] Polybius describes a Roman funeral:

> There could not easily be a more ennobling spectacle for a young man who aspires to fame and virtue. For who would not be inspired by the sight of the images of men renowned for their excellence, all together as if alive and breathing? What spectacle could be more glorious than this? Besides, he who makes the oration over the man about to be buried, when finished speaking of him recounts the successes and exploits of the rest whose images are

present, beginning from the most ancient. By this means, by this constant renewal of the good report of brave men, the celebrity of those who performed noble deeds is rendered immortal, while at the same time the fame of those who did good service to their country becomes known to the people and a heritage for future generations. But the most important result is that young men are thus inspired to endure every suffering for the public welfare in the hope of winning the glory that attends on brave men.[60]

The Roman tradition of crafting *imagines* of the dead was a highly visual practice that, as Polybius indicates, uniquely shaped the orator's eulogy of the dead, joining the deceased with his or her ancestral history and the history of Rome, melding the private and public, the past and the future.

The right to be honored with a wax mask and have the likeness preserved alongside the family *imagines* depended on reaching high office, but, apparently, it also depended on maintaining a certain moral virtue or at least not soiling the family name. After recounting both the patricians and plebeians of a certain family who had reached an office to qualify for ancestral portraits, Cicero advises his friend Paetus that, of two lines of his ancestry on the plebian side, "I think you may well disregard them; for with the exception of that C. Carbo . . . not one of them was a true or loyal citizen."[61] Among the misdeeds Cicero recounts that apparently allow for the exclusion: acting like a clown, being wicked, being a thief, being a factious tribune, ordering an assassination, and committing suicide to escape prosecution.[62] Cicero's advice leads to the conclusion that "he considered Paetus within his customary rights in discriminating against the inclusion among his *images* of certain ancestors who were qualified for the honor because the offices they had held, but were not deemed worthy of it for reasons of conduct and *mores*."[63]

Cicero's insistence on including men of virtue only no doubt has to do with maintaining the family name. After all, it was always up to the eulogizer to portray the dead in the best possible light, and this practice clearly extends to construction of a familial memory and how the more distantly deceased would figure in future eulogies. Cicero's insistence is also likely because of the role of eulogy and *imagines* (as with the epideictic genre broadly) in shaping (Roman) culture: both the eulogy and the legacy embodied in *imagines* were meant as models for imitation.[64] This point is made clearly by Polybius who, after recounting the heroic conduct of one Roman, claims that his actions should inspire "the eager emulation of achieving noble deeds engendered in the Roman youth by their institutions."[65] More humorously but no less to the point, in Cicero's discussion of wit in *De Oratore*, an implicit argument is made that it is up to an individual to live up to the model set by his or her ancestors. Crassus jests with Brutus as a funeral procession passes: "Do you not fear even that dead corpse, and those very images (*imagines*) of your ancestors, you who have not only left yourself no room for the imitation of their virtues, but none in which you can place their statues?"[66] While *imagines* and eulogies may have been meant to inspire youths, they were also the measure of men. In time, the display of the notable ancestors became "a mark of nobility," a "family hall of fame where a family's political pedigree was exhibited to residents and visitors alike."[67]

There is a significant private/public duality to *imagines.* Pernot argues that funeral orations, particularly public eulogies offered by a magistrate, were "eminently political, [and] played an important role in self-affirming strategies of the great families."[68] No doubt this was true of public funerary events such as the procession and the *imagines* as well; however, the display of the *imagines* within the house, coupled with family archives, must have been a constant reminder of the family legacy and the custom of the Roman ancestors.[69] While Polybius discusses the "inspirational" effect of funerary processions on young men, one can only speculate that within the house the *imagines* were a source of emulation for young Roman boys—a kind of constant private education, which offered a way to begin to build their own *auctoritas.*[70] No doubt these private halls of fame became progressively more significant in light of the increasing financial, if not social, mobility of the early empire.[71]

The Greek Paideia, Epicurus, and (Roman) Sculpture

The Roman atrium in the early empire, Pliny tells us, was home to more than just *imagines:* "In the halls (*atriis*) of our ancestors it was otherwise; portraits were the objects displayed to be looked at, not statues by foreign artists, not bronzes nor marbles, but wax models of faces (*imagines*) were set out each on a separate side-board."[72] Pliny is greatly offended, it seems, by the presence of statues of nonancestors, especially those by "foreign," meaning "Greek," artists. These include the "likenesses of strangers" and "statues" that homeowners used to "represent their money, not themselves."[73] Most offensive to Pliny: the "portraits of athletes" and the "likeness of Epicurus."[74] Pliny's displeasure with what he sees as the corruption of the Roman atrium likely stems from several places, including a bit of classism at the displays of financial success that such foreign art denoted, which Pliny clearly finds not in keeping with Roman decorum, which often objected to "luxury." Additionally, inasmuch as the *imagines* served as models of imitation meant to maintain Roman customs, the presence of Greek models represents a foreign influence that does not fit with the traditional *mores maiorum.* There is, no doubt, a healthy dose of Roman xenophobia operating with Pliny as well. Perhaps most offensive to Pliny is the presence of Epicurus, the Greek philosopher and namesake of Epicurean philosophy, who plays an important part in explaining why many Romans had Greek statues and provides another source for considering the significance of imitation.

Art historian Peter Stewart, in light of Epicurean philosophy, explains that, while decoration, particularly sculpture and painting, in private residences was meant to convey the owner's status and to serve as an escape in leisure time, "art was conceived as having a more serious, active role in the intellectual and cultural formation of the patron."[75] The first-century poet Statius describes the sculptures of great men from Greek history found in a particular villa as "the faces of chiefs and bards and wise men of the past, whom you take pains to follow, whose example you take completely to heart, free from cares, composed in your calm virtue and always in control of yourself."[76] Though Stewart suggests the emphasis on imitation of Greek figures was new to the time period, he claims it "compliment[ed] more traditionally 'Roman' portraits such as images of ancestors which had been displayed in the home since republican times, or indeed the portraits of the emperor and his family which were also loyally exhibited in private settings."[77]

Per Stewart's reading of Statius, a homeowner might seek to imitate some characteristic of a famous person whose legacy was represented by a statue, though this practice might work as well with written texts. For example, the Villa of the Papyri, commonly thought to have been owned by Calpurnius Piso Caesoninus, contained numerous statues similar to those described by Statius but also an extensive library, which included scrolls of Epicurean philosophy.[78] Yun Lee Too, specifically considering libraries, has argued that statues could stand in several relationships with texts. Images of the gods or muses could refer to the "literary origination and production" of texts while a statue of "a dead author might be conceived as speaking to a reader in the library."[79] However, Too reads statues such as those owned by Piso in the Epicurean tradition, arguing that ultimately "statues and busts would function as incentives for the viewer to become *like* the represented subjects, who in turn resemble the otherwise unapproachable gods."[80]

The concern with Epicurean philosophy was found in rhetorical education as well. Quintilian takes Epicurus into account in his thinking on imitation when he encourages his students to move past the "façade" of a speech when imitating style: "And even those who have judgment enough to avoid faults should not be satisfied with producing an image of excellence, a mere outer, as it were, or rather a 'shape' like those which Epicurus says are given off by the surface of bodies."[81] While in some ways Quintilian's concern would seem to mirror Isocrates's concerns that statues provide only a shell of a model, the hall of great men found in Augustus's Forum marks a significant change in the practice of imitation, one which largely excises the orator's role so stressed by Isocrates and makes long-private practices public.[82]

The practice of displaying statues of (Greek) philosophers was not unique to adherents of Epicurean philosophy. Paul Zanker explains that "portraits of well-known Greeks have been found almost exclusively in lavish villas and private houses" and yet very rarely in public venues.[83] The presence of statues of Greeks was part of what Zanker broadly terms the "Hellenization" of Roman culture beginning in the second-century B.C.E. It was not uncommon for a learned man such as Cicero, Seneca, Atticus, or Brutus to choose an "intellectual authority" and to erect a statue of that authority, be it Plato, Aristotle, or Demosthenes alongside the household gods.[84] Zanker calls attention to the practice as a manifestation of the "need to inhabit fully the world of Greek *paideia*."[85]

Like Polybius, Zanker claims that such displays have more to do with a desire to show that the homeowner "belonged to the educated class and therefore the upper ranks of society" than an actual concern with education by the time of the principate. This distinction between financial status and education suggests a certain discomfort with social mobility; as Zanker cites, Juvenal complained that "the most uneducated man" had such statues. Still, these displays suggest something significant about the role of visual and material culture in Roman educational and cultural practices.[86] Zanker, following Richard Neudecker, makes the claim that when statues of Greek thinkers were arranged alphabetically, they formed a sort of "encyclopedia" that one "could commit to memory."[87] This practice, along with practices of Epicurean philosophy, alludes to a kind of knowledge or (public) memory embodied or enshrined, in this case, in statues, where the visual and/or material served as a repository or placeholder for knowledge that a Roman could then use not only as a memory aid but also as a source of an exemplar for imitation. Sculpture gardens, in other words, function analogously to encyclopedias or collections like Dionysius's *The Ancient Orators* that were in vogue during the principate.

Imitation and the Summi Viri

While the Forum of Augustus became a venue for the practice of rhetoric traditionally associated with Rome—judicial and deliberative—and eventually Roman imperial rhetoric, the forum was greatly influenced by epideictic rhetorical practices. Suetonius leaves little doubt about the purpose of the "Hall of Great Men" from the Forum of Augustus: "Next to the immortal Gods [Augustus] honoured the memory of the leaders who had raised the estate of the Roman people from obscurity to greatness. Accordingly he restored the works of such men with their original inscriptions, and in the two colonnades of his forum dedicated statues of all of them in triumphal garb, declaring besides in a proclamation: 'I have contrived this to lead the citizens to require me, while I live, and the rulers of later times as well to attain the standard set by those worthies of old.'"[88] The Hall of Great Men, then, in the Forum of Augustus was clearly meant to provide exemplars of virtue for the people of Rome, and not just the common people but "rulers of later times," just as the eulogy of Evagoras composed by Isocrates was meant to provide Nicocles with a lasting exemplar of his father's most admirable traits.

While the origin of the concept for the *summi viri* in the Forum of Augustus is often debated, so too are the literary antecedents and authorship of the *elogia,* the inscriptions that detailed the accomplishments of each man. The Forum of Augustus may have elided the orator in the traditional sense, but it was not without the mediation of words. Each statue of a great figure from republican history would have stood over a *titulus,* an inscription recounting his name and office and a longer *elogium* recounting the deeds for which he was renowned and presumably those worthy of imitation (see fig. 13). In many respects, the *elogia* of the *summi viri* functioned as the eulogy would have in an actual Roman funeral and were likely similar to the archives kept in private houses mentioned by Pliny.[89] As is often the case with Augustan art, the influence of traditional oratory is present, but the orator is physically absent.

13. Re-creation of one of the *summi viri* based on fragments from the Forum of Augustus. Museo dei Fori Imperiali, Rome.
   Illustration, Archive of the Museum of the Imperial Forums, Sovraintendenza di Roma Capitale.

The authorship and influence of the *elogia* is a source of frequent conten-
tion among classicists.[90] Pliny claims Augustus himself wrote the accounts of
the deeds of the *summi viri,* and though this is universally rejected by scholars,
it does evidence how closely Augustus was involved with the building project.[91]
One literary source that bears close resemblance to the hall of fame (and lacks
controversy in the comparison) in the Forum is book 6 of Vergil's *Aeneid.*[92]
Though the Forum Augustum focuses on the past, Anchises tells Aeneas about
the future leaders of Rome who will lead the city to greatness, culminating with
a prophecy about Augustus. In all the discussion of literary precedents for the
elogia, epideictic rhetoric is rarely mentioned. The exception comes in Eduard
Norden's discussion of book 6 when he argues that both the great men in this
passage and the *summi viri* function as models for imitation as in panegyric oratory.[93] I would argue that, without the connection to epideictic discourse, both
our understanding of the *summi viri* and the practice of Roman epideictic is
incomplete.

Suetonius makes clear that the *summi viri* were meant as models of imitation,
but what precisely was the standard to which Augustus, future rulers, and the
Roman people were being held? Henry Rowell argues, based on literary sources,
that all of the *summi viri* were presented in triumphal garb a claim which would
emphasize the military accomplishments of the men.[94] Barbara Kellum, basing
her argument on archeological fragments, claims that most *summi viri* "wore the
civilian toga," which challenges the idea that only military accomplishments or
virtus was meant for emulation in the Forum of Augustus.[95]

The men modeled in the forum were chosen, according to James C. Anderson, first and foremost for offering precedents and parallels to Augustus's own
accomplishments. In other words, they served as points of amplification, a frequent commonplace of panegyric. Following this line of reasoning, the *summi
viri* formed a kind of narrative that the leadership of Rome continued to build,
culminating in Augustus; whereas all roads may lead to Rome, all the *summi
viri* lead to Augustus. In this narrative, the virtue of the great leaders of Rome
certainly mattered, but the *summi viri* were also chosen to justify Augustus's
unusual position as keeping with Roman tradition. According to Kellum, of
the nineteen *summi viri* unrelated to Augustus, fifteen "had held positions of
extraordinary power," such as "multiple consulships" or the title "dictator."[96]

Precedent to justify Augustus's sole rule was not the only significant facet of
the narrative of the history of Rome created by the hall of fame. Men were chosen
who had demonstrated "leadership in civil disturbances," "the religious life of
the people," and "military exploits"; additionally, those who had made material
improvements to the "fabric of the city itself" were honored.[97] The *summi viri,*
then, were well-known civic, military, and religious leaders, but, importantly,

Augustus "matche[d] or surpassed the deeds of all the great men of Roman history," as he was the one being praised, if not eulogized.[98]

Rowell, focusing on the military aspects of Augustus's Forum, reads the *summi viri* together with book 6 of the *Aeneid* and argues that, in contrast to the intellectual prowess of the Greeks, the Romans, who dominated through military skill, should be "merciful in their conquests" with the virtue of "*clementia*" in order "to bring a peaceful order into the world."[99] In keeping with his emphasis on the forum as a military center, Rowell does not focus on the other virtues necessary for Roman statesmen. The hall of fame offered accomplishment that fit with the virtues from the *clipeus virtutis: virtus clementia, iustitia,* and *pietas,* creating an Augustan canon meant to guide the administrators of the empire.[100] Certainly, the Forum of Augustus was designed to impart Roman rulers with virtue, judgment, and civic-mindedness in keeping with Roman customs as they performed their duties, be they military, civic, or religious.

ISOCRATES'S CONCERN ABOUT the use of statues as memorials as opposed to epideictic oratory reveals both a concern about the place of the orator in Greek society and an anxiety about leaving the creation of a legacy up to public memory alone, albeit encapsulated, in a mute statue. The stakes for Isocrates were high. It was the responsibility of the orator not only to memorialize but also to posit an example that displayed the virtues held by a society, virtues needed to make the civil workings of that society run smoothly. While Augustus's administration seems not to have held the same reservations about entrusting legacies to public memory, the places that encapsulated those legacies were carefully crafted and mediated, in this case, through the Augustan political myth as a whole as well as through the *elogia* that accompanied the statue of each great man.

Even the uses of the Forum Augustum show how events in Roman history—the Battle of Philippi and the return of the Roman standards by the Parthians—were enshrined in a structure and then continually recalled through the consideration of war and the successful outcomes of those decisions in that space.[101] The Forum Augustum was also a place for the hearing of court cases. Certainly, one of the laments of the period found in classical authors like Tacitus and echoed in the decline narrative is the notion that rhetoric lost its civic force. The Forum of Augustus offers a specific *locus* of practice to argue that judicial oratory as well as a broader epideictic rhetoric meant to shape *praxis* were alive and well. Jeffrey Walker calls this second type of rhetoric a "culture-shaping *logôn technê* grounded in a broad *paideia,*" which he traces back to Isocrates and the Sophistic tradition of the fifth century B.C.E.[102]

This *logôn technê* operated independently of democracy; instead, it is that which "cultivated the general, cultural consensus on which civil institutions and a public discourse might be based."[103] In other words, this rhetoric cultivated a civic-minded practical wisdom, a shared understanding of justice and decorum, and even an aesthetic of communication. In short, this *logôn technê* produced the practiced reason of good citizens, rulers, and judges and, in doing so, created a culture of citizenship that, in theory, would continue to do so. It is this culture-shaping rhetoric that Isocrates did not wish to trust to statues, and yet, that is precisely what Augustus did in his forum, and it is important to understand Augustus's choice as rhetorical practice that was very much in keeping in the Roman tradition that entwined eulogy and *imagines,* with the educational curriculum, and household statuary. That is, in the principate the plastic arts and Roman oratory were not separate parallel traditions, but merge together into Roman rhetorical practice.

The Forum of Augustus participated in this culture-shaping tradition through visual and material rhetorical practice by establishing a "standard set by those worthies of old" for Augustus and future leaders, forming a contract of sorts between the "citizens" and what they may "require" of their ruler. The most significant change in the government of Rome during the principate was not a shift from republic (more accurately oligarchy) to empire but the establishment of a bureaucracy with many "rulers" from provincial governors, to military generals, to juries hearing trials. All of the people responsible for the administration of the empire passed through the Forum of Augustus, and the forum itself functioned as a venue for deliberations concerning war and trials deemed significant to the well-being of Rome. In many respects, the Forum of Augustus was a visual and material incarnation of a *logôn technê* based equally on visual and material manifestations of the Greek *paideia* found in many Roman villas and on a highly visual tradition of Roman funerary rights. These traditions, as manifest in the Forum of Augustus, were meant to develop the moral character and civic-mindedness of not just the *princeps* but everyone in charge of the civil administration of Rome and its provinces and the citizens themselves, who were responsible for enforcing the standards displayed to them in the Forum Augustum. While elite families had long had access to such models, one can view the Forum of Augustus as a type of public education that functioned analogously to the (traditional) practices of the Roman elite. That is, the Forum of Augustus was the public equivalent of the private atrium.

The Forum of Augustus, then, represents a moment in Roman history when there was an attempt to fabricate a Roman legacy. That legacy was, in keeping with the traditional (though often feigned) Roman abhorrence of everything non-Roman, nonetheless based on the Hellenistic tradition and meant to graft onto, if not replace, the Greek *paideia* with a Roman version.[104] Rowell comments on Vergil's book 6: "Vergil was reminding the Romans that there was more to the statues in the forum than the art which created them. The making of statues, the fashioning of beauty in material things, was the province of the Greeks together with science and oratory. Rome produced men, the kind of men represented in the statues of the forum."[105] But Rowell fails to recognize that the Forum of Augustus was also something beautiful, cited as one of Rome's greatest achievements by Pliny, and though Roman virtues were significantly different from those of the Greeks, and perhaps because they were different, the Forum of Augustus attempts to rival Greek culture, to supplant the Greek *paideia,* including rhetorical practice, and to offer a Roman model.[106]

A century and a half after the completion of the Forum of Augustus, Apuleius would write, if not deliver to the proconsul of Africa, his *Apologia,* a courtroom defense against charges of practicing magic that he allegedly used to bewitch a woman, Pudentilla, for the sake of gaining her fortunes.[107] Jeffrey Walker has written about the text as an allegory that "represent[s] the seduction of "Rome" (Pudentilla and her estate) by Hellenized, sophistic culture (Apuleius)."[108] At the same time, Walker argues that the text "pits the crass, uncultured, provincial Roman against the cosmopolitan, cultured, Hellenized sophist, the man of the *paideia.*" It is one sign, of several, that, at least from the perspective of Apuleius, the end goal of the Forum Augustum—producing civic-minded virtuous rulers, administrators, and citizens to oversee Rome and the provinces—had fallen a bit short.[109] This failure makes the Forum of Augustus no less significant a monument in rhetorical history, nor does it imply that the message of the forum had no impact on the people; quite the contrary, it suggests only that the forum was not used as Augustus intended and that maybe Isocrates had a point.

5

COINS, MATERIAL RHETORICS,
AND CIRCULATION

The Augustan political myth presented on the Ara Pacis argues that Rome had been founded with the favor of the gods, that the people's lack of piety had brought about great suffering and the civil wars, that the Julian line was descended from the gods and destined to restore peace and prosperity to Rome, and that only a successor from the Julian line would be able to continue the peace and prosperity brought to Rome by Augustus. The friezes on the altar narrate this myth and offer models of Augustan citizenship meant for emulation, but not all Roman citizens lived in Rome where they could view the Ara Pacis or the models of citizenship offered subsequently in the *summi viri*.[1] The problem of circulation described by Isocrates that led him to disparage statues as memorials was a very real problem for the Augustan political myth as displayed on the Ara Pacis, which was even more difficult to replicate and circulate than a single statue. Still, the static incarnation of the political myth on the Ara Pacis could serve as a repository of meaning, literally a source of invention for other rhetorical media, which could then be circulated more broadly. The Augustan political myth as represented on the Ara Pacis in 13 B.C.E. continued to evolve until the end of Augustus's reign in 14 C.E. Roman coinage displays this evolution.

The role of coins as a communication medium is summarized by numismatist Harold Mattingly: "The accession of a new Emperor, the adoption of successor, important concessions to the Senate or people, building of temples, roads or harbours, journeys in the provinces or victories over the foreign foe—one and all are brought to the public notice on coins."[2] As the most broadly circulating medium between the emperor and the Roman people, then, coins functioned as visual and material rhetorical artifacts; however, coins were not just a means to show the people the emperor's accomplishments, but as Mattingly stresses, coins showed which events the emperor wished to be known for, which acts he chose to ignore, and how he wanted to be seen by the people.[3] As such, coins often reveal the rhetorical strategy of Augustus's administration, and those produced by the imperial mint are clear examples of state-sponsored rhetoric meant for mass circulation to publicize the *princeps,* his administration, his accomplishments, and the Julian line.

Coins functioned rhetorically in two ways in the principate: first, coins functioned as a material rhetoric. There is an old saying that the more of the emperor you have in your pocket, the more he has you in his, referring to the image of the emperor on the obverse of coins. While this saying may not at first seem to denote the rhetorical properties of currency, Augustus created a political myth that promised the people of Rome prosperity with currency functioning as one tangible outcome of the myth. In other words, coins were one material result of the promise of prosperity made in the Augustan political myth. Second, coins offered a way to disseminate information to the people, and though often a material rhetoric, coins were also a significant form of visual communication.[4]

Though there are vast numbers of coin types from Augustus's reign, imperial and senatorial coins communicate different versions of the principate. Even as early as 13 B.C.E., coins emphasize the conclusions of the Augustan political myth, the arrival of the golden age, and look forward to continued prosperity while assuming a familiarity on the part of the viewer with the myth. Evolutions in the depiction of the themes of the Augustan political myth, particularly succession, reveal changes in the myth, including more of an emphasis on the *princeps* as sacrosanct, rather than as an actor caught up in his mythic destiny (as he is shown on the Ara Pacis). Over time, coins also show an increased emphasis on generalized piety, peace, and prosperity that denote the fulfillment of the Augustan political myth. These shifts, I would argue, signify a change in rhetorical strategy of Augustus's administration that suggest (at least the perceived) acceptance of the Augustan political myth by the people of Rome.

REPUBLICAN COINAGE AND AUGUSTAN STANDARDIZATION

In the Roman republic, coins were primarily minted either by the *tresviri monetales,* the Office of Three Moneyers, at the "senatorial mint" at Rome, or through *imperium* power, that is, the power awarded to military generals in order to pay troops when away from Rome.[5] Mints established through imperial power are sometimes referred to as "imperial mint(s)," though the term comes to mean the mint of the Roman emperor. Coins were also minted in a third way, though only in provinces such as Gaul, Spain, and Africa, where a number of "provincial mints" were established for the creation of local currency.[6]

There were a number of problems with currency that fell to Octavian to solve when he gained sole power. By 31 B.C.E., the mint at Rome was no longer issuing coins.[7] New silver and gold issues were being struck only through *imperium* power for the purpose of paying troops, and bronze coinage was not of a standard weight. No denomination had been struck regularly at Rome since 82 B.C.E.[8] One of Augustus's most significant, though perhaps not most challenging reforms, was the standardization of the weights of all currency. Additionally, Augustus took control of the gold and silver coinage and turned control of the bronze coinage over to the senate.[9]

This standardization under Augustus led to the following divisions of currency. Gold: the aureus (400 Asses) and the gold quinarius (200 Asses); silver: the denarius (16 Asses) and the silver quinarius (8 Asses); and the four denominations of the As: the brass or *orichalcum* sestertius (4 Asses), the brass dupondius (2 Asses), the copper As, and the copper quardrans (1/4 As).[10] Coins were struck by hand with metal dies; the designs of these coins were decided on by the *tresviri* or *imperator,* fashioned by skilled artists, *sculptores,* and then struck by a variety of unskilled workers.[11] The front of coins is referred to as the obverse, the back the reverse.

Though it took several phases, around 15 B.C.E., mint locations and circulation were more or less settled. The mint at Lugdunum (Lyons) supplied gold and silver coinage to Rome and the West; the mint at Antioch supplied/supplemented silver coinage to the East; Rome and Italy got bronze coinage from the mint at Rome, and these issues may have been restricted only to Italy while the provinces minted their own supply of smaller denominations.[12] Though it seems mints supplied certain regions with coins, there is some disagreement among numismatists as to how widely coins circulated. That is, there is debate whether a specific series was minted with a region and audience in mind, which is the position of Harold Mattingly, or whether, as C. H. V. Sutherland argues, coins circulated so widely that those outside the "intended audience" routinely saw them.[13] Assuming that Sutherland's position is correct, the contexts that led to a coin's creation are significant inasmuch as understanding the rhetorical situation of a "text" is significant.

Numismatists have noted significant changes in the types of coins minted at both the senatorial and imperial mints from republic to empire. The main changes in types during the principate can be broadly summarized as such: (1) references to the aristocratic families, usually those of the moneyers, are replaced with images of the emperor and his family; (2) this replacement is accompanied by an increase in portraiture of living people, usually the emperor, which was uncommon if not unheard of before Julius Caesar; (3) old mythology fades away, with the exception of references to the Julian line, and is replaced with personified virtues; and (4) inscriptions on the coins are changed to suggest minting by the emperor for imperial coins and, on occasion, by the moneyers for senatorial coins.[14] While this description of changes is certainly accurate, many of the changes represent incarnations and evolutions of the Augustan political myth and deserve closer examination with an emphasis on rhetorical significance.

THE CIRCULATION OF THE POLITICAL MYTH: THE SENATORIAL MINT AFTER 13 B.C.E.

Many of the senatorially issued coins from the time at which the Ara Pacis was commissioned focus tightly on the themes of the Augustan political myth, so much so that it seems one of the chief goals of the coins was to circulate the myth to broader audiences. The iconography of the coins offers a variety of techniques for overcoming the limited space available, including slight changes in similar issues to stress a point, reading issues serially, and the use of complex iconography. All of these techniques assume some familiarity with Augustan iconography on the part of the viewer.

Piety

The Augustan political myth emphasized Augustus's piety as the virtue that brought the return of the favor of the gods to Rome and modeled piety as an important virtue for the people to emulate. In other words, in the principate, a good citizen was a pious citizen. *Pietas* in the Augustan political myth had both filial and religious significance. Both aspects were portrayed in the figure of Aeneas, whom Augustus often used to amplify his own deeds. Augustus's own religious piety was often stressed as it is on the Ara Pacis, where he is shown with his toga drawn over his head and as a member of the four colleges of state priests (see fig. 4). Other products of the Augustan building program such as the Temple of Mars Ultor clearly emphasized Augustus's filial piety in avenging the murder of his adopted father. It is perhaps not surprising, then, given the prominence of piety in Augustan rhetoric, to find the theme of piety displayed prominently on the coinage of 13 B.C.E.

While the theme of piety is depicted in a variety of manners on coins, piety as depicted on the Ara Pacis seems to have specifically influenced some coin types. The moneyers C. Marius and C. F. Tro, who often stress piety as a theme on their coin types, depict Augustus with his toga drawn over his head with a *simpulum* in his right hand on the reverse of a denarius in a manner very nearly identical to the depiction of the Augustus on the Ara Pacis (see fig. 14.).[15] At the time at which the coin was minted, the Ara Pacis was not yet available to the

14. Denarius of C Marius and CF Tro, 13 B.C.E.
Obv. not shown, as in fig. 15; rev. Augustus
as priest holding a simpulum. American
Numismatic Society, Reg. 1937.158.389.
*Photograph courtesy of the American
Numismatic Society.*

people of Rome.[16] Still, the plans for the Ara Pacis seem to have influenced the minting of this coin—literally providing a place to turn for a means of invention. It is possible, if not probable, that the coin was intended to publicize the construction of the Ara Pacis and to circulate its narrative, overcoming the static nature of the Augustan building program and Isocrates's complaint about static, unmoving memorials. Still, it is important to realize that the coin could be understood without reference to the larger narrative found on the Ara Pacis, especially as other accounts of the myth such as Virgil's *Aeneid* were likely becoming widely known.[17] This certainly suggests that, while the Ara Pacis was the culmination of the Augustan political myth, the myth was already well known by 13 B.C.E. Though the depiction of Augustus's piety on the denarius can stand alone, it can also be read against others in the series, which provide many of the themes of the Augustan political myth.[18] Still, the simple depiction of Augustus with his toga drawn over his head, a demonstration of his piety, held significance even without the use of amplification, and was likely circulated as a model for emulation.

This denarius was not the only issue by C. Marius and C. F. Tro. to emphasize piety. Perhaps because of the limited space provided by coins, various types stress different aspects of piety found in the Augustan political myth. Another coin issued by C. Marius and C. F. Tro. shares the same obverse as the denarius discussed above, Augustus bare-headed with the *lituus,* which suggests his role as *princeps,* first citizen, with the priestly tool the *lituus,* curved staff, which could denote Augustus's role as priest and mediator of the gods' will and favor (see fig. 15).[19] At the time at which this coin was struck, Augustus was not yet chief priest, *pontifex maximus,* but he was a member of the four priestly colleges of the state, Mars, Jupiter, Deified Caesar, and Quirinus, a point emphasized on the Ara Pacis. In addition, if a *lituus* is shown under the hand of Augustus on the Ara Pacis, as Niels Hannestad argues, the symbol of the *lituus* on these coins again references that monument.[20] At the same time, the *lituus* may serve as a

15. Denarius of C Marius and CF Tro, 13 B.C.E. Obv. portrait head of Augustus
with lituus; rev. Augustus (left) wearing laurels and Agrippa wearing the
mural and rostral crown, both holding scrolls with a capsa below. The British
Museum, London. Reg. R.6048. *Photograph © the Trustees of the British Museum.*

subtle point of amplification, drawing a comparison to historical Roman rulers,
specifically Romulus.[21]

    The obverses of both denarii predominantly depict Augustus in his civic role
while the reverses emphasize his role as priest or mediator of the gods' will. The
reverse of this second issue shows Augustus (on the left) with his toga drawn
over his head as a priest and holding a scroll in his left hand and Agrippa (on the
right) wearing the combined mural and rostral crown (see fig. 15). Below them
is a *capsa,* a repository often used for holding scrolls.[22] While certainly the coin
makes a statement about Agrippa's intended succession of Augustus, a theme
discussed shortly, the obverse shows Augustus as the leader of the Roman people
while the reverse stresses Augustus's piety. This piety has allowed Augustus to
rule with the gods' favor and also has led to military victories, his own as well as
Agrippa's, both at land and at sea, which are denoted by Agrippa's crown.

    Virgil writes of the relationship between Augustus, Agrippa, and the gods
while describing the battle of Actium in the *Aeneid*: "On the one side Augustus Caesar stands on the lofty stern, leading Italians to strife, with Senate and
People, the Penates of the state, and all the mighty gods; his auspicious brows
shoot forth a double flame, and on his head dawns his father's star. Elsewhere,
favored by winds and gods, high-towering Agrippa leads his column; his brows
gleam with the beaks of the naval crown, proud token won in war."[23] Here it is
not only Augustus who is favored by the gods, including his deified, adopted
father Julius Caesar, but also Agrippa who has gained the gods' favor and whose

military prowess has made the Augustan peace possible. Agrippa's prominent position was emphasized when he was bestowed *tribunician* power for a second time in 13 B.C.E., the only man to share this power with Augustus at this point.[24] Augustus's piety functions as the mediating force for the success of Roman military ventures and for the prosperity these ventures bring to the Roman people.

In addition, the alternate obverse of this coin from the same date and moneyers features a portrait head of Augustus, bare, with the legend AVGVSTVS DIVI F rather than merely AVGVSTVS with the whole obverse surrounded by an oak-wreath. This coin, like the passage from the *Aeneid,* makes reference to Julius Caesar through the inscription referencing Augustus's status as the son of the deified Julius, or literally "son of the divine," while the passage uses the symbolism of the comet that appeared after the death of Caesar, which was believed to signify his deification.[25] This alternate obverse more explicitly connects the gods' favor to the Julian line, but it also shows a limitation of coins: there is only so much space. This coin demonstrates that, in order to overcome limited space, slight differences in iconography or inscription could be used to highlight variations on similar coins to express an array of messages, especially if the coins are read in relation to one another or serially.

The moneyers C. Marius and C. F. Tro. were not the only ones to take up the theme of piety. There are several more generalized images of piety on the coins from 13 B.C.E. such as the aureus and denarius of C. Antistius Reginus. The aureus features the portrait head of Augustus wearing an oak wreath on the obverse and depicts two priests, with their togas drawn over their heads, holding a pig

16. Aureus of C. Antistius Reginus, 13 B.C.E. Obv. portrait head of Augustus wearing oak wreath; rev. two priests holding a pig over an altar. The British Museum, London. Reg. 1864,1128.22.
Photograph © the Trustees of the British Museum.

over an altar on the reverse (see fig. 16). The denarius has the bare portrait head of Augustus on the obverse with the priestly implements the *simpulum, lituus,* tripod, and *patera* shown on the reverse (see fig. 17).[26] The imagery differs somewhat from the themes of piety depicted on the Ara Pacis or circulated in Virgil's account. Rather, as Mark Fullerton argues, the emphasis of priestly implements denotes the Gabines, the people of a city near Rome, and their "association with augury" from which the moneyer's family was descended, marking these issues as the last "republican types" to make such a reference.[27]

Of these so-called republican types of general piety by Reginus the depiction of priestly tools is a repeated type from 18 B.C.E.; the repetition in 13 B.C.E. is intriguing. Overall, the types from Reginus fit well with the pious tone Augustus advocated as the people's role in supporting the Augustan political myth, making the types appropriate to the period. Rather than seeing these types as anomalous, as Fullerton does, these types can be read as examples of how Reginus (and his family) fit with the Augustan political myth, that is, how his family embodies the practices of citizenship stressed by the Augustan political myth making the repetition of these types appropriate.

Beginning in 9 B.C.E., bronze issues prominently feature the *lituus, simpulum,* and altars, possibly influenced by the issues of Reginus. While the plans for the Ara Pacis seem to have influenced some moneyers, the persistence of republican types connected to a specific moneyer's family does suggest Augustan

17. Denarius of C. Antistius Reginus, 13 B.C.E. Obv. portrait head of Augustus; rev. priestly tools. The British Museum, London. Reg. R. 6050.
   Photograph © the Trustees of the British Museum.

iconography was not always "top down"; expressions of citizenship that fit with the Augustan political myth were circulated widely. While Reginus's types may not strictly be examples of imitation, they do offer an example of ideal citizenship as stressed in the Augustan political myth.

The senatorial issues of 13–12 B.C.E. in gold and silver, then, use the theme of piety rhetorically in ways that are similar to the Augustan political myth as represented on the Ara Pacis: it is Augustus's piety that brings about the goodwill of the gods, allowing for military victories and civic stability; Augustus's relationship with the deified Julius contributes to the gods' favor; his role as *pontifex maximus* after 12 B.C.E. allows for further mediation of the gods' favor; and the instruction that the people imitate Augustus's piety offers one way to participate in the new government of the principate. While any of these scenes of generalized piety could be interpreted in relation to any or all of these themes, the more generalized scenes of priestly tools or sacrifice at a nondescript altar, as in other Augustan media, leave much to the viewer, suggesting it is their job to take up religious duties.

Three aspects of the issues dealing with piety stand out as significant advances in the use of coins as rhetorical media. First, at least with some issues, it is likely that the Ara Pacis influenced the selection of motifs. This suggests that the Augustan building program was influencing invention in other media, while at the same time more transitory media such as coins were being used to overcome the problem of circulating static or fixed rhetoric media. Second, the obverse and the reverse do not just portray Augustus and some act or deed for which he is responsible (a building, the grain distribution, a road) as done earlier in the principate, but rather they depict two aspects of his role as ruler—civic and religious. This is a significant shift in the Augustan political myth and likely reflects a shift in rhetorical strategy of Augustus's administration. Though the shift is subtle, the emphasis is on Augustus's character or person, placing him as the mediator of the people's fortunes rather than as an actor caught up in his destiny. In other words, there is a shift from justification of Augustus's rule to a perceived acceptance that stresses the people's role in the principate. Third, the practice of altering images slightly to call attention to the differences in iconography is also an important rhetorical technique. The images on coins were so frequently seen that variation keeps them from becoming overlooked by a viewer due to monotony. In other words, what might become mundane through repetition is altered for greater impact. The tactic of altering types slightly is also a strategy to deal with the limited space provided by the medium. Perhaps most significantly, the coins dealing with piety instruct the Roman people how they might practice citizenship by offering models for imitation (Augustus and Agrippa), creating a generally pious tone, and prominently featuring those who practiced piety (priests and the types of Reginus).

Succession

The coin types dealing with piety from 13 B.C.E. offer a snapshot of how themes from the Augustan political myth were circulated and of how emulation both of the *Ara* Pacis and of Augustus's model of citizenship played into type selection at one time. The theme of succession offers a much different example in that it was possibly the most problematic aspect of Augustus's reign and, as such, continued to demand attention over the remainder of the principate. Because of Augustus's difficulty in finding an heir, the theme of succession continues to develop nearly to the end Augustus's reign, offering an opportunity to see how the Augustan political myth evolved.

The ultimate goal of the Augustan political myth was to ease the process of succession for a designated heir. Augustus had experienced the challenges of establishing himself based on his status as Caesar's heir. For Augustus, then Octavian, the problem was multifaceted; Augustus's status as Caesar's heir had not been publicly recognized before Caesar's assassination, and there was the general dislike of monarchs and dynastic succession by the Roman people. The Augustan political myth suggests a rhetorical strategy for overcoming the constraints Augustus faced after the assassination of Caesar; however, this strategy, as coins show, changed over time and with each successor. Unfortunately, it was not only rhetorical constraints that complicated Augustan succession—Augustus outlived a number of chosen successors in his seventy-five years.

Many of the strategies used by Octavian to legitimate his own succession appear in his own designation of a successor. A number of early issues emphasize Julius Caesar as divine, thus marking Octavian as "son of the divine" through both inscriptions and iconography, particularly the use of the comet thought to signify the ascent of Caesar.[28] The importance of Octavian's status as son of the deified Julius was, at times, as C. H. V. Sutherland suggests, "the only legitimate power the young man held."[29] These early issues featuring references to Julius Caesar and Octavian established the practice of showing the (posthumous) ruler and the heir on opposite sides of the coin.

At the time of the creation of the Ara Pacis, Agrippa was the heir apparent and had already been publicly designated as such through the grant of *tribunician* power to him in 18 B.C.E. and again in 13 B.C.E.; through his marriage to Julia, Augustus's daughter, in 21 B.C.E.; and through the adoption of their children by Augustus in 17 B.C.E.[30] The coins of 13 B.C.E. mark the first unambiguous statement of Augustan succession in the media and a clear push to publicize the imperial family.[31] The convention of showing the portrait head of the ruler on the obverse and of the successor on the reverse, established on the early issues of Octavian to mark him as Caesar's successor, continued throughout Augustus's reign.

18. Aureus of C. Sulpicius Platorinus, 13 B.C.E. Obv. portrait head of Augustus
wearing oak wreath; rev. Agrippa wearing the mural and rostral crown. The
British Museum, London. Reg. 1864,1128.22.
Photograph © the Trustees of the British Museum.

This practice of showing the ruler on the obverse and the heir on the reverse
was adopted on senatorial issues denoting Agrippa as Augustus's successor. On
the aureus of the moneyer C. Sulpicius Platorinus, Augustus is shown on the
obverse wearing an oak wreath while the reverse shows Agrippa wearing the
mural and rostral crown (see fig. 18). The iconography is more complicated
than simply showing the ruler and his heir, and it plays heavily on the Augustan political myth. As Fullerton notes, Agrippa was both "Augustus' partner in
war . . . [and also] in the propagation of the dynasty. The most obvious result
of Augustus' and Agrippa's partnership was the Pax Augusta. . . . That Pax in
the form of respite from the civil war was the accomplishment of Augustus and
Agrippa" and one of the most significant outcomes of the Augustan political
myth.[32] While the aureus of Platorinus specifically references the military aspect
of the partnership, that relationship has ramifications for the peace and prosperity enjoyed by the people as well.

The iconography of other coins from this period such as the denarius by C.
Marius and C. F. Tro., which shows Augustus with his toga drawn over his head
and Agrippa in the rostral and mural crown, denotes that the success of Agrippa
is due in part to the piety of Augustus but also promises that Agrippa could continue the prosperity of the Augustan political myth (see fig. 15). While Augustan
rhetoric from 13 B.C.E. aggressively sought to establish Agrippa as an heir, he died
shortly after the Ara Pacis was commissioned, though the same type minted by
Platorinus was repeated honorifically.

19. Denarius from the Imperial mint at Lugdunum, 2 B.C.E.–4 C.E. Obv. portrait head of Augustus, laureate; rev. Gaius and Lucius Caesar with shield, spear, simpulum, and lituus. The British Museum, London. Reg. 1920,0614.2.
Photograph © the Trustees of the British Museum.

The method showing the *princeps* and heir on the obverse and reverse was repeated on the coins issued at the imperial mint at Lugdunum beginning as early as 2 B.C.E., designating as heirs Gaius and Lucius Caesar, the sons of Agrippa (see fig. 19). The obverse of the coin shows Augustus laureate with the inscription "Caesar Augustus, Son of the Divine, Father of the Country."[33] The legend on the obverse again establishes Augustus as the "son of the divine" in reference to Julius Caesar but also adds the title *pater patriae*, "Father of his Country," which Augustus received from the senate and the Roman people in 2 B.C.E. The legend on the reverse, "Gaius and Lucius Caesar, sons of Augustus, consuls designate, first of the knights," establishes Gaius and Lucius Caesar as heirs apparent through the designation *princeps iuventutis*, sometimes translated as "chief of the knights," though this is the first time this title is used to designate an heir.[34]

The symbols between the two young men rely heavily on the iconography of the Augustan political myth, as do the depictions of the two youths. Both are shown wearing the *toga virilis*, the toga given to a youth to denote manhood, while the weaponry signifies their knighthood and possibly their military campaigns. Both are shown with their togas drawn over their heads as Augustus was often depicted, but their dress and the priestly tools also denote their (or at least Gaius's) priesthood(s). The reverse can be read as the promise by Augustus that Gaius and Lucius both possess the military virtue and the relationship with the gods necessary to continue Augustus's reign of prosperity. In addition, because the iconography symbolizes various titles and positions given to the youths, there is the sense that, because Augustus's heirs' virtues have been publicly recognized and therefore legitimized, it would be difficult for the senate and Roman people to turn their backs on the young men, particularly, as the inscription denotes, after designating them as future consuls. The young men were not depicted on senatorial issues; however, they were so popular with the people of Rome that a bronze issue at Rome may have been unnecessary. Lucius and Gaius were no more successful than Agrippa in succeeding Augustus, with the former dying in 2 C.E. and the latter in 4 C.E., though again, as with Agrippa, the coin type continued honorifically.[35]

Whereas Agrippa was shown as a partner to Augustus, sharing in the gods' favor, and Lucius and Gaius were shown as sharing certain characteristics with the *princeps,* not unlike the *summi viri,* the rhetorical strategy for denoting a suitable successor shifts again with Tiberius. Tiberius, the son of Augustus's wife Livia from her first marriage, was Augustus's last option for a successor in many respects, and though already a successful general, former consul, and recipient of *tribunician* power, the push for recognition as heir came late in Augustus's reign and only after the death of Gaius.[36] The coins that promote Tiberius as an heir sometimes use the strategy of depicting Augustus on the obverse and Tiberius on the reverse, but at times more literally show Tiberius in place of Augustus on the obverse.[37] This strategy is clearly seen on coinage from the imperial mint at Lugdunum. For example, two dupondii depict either Augustus or Tiberius on the obverse and the Altar of Rome and Augustus at Lugdunum (Lyons), which was dedicated as part of the *consilium Galliarum* in 10 B.C.E. on the reverse (see figs. 20 and 21).[38] The legend on the obverse of the dupondius featuring Tiberius reads, "Tiberius Caesar, son of Augustus, Imperator for the fifth time,"[39] calling attention to Tiberius's familial relationship with Augustus. Similarly the inscription on the obverse of the dupondius featuring Augustus reads, "Caesar Augustus, son of the divine, Father of the Country,"[40] calling attention to the familial relationship between Caesar and Augustus. While Augustus is not yet divine, the similarity between the inscriptions foreshadows that the "D" (signifying deification) appended to Augustus's name is not far off. While Tiberius is shown in place of Augustus, the title "Imperator" on the dupondius does allude to Tiberius's military prowess and his role in maintaining the peace abroad, again emphasizing a characteristic that will potentially allow Tiberius to continue the prosperity brought to Rome by Augustus.

These shifts in how succession was handled on Augustan coinage hints at Augustus's rhetorical strategy in creating support for his heir and the importance of various rhetorical audiences. While it would seem that one of the apparent goals of the senatorial issues of 13–12 B.C.E. was to promote the Julian line

20. Dupondius from the Imperial mint at Lugdunum, 9–14 C.E. Obv. portrait head
of Augustus, laureate; rev. Altar of Lugdunum. The British Museum, London.
Reg. R.6278. *Photograph © the Trustees of the British Museum.*

21. Dupondius from the Imperial mint at Lugdunum, 8–10 C.E. Obv. portrait
head of Tiberius, laureate; rev. Altar of Lugdunum. The British Museum,
London. Reg. 1919,0307.320. *Photograph © the Trustees of the British Museum.*

and the succession of Agrippa via the Augustan political myth, there is a fundamental need to have the legitimacy and support of the senate in backing the
process of dynastic succession. This support was, in part, created and publicized
by the circulation of coins minted by the *tresviri*. No bronze issues were minted
during the period when there was a push for support for Agrippa, making his
absence on bronze issues unsurprising; however, bronze issues resumed in 9

B.C.E. in Rome. Gaius and Lucius were never depicted on a bronze issue, making it perhaps significant that Tiberius's image was chiefly circulated on bronze issues prior to Augustus's death.[41]

At the time when Gaius and Lucius were the heirs apparent, a push for popular support may have been unnecessary because the boys had been thoroughly ensconced by other means including games, titles, and offices to the point of reaching cult-like status at Rome.[42] Tiberius, on the other hand, though a victorious general, had not received the degree of attention from Augustus or public accolades that the two youths had. Tiberius left public life and Rome, seemingly out of jealousy over the advancement of Gaius and Lucius or to avoid giving offense to the two princes, which prompted public conjecture and scorn from Augustus.[43] The circulation of Tiberius's image on bronze issues can be read as an attempt to gain and/or further the support of the urban populace who were, undoubtedly, a key rhetorical audience in the circulation of bronze coins. The emphasis on Augustus's *tribunician* power on many bronze issues highlights the plebian audience who would have traditionally found some political representation through the office of the tribune. The need then for support in the form of bronze coinage carrying the "SC" legend, which translates to both senatorial and popular support, is not altogether surprising when it came to promoting Tiberius's succession.

The issues dealing with the heir of Augustus, on the whole, show several important rhetorical strategies for overcoming the problems Augustus had faced in succeeding Caesar, as the issues addressing the succession of Agrippa, Gaius and Lucius, and Tiberius each mark a change for showing a successor as worthy. These coins establish the familial relationship between Augustus and the potential heir, thus connecting the heir to the Julian line. The coins also serve to show that the potential heir, in large part due to their membership in the Julian line, as capable of continuing the gods' favor, resulting in a continuation of the peace, prosperity, and stability created by Augustus. In other words, the heir possesses the ability to continue the Augustan political myth through military prowess, priesthoods, and the like. While most coins dealing with succession share these characteristics, there is a subtle evolution over time: Agrippa was Augustus's partner in the political myth, Gaius and Lucius are shown as possessing similar traits or even as imitating Augustus, and Tiberius is shown in place of the *princeps*. This reflects a changing attitude, or the perception of a changing attitude by the creator of the coins and a response in rhetorical strategy. That is, as Augustus became more and more sacrosanct, the merits of his heir mattered less than the heir's association with Augustus. Interestingly, it would seem that, while this is most true for Tiberius, perhaps to correct his absence from Rome, a last-ditch effort to gain popular support was also crucial. In all cases, senatorial issues served to legitimize the heir and gain public support for the accomplishments, offices, and honors of the potential heir. It would be significantly harder for the senate and people of Rome to turn on Augustus's heir after recognizing him so prominently.

Peace, Victory, and Prosperity

Just as there is an evolution in the iconography associated with succession, which signifies corresponding changes in the political myth and rhetorical strategy of Augustus, so too there is a shift in the iconography associated with peace, victory, and prosperity on coins. Three significant changes occur in the iconography dealing with peace, victory, and prosperity. First, the practice of crediting the greater gods and heroes on the obverse of coins fades away and is replaced by the portrait head of Augustus. Second, whereas early in Octavian's rule, peace, victory, and prosperity were often tied to a single event, this imagery becomes increasingly generalized by referring to Augustus's rule broadly. Third, this imagery becomes increasingly complex. Each of these changes suggests the acceptance and refinement of the political myth and an increased literacy in the iconography of the myth among Roman citizens.

Early in Octavian's rule, coin types often depicted his mythic lineage showing, for example, Octavian's portrait head on the obverse and the flight of Aeneas on the reverse or a portrait head of Venus on the obverse and Octavian holding a spear on the reverse (see fig. 22).[44] These images tie specific military victories, Philippi and Actium respectively, to Augustus's lineage and the gods. The denarius from an Italian mint featuring Venus on the obverse goes as far as to credit Venus with Octavian's success at Actium while highlighting Julius Caesar's divine status with the inscription CAESAR DIVI F on the reverse of the coin. If these early issues can be read as the gods' mediating the successes of Octavian, then later issues such as those dating from 13–12 B.C.E., which almost always feature the portrait head of Augustus, suggest that it is the *princeps* mediating the fortunes of the Roman people.

Domination of the obverse with the portrait of Augustus and portraiture more generally is significant because it denotes the rise of an individual leader, rather than a republican system. The domination of portraiture also marks advancement in the Augustan political myth. Even the coins that correspond to the same period as the Ara Pacis no longer emphasize Augustus's fate but rather Augustus as an actor with control of his destiny, and, with the exception of references to Julius Caesar, coins no longer look back or emphasize the mythic history of the city. This shift away from the greater gods, also coincides with a move towards depictions of the personified deities Peace and Victory, who appear early in Octavian's issues. These depictions of Peace and Victory also undergo a

22. Denarius from an Italian mint, 32 B.C.E.–29 B.C.E. Obv. Venus; rev. Octavian in military dress holding a spear. The British Museum, London. Reg.
1866,1201.4185. *Photograph © the Trustees of the British Museum.*

shift in the period of 13 B.C.E. in that they are no longer tied to the greater gods,
but instead associated with the *princeps*.[45]

Perhaps the most significant change in coins that depict the imagery of
peace and prosperity is that the images are significantly more generalized. With
Augustus's position firmly entrenched, the political myth turns to the promise of
continued prosperity through dynastic succession. By 9 B.C.E., senatorial issues
feature only vague images of prosperity. This shift, like the shift from portraying
specific victories, suggests that, rather than the coming of a golden age, the *pax
Augustae* is upon the Roman people.

The Augustan political myth comes together by reading the coins of 13 B.C.E.
in relation to one another, although certain coins seem to encapsulate the entire
myth through complex iconography. This is not to say that there was not exceedingly complex iconography prior to this period, but the moneyers of 12 B.C.E.
seem to have assumed a level of proficiency among Roman viewers that would
have required a thorough understanding of Augustan iconography (and history).[46] The denarius of L. Lentulus, dating to 12 B.C.E., shows how all encompassing and generalized, not to mention complicated and involved, both the
Augustan political myth and the iconography thereof have become (see fig. 23).
The obverse shows a portrait head of Augustus, bare, and the reverse shows two
figures, presumably one a statue of Caesar holding Victory and the other Augustus crowning the statue while his hand rests on the Shield of Virtues. Fullerton's
reading of the coin demonstrates the complexity of the iconography:

The figure to the right is quite clearly Augustus; the shield inscribed C.V. can only be the golden "clipeus . . . virtutis, clementiae, iustitiae, pietatis," voted to Augustus in 27 B.C. and dedicated in the Curia Iulia.[47] The figure to the left with the star over his head is encountered elsewhere on monuments of Augustan and Julio-Claudian date—on the Ravenna relief, a relief from Carthage, and on a cuirass statue in Cherchell. Here, as there, it must be a representation of Divus Julius.

The coin does not represent the consecration of a particular statue; it represents Augustus as son of Caesar-DIVI F. The shield is there both as an attribute to identify Augustus and as a monument to Augustus's *pietas.* That Augustus considered it especially connected with his membership in the gens Iulia is shown by the fact that he dedicated it in the Curia Iulia. The relevance of this message in a context of 12 B.C. is not difficult to discern. When writing about his election as *pontifex maximus.* . . . It is clear from this passage[48] that Augustus considered Lepidus to be an illegal usurper of the high priesthood and himself to be the legal successor to his own father in the office. . . . Augustus was "ortus ab Aenea" ["descended from Aeneas"][49] only through his membership in the gens Iulia, that is, through his adoption by Caesar. He was entitled to his office less as son of Julius Caesar, *pontifex maximus,* than as son of Divus Iulius, descendant of Aeneas and Venus Genetrix. L. Lentulus was therefore entrusted with the striking of an issue of

23. Denarius of L. Lentulus, 12 B.C.E. Obv. portrait head of Augustus; rev. Augustus with the *clipeus virtutis,* crowning a statue of the Deified Julius holding victory. The British Museum, London. Reg. 1844,0425.448.
Photograph © the Trustees of the British Museum.

denarii commemorating Augustus's election as *pontifex maximus.* This issue may have been commissioned to supply the *congiarium*[, gift of money] distributed by Augustus upon his assumption of the office.[50]

As Fullerton's reading reveals, to understand this coin involves knowledge of the symbols such as the comet to identify the statue of the divine Julius, the CV to identify the Shield of Virtues, and the connection the of shield with the Curia Julia. If Fullerton is correct that the coin was part of a distribution of money to the people by Augustus to celebrate his election as *pontifex maximus,* the iconography would easily be tied to this occasion and the role of the coin as a material rhetoric. However, a full understanding of this coin's iconography requires a great deal of social knowledge, familiarity with other Augustan monuments, and awareness of the events that prompted their building in order for the viewer to construct an enthymematic argument. While Fullerton has used sources such as Ovid and the *Res Gestae* for context, his reading of the coin was likely not outside the grasp of the Roman viewer who might have been familiar with the events and monuments referred to on the coin, though one wonders how effective the iconography of this coin would have been outside of Rome.

Like the coin of Lentulus, issues minted after 13 B.C.E. continued to stress Augustus as fulfilling a (divine) mission, but the reason for his accomplishments shifted somewhat. If the descent of the Julian line from divine ancestry is represented, it is done so only through references to the divine Julius. The rest of the narrative, if there is any, must be filled in by the viewer. The role of Augustus as mediating the relationship between the gods and the people, in part through the

24. Sestertius of C. Cassius Celer, 16 B.C.E. Obv. "Ob Civis Servatos" with oak wreath; rev. SC with name and title of the moneyer. The British Museum, London. Reg. R.6202. *Photograph © the Trustees of the British Museum.*

25. Dupondius of C. Plotius Rufus, 15 B.C.E. Obv. "Augustus Tribunic Potest" in oak wreath; rev. SC with name and title of the moneyer. The British Museum, London. Reg. R.5086. *Photograph © the Trustees of the British Museum.*

divine Julius, shifts with the replacement of the great gods by the *princeps* portrait and the appearance of personified virtues; Augustus is no longer a hapless character fulfilling his fate; he creates the favor that leads to the prosperity of the Roman people. The coins of 13–12 B.C.E. stress both the deification of Caesar and Augustus's succession of Caesar perhaps as parallel arguments for future events. The peace, prosperity, and victory on coins after 13 B.C.E. is more generalized, allowing for greater interpretation on the part of the viewer but also suggesting the fulfillment of the Augustan political myth by Augustus. These shifts, particularly the replacement of the great gods of Roman mythology with the divine Julius, the Julian family, and personified deities is, perhaps, the most rhetorically significant because the coins dealing with peace, victory, and prosperity suggest that the Augustan political myth has succeeded with the people, and, to a degree, supplanted the city's mythology.

BRONZE COINS AFTER 9 B.C.E.

Like silver and gold coinage, production of bronze coinage at the senatorial mint also ceased, though for a broader span of time with a gap in production at Rome from 16 to 9 B.C.E. Prior to 9 B.C.E. there were a limited number of types. The reverse of almost all senatorial issues features the large SC in the middle with the name and title of the moneyer around the edge of the coin (see figs. 24, 25, and 26).[51]

The obverse varies by denomination. For the sestertius, the obverse features the iconography of the restoration of the republic, including the *corona civica*, an oak wreath traditionally given to a soldier for saving the life of another, between two laurel branches with the inscription OB CIVIS SERVATOS, "For the citizens he saved" (see fig. 24).[52] For the dupondius, the obverse is inscribed AVGVSTVS TRIB-VNIC POTEST inside the *corona civica* (see fig. 25). For the As, the obverse shows the portrait head of Augustus with the inscription CAESAR AGVSTVS TRIBVNIC POTEST. There are variations in abbreviations and punctuation with nonstandard types (so called "republican types") dropping out over time, but essentially the iconography of bronze issues remained virtually unchanged from 23 B.C.E. until 9 B.C.E.

The bronze coinage before 9 B.C.E. communicated three central ideas. First, the Civic Crown on both the sestertius and dupondius refers to the restoration of the republic but also to the safety and security of the people. The latter message is emphasized not only through the use of the Civic Crown, which was granted to Augustus by the senate when he "returned the Republic to their control" for saving the lives of many citizens, but also is emphasized with the legend OB CIVIS SERVATOS (see fig. 24). Though the crown was traditionally given to a soldier for saving another soldier's life, the legend suggests Augustus saved many lives and ties the notion of safety and security to the *princeps* and to the restoration of the republic. Pliny discusses the conditions under which the crown had historically been bestowed: "These laws are to the effect that the life of a fellow-citizen must be preserved, and an enemy slain; that the spot where this takes place must have been held by the enemy that same day; that the person saved shall admit the fact, other witnesses being of no use at all; and that the person saved shall have been a Roman citizen."[53]

26. As of L. Naevius Surdinus, 15 B.C.E. Obv. portrait head of Augustus; rev. SC with name and title of the moneyer. The British Museum, London. Reg. 1847,0309.61.
Photograph © the Trustees of the British Museum.

Augustus, in his *Res Gestae,* explains the conditions under which he was awarded the Civic Crown, which are quite different from the circumstances described by Pliny: "In my sixth and seventh consulships [28–27 B.C.E.], when I had extinguished the flames of civil war, after receiving by universal consent the absolute control of affairs, I transferred the Republic from my own control to the will of the Senate and the Roman people. For this service on my part I was given the title Augustus by decree of the Senate, and the door posts of my house were covered with laurels by public act, and a Civic Crown was fixed above my door, and a golden shield was placed in the Curia Julia whose inscription testified that the Senate and the Roman people gave me this in recognition of my valour, my clemency, my justice, and my piety."[54] By Augustus's account, he received the crown for ending the civil wars and possibly for his clemency, as these are the acts that saved citizens' lives at the time, though conceivably Augustus saved many lives by stabilizing the "Republic" before transferring control back to the Senate and Roman people.

The second main concept communicated by bronze coinage before 9 B.C.E. is typified by the inscriptions referring to the *tribunician* power of Augustus (see figs. 25 and 26).[55] Both coins stress Augustus's *tribunician* power and his role as representative of the people's interests. Augustus, in his *Res Gestae,* recounts that he was granted this power "by decree of the Senate" in 23 B.C.E. "for life."[56] Traditionally, the office was held by two plebeians meant "to protect the common people against abuse by magistrates or by the Senate. They had wide powers of vet, they could initiate legislation, and their persons were sacrosanct."[57] However, W. Eder explains that in accepting this power for "the populace . . . the paramount issue was the extent to which Augustus actually realized what they had always expected from the tribunes of the plebs—that is, the improvement of their quality of life."[58] Then the references to Augustus's *tribunician* power on the bronze issues of 23–17 B.C.E. suggest both the basis of his power and the obligation he has to the urban plebs of Rome. Significantly, then, the prominence of Augustus's *tribunician* power suggests the rhetorical audience for bronze coinage was the urban plebs represented by that power.

Finally, the third major concept conveyed by bronze coinage is embodied by the SC, which is featured prominently, serving both to show that the senate, and therefore the republic, are still intact. The meaning of *senatus consultum* as well as the role of the moneyers, *tresviri monetales,* at the senatorial mint in Rome bring up questions as to how independently the mint functioned. Though there is limited consensus among numismatists, many suggest that the senatorial mint had little to no actual authority.[59] While many see the SC of the senatorial coinage as predominantly for show, Sutherland suggests that the SC does not indicate "senatorial coinage," but instead that "SC primarily called universal attention to the honours, titles, and powers which Augustus had received from the Senate."[60] As part of the promotion of the Augustan political myth, the SC indicates senatorial involvement for the sake of legitimating Augustus's power and continuing Roman tradition.

New bronze types began in 9 B.C.E. Perhaps because the iconography of the bronze coinage was essentially the same from 23 B.C.E. to 17 B.C.E., the new types are quite striking. In 9 B.C.E., much like the gold and silver coinage of 13 B.C.E., the new types stress peace, prosperity, and piety, the themes of the political myth of Augustus. Three new types are introduced on the quadrans of 9 B.C.E. The obverses feature either: (1) clasped hands holding a caduceus; (2) the priestly implements, the *simpulum,* ladle, and *lituus,* curved staff; or (3) the cornucopia with the SC on either side. The inscriptions on the obverses feature the name of the *tresviri* of that year. The two reverse types include: (1) the traditional SC and (2) the so called "altar type," which shows a garlanded altar used as a reverse to the cornucopia obverse.

The type with the *simpulum* and the *lituus,* Mattingly argues, "refer[s] . . . to Augustus as *pontifex maximus.*" He calls "the clasped hands, caduceus, and cornucopia, trite symbols of concord and prosperity," and the altar a "general religious type."[61] In this case, reading the iconography as discrete images seems to undercut the relationship of these coins to the political myth of Augustus, which despite the absence of his image, is quite strong. It is perhaps easiest to tie the concept of religious piety resulting in prosperity to the type which features the cornucopia on the obverse and the altar on the reverse.

It is even tempting to suggest the altar is an altar of the *lares Augusti,* as Augustus's reformations of the cult coincide with the dating of these coins, and altars dedicated to the Lares would have been springing up like mushrooms all over urban Rome. Such a reading is enticing because the prior inscriptions on bronze coins stress Augustus's *tribunician* power, that is, the office which traditionally represents the urban plebs of Rome, who, in part, likely made up the adherents of the cult, making it possible to speculate they were the intended audience of the bronze issues. Still, without identifying iconography or inscriptions associated with the altars, the coins can be read as a generalized message about piety: piety demonstrated by sacrifice to the gods at an altar would result in prosperity represented on the obverse by the cornucopia. In other words, the piety of the people inspired by Augustus's own piety has restored the gods' favor and brought prosperity. Just as on the Ara Pacis, these bronze issues instruct the citizens of Rome how to participate in the principate.

The emphasis of the bronze issue prior to 9 B.C.E. centered on the safety of the populace due to Augustus's restoration of the republic, the *princeps* relationship with the plebs, and the role of the senate, both as a continuing Roman institution and as a legitimizing body for Augustus's reign. However, the issues

27. Quadrans of Livineius, 8 B.C.E. Obv. simpulum and lituus; rev. SC with title of the moneyer. The British Museum, London. Reg. 1904,0203.60.
   Photograph © the Trustees of the British Museum.

28. Quadrans of Livineius Regulus, 8 B.C.E. Obv. SC with cornucopia; rev. altar with garland. The British Museum, London. Reg. 1843,1024.4.
   Photograph © the Trustees of the British Museum.

after 9 B.C.E. mark a shift similar to the silver and gold coins in that all the images become more generalized. While all relate to the political myth, the bronze types after 9 B.C.E. emphasize prosperity and piety above all else. Again, these changes suggest the political myth had become popular enough among the people that it no longer needed to be explained or argued for. Rather it fell to the viewers to interpret vague images of peace and prosperity and make whatever associations they saw fit.

29. Quadrans of Livineius Regulus, 8 B.C.E. Obv. clasped hands with caduceus
with the name of the moneyer; rev. SC with title of the moneyer. The British
Museum, London. Reg. R.6226. *Photograph © the Trustees of the British Museum.*

DIVERGENCE: THE INFLUENCE OF TYPES
FROM IMPERIAL MINTS

A frequent discussion among numismatists centers on how free the senatorial
mint was to choose types. Certainly it seems that as Augustus's reign continued
there was more uniformity of coin types, be it from compulsion or the prevalence of Augustan imagery dominating the inventional process and crowding
out other types. Still, there is some divergence in imagery between the imperial
and senatorial issues, suggesting perhaps Roman audiences found certain iconography more appealing than others.

Much of the iconography on bronze coins prior to 9 B.C.E. deals with the
honors given to Augustus by the senate and the Roman people in 27 B.C.E. for
restoring the republic. This iconography includes the laurels placed outside his
home, the Civic Crown, and the Shield of Virtues, which recognized Augustus's
piety, clemency, military virtue, and justice.[62] While the iconography of the restoration of the republic is markedly less present, actually almost absent, on silver and gold issues from the senatorial mint before 9 B.C.E., the iconography of
bronze issues often depicted the Civic Crown and the laurels, but almost never
the Shield of Virtues. The Shield of Virtues appears rarely on senatorial issues
(see figs. 23 and 30). This is surprising given the frequency of types that feature
the shield minted at the imperial mint in Spain and date from 19 to 16 B.C.E.

The use of the Shield of Virtues or lack thereof leads to two interesting points
regarding the relationship between Augustus, the principate, and the people of

30. Aureus of Q. Rustius, 19 B.C.E. Obv. Fortuna Victrix and Fortuna Felix; rev.
Victory with *clipeus virtutis.* The British Museum, London. Reg. 1864,1128.25.
Photograph © the Trustees of the British Museum.

Rome. First, it suggests that, for Roman audiences, the laurels and Civic Crown
were somehow more appropriate to symbolize the "restoration of the Republic."
There are several reasons this could be the case: both the Civic Crown and laurels
had long traditions in republican Rome, while the Shield of Virtues was a new
honor. Second, Roman audiences were, at least initially, likely more concerned
with the peace symbolized by the Civic Crown and laurels than with the emper-
or's virtues. That is, the people were more concerned with the tangible benefits
of the Augustan political myth than how that prosperity was created. Finally, the
civic crown and the virtues represented on it may have been targeted by Augustus's administration specifically to those taking on administrative positions and
less so to the Roman masses.

Second, the Shield of Virtues was prevalent in the iconography on the types
of coins produced at various imperial mints in Spain between 19 and 16 B.C.E.,
but the scarcity of such types in Rome brings up the question of influence. Some
types clearly began at imperial mints and then were used by the senatorial mint
at Rome. This is certainly not always the case. The clearest example of a type
from an individual moneyer at the senatorial mint having great influence over
later bronze types occurs with the use of the priestly implements by C. Antistius
Vetus in 18 B.C.E. and repeated by his family member in C. Antistius Reginus in
13 B.C.E. In this case, what may have started off as a type of significance to the
family of the moneyer was appropriated for broader continued use in the principate, likely because it fit with the Augustan political myth so well. The changes
in types beginning in 13 B.C.E. in gold and silver issues, and 9 B.C.E. for bronze

issues, suggest either more control on the part of Augustus's administration over the types, or that the Augustan political myth had already taken hold and had influenced the moneyers' selections. While either claim could be argued, it is fairly clear that the moneyers at the senatorial mint in Rome had some selection in types, especially prior to 13 B.C.E.

THE UNIFICATION OF THE AUGUSTAN POLITICAL MYTH

In 7 B.C.E. "triumphal" coinage, which is the most complete illustration of the Augustan political myth on a bronze coin as well as the highest quality artwork, was issued at the senatorial mint. The obverse of the triumphal As features a portrait head of Augustus laureate, sometimes over a globe, with victory standing behind the portrait head holding a cornucopia touching the laurel wreath (see fig. 31).[63] The reverse is the usual SC with the name and title of the moneyer. The occasion for the triumphal issue may have been Tiberius's triumph of 7 B.C.E. Tiberius at this time was also given the title "Imperator" and made consul for the second time.[64] If the coin was minted in association with Tiberius's triumphs of the year for the campaign in Germany, these were also Augustus's victories. As Dio tells us, "He also granted Tiberius the honour of a triumph; he did not wish to celebrate one himself."[65] And although Tiberius would leave political life at Rome and retire to Rhodes in just the next year, he received many honors and titles in 7 B.C.E. Historian Colin Wells describes his position as "clearly marked out as the second man in the state" in this period.[66] The triumphal As can then be

31. Dupondius or As of M. Maecilius Tullus, 7 B.C.E. Obv. portrait head of Augustus, laureate; rev. SC with name and title of the moneyer. The British Museum, London. Reg. R. 6232. *Photograph © the Trustees of the British Museum.*

read in association with the triumph of Tiberius or as representing the Augustan political myth more broadly, encompassing the themes of succession and victory.

Either way, the triumphal As is the best example of the unification of iconography dealing with the political myth of Augustus on a bronze coin, if not on any coin of the period. The portrait head of Augustus is shown laureate, depicting Augustus as victorious, with Victory herself standing behind him, touching the laurels. In her hand is a cornucopia. While the images of Roma seated on spoils and "Tellus" depicted in a scene of abundance on the Ara Pacis convey a similar message, here the iconography is abbreviated. Augustus, Victory, and Plenty as represented by the cornucopia are all interdependent. In addition, on some issues there is a globe shown below the portrait bust of Augustus, denoting that Augustus has fulfilled his role as ruler of Rome by restoring the city to its rightful place ruling the world. If the occasion for the issue was the triumph of Tiberius celebrated in 7 B.C.E., then this would serve to connect the iconography of the coin to Tiberius, showing he could carry on the political myth of Augustus.

While the triumphal As of 7 B.C.E. is perhaps the most complete depiction of the Augustan political myth on a coin type, it also shows many of the changes in the Augustan political myth that occurred in a relatively short five-year period from the circulation of the political myth on the coins of 13–12 B.C.E. On the triumphal issue, victory is the prevalent theme rather than piety, as is the case on other issues of the period; however, the cornucopia persists as a sign of generalized prosperity. On the triumphal issue, a personified deity, debatably an aspect of Augustus's own character, is responsible for the victory, rather than a great god like Venus or Apollo. However slight the shift, the political myth evolved from making Augustus's destiny part of a larger narrative to emphasizing the *princeps* own responsibility in creating Rome's future.

It is this shift to an emphasis of the person of the *princeps* that is most evident on coins dealing with the themes of the political myth. This change on coin types after the issue of 13–12 B.C.E. is reflected in a number of ways: Augustus is continually shown as mediating the fortunes of the people; however, that mediation becomes more and more dependent on the Julian line and less so on the greater gods; the rhetorical strategy of designating a successor depends less on showing the heir as similar to Augustus and shifts to associating him with the *princeps* or even as Augustus; and the iconography of the restoration of the republic, the laurel and civic crown, begin to include the shield of virtues on senatorial issues, again suggesting an emphasis on the character of the *princeps* himself. All of these changes in the political myth suggest a populace that had been exposed to and taken up the political myth of Augustus and the principate itself.

The same arguments hold in examining the specific rhetorical techniques found on coins. For example, while techniques like imitation and amplification

found on the Ara Pacis still operate on coins, likely because of spatial limita-
tions, the exemplar is often missing, requiring the audience to fill in the model
of emulation. Similarly, generalized images of peace and prosperity again rely on
the viewer to customize the outcome of the political myth to their own experience. This would be a risky rhetorical strategy if the Augustan political myth as
depicted on the Ara Pacis had not become firmly entrenched by this period.

6

THE AUGUSTAN POLITICAL
MYTH IN VERNACULAR ART

Paul Zanker argues of the principate that, because of "the dominance of the official imagery, it became impossible to find a means of individual artistic expression."[1] Writing about the same period, Tacitus mentions a lack of freedom of speech, though one that was driven more from sycophancy than imposed by censorship.[2] These stances, no doubt, contribute to the narrative that Augustus was a "tyrant."[3] It would seem, according to widely held belief, that across media from art to oratory there was little in the way of comment on, let alone voiced opposition to, the reign of Augustus or the principate generally. Given the vastly new and ideologically foreign structure of the principate compared to the constitutional republic, this silence seems somewhat surprising.

The views expressed by Zanker, Tacitus, and Bizzell and Herzberg are significant when it comes to examining Augustan rhetoric because of the way many scholars of rhetoric think about and define (the practice of) rhetoric. Richard Leo Enos says of rhetoric in the transition from republic to principate, "It is clear that rhetoric in Rome functioned well when the society had a public that was empowered to fully use it in the administration of legal and civic affairs. Denied that power, the utility of rhetoric as a social force quickly eroded."[4] Enos reveals an underlying belief that seems to trace back to Lloyd Bitzer's rhetorical situation; that is, in order for a rhetorical act to take place, a rhetor must be addressing a rhetorical audience, that is, an audience "capable of being influenced by discourse and of being mediators of change."[5] However implicitly, the grounds for denying the presence of rhetoric in the principate is often tied to the belief that there were no rhetorical audiences and additionally that there was no freedom of speech.

While Tacitus does imply that there was a lack of freedom of speech, he suggests it was not censorship, but the desire for political advancement that silenced many.[6] Ovid is the obvious example to the contrary.[7] As classicists K. A. Raaflaub and L. J. Samons II argue, "Ovid's banishment could scarcely have been indicative of a concerted policy on the part of Augustus to repress freedom of speech and never had found its way into the extent sources. Modern scholarship is guilty of interpreting this event in a way the ancient authors never did."[8] The denial of the existence of rhetorical audiences and the belief that the populace was silenced in the principate both lack adequate support. Popular expressions of citizenship in the principate suggest that rhetorical audiences and individual expression not only existed but were significant in reifying the Augustan political myth and creating a public memory of the principate.

I have considered the construction of the Augustan political myth by the state on the Ara Pacis, a second incarnation of the myth with an emphasis on citizenship in the Forum of Augustus, and the dissemination of that myth by the imperial and senatorial mints on coins, all representing official discourses. But the iconic images of the Augustan political myth—Augustus as priest, the *corona civica* (Civic Crown), *clipeus virtutis* (Shield of Virtues), and laurels—were also appropriated and merged with the iconography of the cult of the Lares to form depictions of citizenship on altars constructed by the people of Rome. Seven of the remaining altars of the *lares Augusti,* which were constructed by the priests of the cult comprised of urban freedmen, as well as other adherents including women and slaves, serve as examples of displays of vernacular discourse from the principate.[9]

My reading of the altars of the Lares suggests that, while the use of the *corona civica, clipeus virtutis,* and laurels shows an acceptance of the principate and Augustus's reign, this acceptance was not a complete adoption of the dominant discourse. Rather the motifs on the altars of the Lares, though drawn selectively from state iconography, exemplify the characteristics of a vernacular rhetoric, stressing the subject position of the plebs, emphasizing their agency as citizens and supporters of Augustus. Though the altars resemble state art, they are not identical and show a (rhetorical) audience that filtered and selectively accepted state messages and in turn created images, which put them in communication with the *princeps.*

The iconography of the altars both masks and undermines the subject position created in the altars, reinforcing Augustus's account of the principate. Specifically, because the adherents of the cult rely on the iconography of the principate, the vernacular rhetoric of the adherents of the cult reifies the state rhetoric of the principate and Augustan ideology. This reification demonstrates how state art served to limit the inventional means available to the people of Rome, how some nonelite urban residents of Rome responded to the rhetorical strategy of imitation used by Augustus's administration, as well as how Augustan art shaped public memory. In other words, though the Altars of the Lares prove there were rhetorical audiences in the principate, the similarity between vernacular and state iconography masks the agency of the adherents of the cult of the Lares, creating an overwhelming uniformity in motifs, obscuring individual expression and leading to the mistaken conclusion that there were no rhetorical audiences.

THE ALTARS OF THE *LARES AUGUSTI*

Context and Production of Use

The production of the Altars of the Lares began because of Augustus's official religious reforms, which included the revitalization of the longstanding cult of the *lares compitales* with the new addition of the *lares Augusti* and the *princeps' genius,* the household gods and the divine essence of the head of the Julian household, throughout the neighborhoods of Rome in 7 B.C.E. These reforms included the division of the city into fourteen *regiones* (districts) and 265 *vici* (wards) and the creation of a college of priests to oversee the cult in each ward. The priests of each ward, the *vicomagistri,* selected from freedmen, were responsible for constructing the official altar for their ward, as well as performing sacrifices at the altars, though additional altars were built by the *vicoministri* as well as other adherents of the cult.[10]

The new cult of the *lares Augusti* was based on a cult dedicated to the spirit of the crossroads, the cult of the *lares compitales,* which had a long history in the neighborhoods of plebian Rome, but was in disuse at the time of the principate.[11] The cult as revised by Augustus served political, religious, social, and rhetorical functions in the principate. Politically it functioned to create support among nonelites for Augustus and the Julian line, religiously to return the gods to their privileged place in Roman society and Rome to its privileged place with the gods, and socially to provide the prosperity promised by Augustus under the principate by delivering basic firefighting and policing services, thus improving the living conditions in urban Rome.

While an argument could be made that many of the political, social, and religious aspects of the cult functioned rhetorically, the cult of the Lares also functioned to direct the political myth of the principate and the Julian line to a specific segment of the population while shaping their collective identity.[12] The cult met these political, social, and rhetorical functions precisely because of its long history in the city. Augustus's actions were constantly constrained by both the constitutional republic that had governed Rome for the previous five hundred years, and the *mores maiorum,* ancestral traditions that bound Roman conduct. These constraints shaped most of Augustus's reforms, which as Karl Galinsky argues, were often marked by the combination of "restoration and innovation."[13] The cult of the Lares was not a "new" entity, and therefore fairly unobjectionable; however, the Augustan reforms were both many and drastic, radically changing the nature of the cult.[14]

The fulfillment of Augustus's political myth, that "the *gens Iulia* [Julian line] brought peace and prosperity to the world through Augustus, and this favorable state of affairs could persist only with the continued leadership of the *gens Iulia*—through the *domus Augusti* [house of Augustus]," was dependent on the people feeling the material benefits of the principate as opposed to the strife and suffering of the civil wars.[15] The cult of the Lares, with its newly revised structure, along with many other Augustan reforms, created stability in the city of Rome both by ending the organized crime of the former *collegia* and providing policing and firefighting services. The improvement in living conditions created by the cult played directly into the Augustan political myth by showing that Augustus had restored the favor of the gods to the city and that the favor of the gods brought material prosperity to the city.

Classicists and art historians give brief attention to the altars, which, on the whole, are not particularly aesthetically pleasing.[16] As Galinsky explains, the quality of the altars is largely due to their "sponsorship by the *vicomagistri* and the sudden and large demand for them after the reorganization of the cult [which] precluded the level of craftsmanship," suggesting that the financial standing of the sponsors, the skill of the sculptors, as well as haste played a role in the final appearance of the altars.[17] Nonetheless, classicist Inez Scott Ryberg describes the altars as having "historical value," particularly as a source about daily religious practices.[18]

Perhaps more importantly from a rhetorical standpoint, Galinsky emphasizes the adherents of the cult's control in the construction of the altars: "Nor were they simply copies of a mandated prototype. In accordance with the workings of Augustus's *auctoritas,* their basic themes suggested themselves instead of being regimented in every aspect. The shaping of these themes depended on the imagination and quality of the workshops and on the sponsors' initiative."[19] It is precisely the relationship between the altars and their sponsors alluded to by Galinsky that gives the altars their great rhetorical significance. Because they were not state sponsored, the altars of the Lares offered an often-overlooked vernacular voice of sorts, albeit of the most privileged urban plebs, in response to the Augustan political myth disseminated through state art.[20]

The altars were constructed by the priests of the cult, and at times other adherents, who, aside from their right to vote in popular elections, were because of their class standing largely alienated from political practices in Rome.[21] Traditionally, freedmen, though considered plebeians, were barred from holding religious office in Rome because of their servile past. By contrast, the plebs were also a significant power base for the new *princeps*; as Millar argues, "it was precisely this two-way relationship between *princeps* and *plebs* which broke up the Republic."[22] The altars, as vernacular discourses, offer insight into the ways the political myth of Augustus was taken up among nonelite Romans, and how they created their own subjectivity in the principate, and how state art was received by a portion of the populace of Rome. In addition, the altars of the Lares also give a voice to those excluded from the traditional practice of rhetoric in ancient Rome, who are rarely, if ever, (self-)represented in the literary record.

Rhetorical Features of the Altars

The actual construction and design of the neighborhood altars to the Lares fell to the *vicomagistri* or, in the case of unofficial altars, the adherents who commissioned them. The subject matter of the surviving altars can generally be divided into four categories: (1) depictions of the Lares and Genius; (2) simple motifs dealing with the restoration of the republic, including the *corona civica* (Civic Crown), laurels, and the *clipeus virtutis* (Shield of Virtues); (3) scenes depicting the emperor and his family, and (4) scenes representing the *vicomagistri* or other adherents. There are two main rhetorical features of the altars. First, the iconography of the Altars of the Lares deals with the restoration of the republic, showing that, while state iconography certainly influenced and possibly constrained the altars of the Lares, the altars show the role taken up by some plebs in the principate as constructed by the Augustan political myth. Second, there was a virtual absence of dynastic themes on the altars as well as repeated depictions of the adherents of the cult as emphasizing the agency of the nonelite citizens of Rome, both in participating in a cult meant to maintain the favor of the gods and the well-being of the Julian line, and in influencing matters of succession.

The Shield of Virtues, Civic Crown and Laurels: The Iconography of the Principate

Most of the altars of Lares were constructed between 7 B.C.E. and 2 B.C.E. Though elements of the Augustan political myth circulated very early in Octavian's political career, Virgil's *Aeneid,* published in 19 B.C.E., followed by the construction of the Ara Pacis, which was commissioned in 13 B.C.E. and completed in 9 B.C.E., mark the fullest representations of the formation and the fruition, respectively, of the Augustan political myth. The basic themes of the myth as found in visual format on the Ara Pacis were circulated on the gold and silver coins of 13–12 B.C.E. with somewhat revised themes of generalized piety and prosperity disseminated on the bronze coinage after 9 B.C.E. Coin types evolve over time,

32. Altar of the Lares from the Vicus
    Sandaliarius. Victory with shield
    (side) and *corona civica* with lau-
    rels (front). Galleria degli Uffizi,
    Firenzc. Inv. Sculture n. 972.
    Photograph, Neg. 141577, su conces-
    sione del Ministero per i Beni e le
    Attività Culturali.

focusing on Augustus and imbuing him with the responsibility of mediating the
fortunes of the people, putting less emphasis on fate or the gods.

The cult of the Lares, too, emphasizes the role of the Julian line in mediating
the fortunes of the Roman people. The iconography of the altars takes up the
themes of the restoration of the republic of 27 B.C.E. and is remarkably similar
across altars, suggesting a fairly consistent iconology, if not ideology, among the
adherents of the cult who produced the altars (see fig. 32). The *clipeus virtutis*
(Shield of Virtues), *corona civica* (the Civic Crown), and laurels are the most
frequent motifs on the altar of the Lares, all of which originate from the same
event in 27 B.C.E.—the "restoration" and return of the republic to the senate and
Roman people by Augustus following the Battle of Actium, where he defeated
Antonius.[23] From 27 B.C.E. on, Augustus reconstituted all three symbols, the *clipeus virtutis, corona civica,* and laurels, to symbolically invoke his deed of restoring the republic, but also as a type of proof, confirmed by the senate and Roman
people, that he actually had done so. That is, the *clipeus virtutis, corona civica,*
and laurels become the iconic symbols of Augustus's reign, but also proof, vali-
dated by the senate and Roman people, that his reign is what he claims, a restoration of the Roman republic. Dio discusses the same events: "At that time the
privilege of placing the laurel trees in front of the royal residence and of hanging
the wreath of oak leaves above them, was voted in his honour to recognize in
perpetuity his status as victor over his enemies and savior of the citizens."[24]

33. Altar of the Lares dedicated by slaves.
Laurel. Musei Capitolini, Centrale
Montemartini, Rome. Inv. MC 2144/S.
Photograph, Faraglia, Neg. D-DAI-Rom
35.211.

All three symbols were used on coins beginning after 25 B.C.E., but the *clipeus virtutis* was not used frequently on coins minted at Rome, appearing predominantly on coins from the imperial mint (see fig. 34 and 35).[25] The shield was displayed in the Curia Julia and the Civic Crown and laurels stood outside Augustus's house. Coins circulated the images of these fixed icons of the restoration of the republic for nearly twenty years prior to their being taken up by the cult of the *Lares Augusti.* Given the wide and repetitive circulation of these iconic images, a Roman would have been hard pressed to have avoided contact with them by the time the new cult of the Lares was established.

Prior to Augustus's appropriation and reconstitution of these symbols, the *corona civica* and laurels had long histories in Rome that added more depth to their significance. The *corona civica* was the honor for a soldier "presented for preserving the life of a single citizen"; however, as the inscriptions indicate, Augustus was awarded the honor for saving many lives by ending the civil wars and because of his clemency.[26] The laurel trees, "a symbol of Apollo[,] . . . signified victory as well as peace" and allowed Augustus some association with that god.[27] Ryberg argues that, since the Civic Crown and the laurels were displayed outside Augustus's house, they formed "an allusion to the house of Augustus," adding another dimension to the imagery.[28] In addition, because there was a connection between the conversion of Augustus's house to *domus publica,* the

34. Denarius from Spanish mint, 19–18 B.C.E. Obv. portrait head of Augustus wearing oak wreath; rev. *clipeus virtutis* between laurels. The British Museum, London. Reg. 1904,0203.17. *Photograph © the Trustees of the British Museum.*

35. Denarius from Spanish mint, 19 B.C.E. Obv. portrait head of Augustus; rev. victory with wreath and *clipeus virtutis.* The British Museum, London. Reg. BNK,R.227. *Photograph © the Trustees of the British Museum.*

home of the *pontifex maximus,* and the insertion of the *genius Augusti* into the cult of the Lares *compitales,* Augustus's physical house had special significance to the cult of the Lares, making this iconography especially appropriate.

The *clipeus virtutis,* however, was more innovative. The combination of the four virtues, *virtus, clementia, iustitia,* and *pietas* (valor, clemency, justice, and piety), though all distinctly Roman, was uniquely Augustan. The shield was often, though not always, shown with a winged personification of Victory in reference to Actium.[29] Therefore, the shield referred to Augustus's victory over Antonius, which marked the end the civil wars and the return of the *res publica* to the senate and Roman people. While the laurels and *corona civica* also referred to these events, they had a broader range of meaning in the iconography of the period and signified Augustus's election as *pontifex maximus* and the opening of his house and his household shrine to the public.

The frequent popular use of the symbols associated with the restoration of the republic as put forth in state art suggests acceptance of the claim of the "restoration of the republic" by Augustus on the part of some plebs. There is some textual evidence in support of this reading. Velleius Paterculus, Roman soldier, *quaestor,* and eventually *praetor,* writing early in the first century C.E., says of the events of 27 B.C.E.:

> The civil wars were ended after twenty years, foreign wars suppressed, peace restored, the frenzy of arms everywhere lulled to rest; validity was restored to the laws, authority to the courts, and dignity to the Senate; the power of the magistrates was reduced to its former limits, with the sole exception that two were added to the eight existing praetors. The old traditional form of the Republic was restored [*Prisca illa et antiqua rei publicae forma revocata*]. Agriculture returned to the fields, respect to religion, to mankind freedom from anxiety, and to each citizen his property rights were now assured; old laws were usefully emended, and new laws passed for the general good; the revision of the Senate, while not too drastic, was not lacking in severity. The chief men of the state who had won triumphs and had held high office were at the invitation of Augustus induced to adorn the city."[30]

The repetition of the symbols associated with 27 B.C.E. on the altars of the Lares suggests that adherents of the cult, like Velleius, had adopted Augustus's account of history and the principate as an extension of the republic.[31] The Altars of the Lares, however, stress that Augustus's accomplishments were not his alone, but that the people were an active part of the principate.

State and Vernacular Representations of Augustus's Political Myth: The Julian Line and the Plebs

It would seem reasonable given the pervasiveness of Augustus's myth in virtually every instance of state-sponsored art and the religious nature of the cult to find the political myth taken up directly in the iconography of the altars of the Lares; yet, this is the case on only two of the altars, the one now in the Vatican Museums and the one from the *vicus Sandaliarus.*[32] Rather, as Galinsky has noted, the altars repeatedly tend towards representations of the priests or other adherents of the cult of the Lares who commissioned the altars.[33]

The altar now in the Vatican most directly reflects the Augustan political myth, though it may have been state sponsored, as classicist Lily Ross Taylor argues, to show the founding of the cult in 12 B.C.E.[34] The altar shows four scenes that when taken together recall the myth of the Julian line in much the same way as the Ara Pacis. These scenes include an Aeneas scene, a depiction of the apotheosis of Julius Caesar, Augustus handing his household Lares over to the *vicomagistri,* and Victory with a shield, possibly the Shield of Virtues (see figs. 36, 37, 38, and 39). Together these scenes suggest that Rome was founded by Aeneas with the favor of the gods. Julius Caesar continued this god-given mission and was rewarded with deification; because of the gods' favor, Augustus was able to defeat Antonius at Actium, bringing peace and stability to Rome. Finally, the *vicomagistri* and the adherents of the cult are able to ensure the continuation of the gods' favor along with peace and stability by their worship of the household gods of Augustus. While the Ara Pacis conveys a similar message, the altar now in the Vatican explicitly incorporates some plebs into the principate of Augustus, making them responsible for the well being of the emperor's family and, in turn, the city, making the altar now in the Vatican, as Ryberg notes, a popular version of the Ara Pacis.[35]

While the content of the altar, as well as the quality of the workmanship, suggests state sponsorship, there are other explanations. Ryberg, unlike Taylor, believes this altar was commissioned by the priests of the ward, like the other altars, but that it was influenced heavily by the plans for the Ara Pacis, which

36. Altar of the Lares (formerly the Belveder Altar), 7 B.C.E., Aeneas and Prophet. Musei Vaticani, Museo Gregoriano Profano, Inv. 1115.
Photograph, Rossa, Neg. D-DAI-Rom 75.1286, per concessione dei Musei Vaticani.

37. Altar of the Lares, 7 B.C.E.,
Apotheosis of Caesar (center),
Venus with Gaius and Lucius
Caesar (right) and Augustus
(left). Musei Vaticani, Museo
Gregoriano Profano, Inv. 1115.
*Photograph, Rossa, Neg. D-DAI-
Rom 75.1289, per concessione dei
Musei Vaticani.*

38. Altar of the Lares, 7 B.C.E.,
victory with shield between
laurels. Musei Vaticani, Museo
Gregoriano Profano, Inv. 1115.
*Photograph, Rossa, Neg. D-DAI-
Rom 75.1285, per concessione dei
Musei Vaticani.*

was under construction at the same time.[36] According to Ryberg, then, the altar
was not state sponsored but the inventional process for the altar was heavily
influenced by state art. Like the coins of 13–12 B.C.E., the Ara Pacis may again
have served as a locus for invention for the altar now in the Vatican. Assuming
the altar was not state sponsored, it may reflect the intensity of the Augustan
campaign for the Julian line at the time of its construction.

The later altars, generally dating between 7 B.C.E. and 2 C.E., do not repeat imagery dealing with the Julian line, with one exception, suggesting that as time wore on, this theme lost its resonance, or was crowded out by other subject matter, though the actual religious practices of the cult were based around the well being of the Julian family, perhaps making the theme unnecessary or repetitive. Only one of the later altars, from the *vicus Sandaliarius* dating from 2 C.E., depicts a dynastic scene (see fig. 40). The altar shows Augustus holding the *lituus,* the priest's curved staff. On his right is a female figure, probably his wife, Livia; to his left is Lucius Caesar, one of Augustus's two adopted sons, who was at the time heir apparent with his brother Gaius, while a chicken of disputable significance feeds on the ground.[37]

Though the identity of every person in this scene is debated, there is general consensus that Augustus's family is shown and that there is some dynastic aspect to the image. Ryberg comments, "This altar is unique, since it goes beyond the province of the cult of the Lares and Genius Augusti for subject matter, to commemorate a family event of dynastic import."[38] The other three sides of the altar show the Lares, Victory with the *clipeus virtutis,* and the *corona civica* along with two laurel trees and priestly symbols. While the altar most closely mirrors the subject matter of the Ara Pacis and altar of the Lares now in the Vatican, it has a vague similarity to a coin type that was begun in 2 C.E. that featured Gaius and Lucius Caesar with weapons and priestly implements, though it also uses much

39. Altar of the Lares, 7 B.C.E., Augustus
    handing his Lares to the priests of
    the cult. Musei Vaticani, Museo Gre-
    goriano Profano, Inv. 1115.
    Photograph, Rossa, Neg. D-DAI-Rom
    75.1290, per concessione dei Musei Vaticani.

40. Altar from the vicus Sandaliarius, Augustus, Lucius, and Livia. Galleria degli Uffizi, Firenze. Inv. Sculture n. 972. *Photograph, Rossa, Neg. D-DAI-Rom 75.293, su concessione del Ministero per i Beni e le Attività Culturali.*

of the iconography typical of the later altars (see fig. 19). Galinsky has suggested one explanation for the atypical iconography of the altar: it stood in the *vicus Sandaliarius,* a ward that had recently received a gift of money from Augustus to build a cult statue to Apollo Sandaliarius.[39] The dynastic motif of the altar of the Lares from the *vicus Sandaliarius* can then be read as atypical in that the people of the ward may have felt closer to, if not indebted to, the *princeps,* leading to subject matter on the altar that was more typical of state than popular art. If this is the case, the altar from the *vicus Sandaliarius* again demonstrates the freedom the adherents of the cult had in selecting the motifs for the altars. The altar from the *vicus Sandaliarius* is atypical because of its depiction of Julian family outside of their relationship to the cult of the Lares, but more so because there is no representation of the adherents of the cult as on the other five altars.

On each of the other altars, the adherents responsible for the dedication of the altar are shown, with the exception of the altar dedicated by slaves, which lists the names of those who dedicated the altar. The way in which the adherents of the cult chose to depict themselves suggests that Augustus's technique of imitation was a very effective strategy in reaching a nonelite audience in Rome. Augustus, who modeled his piety on that of his mythical ancestor Aeneas, was

41. Altar of the Lares dedicated by
slaves. Wreath with names of
the dedicants. Musei Capitolini,
Centrale Montemartini, Rome,
Inv. MC 2144/S.
Photograph, K Angler, Neg. D-DAI-
Rom 2001.2180.

often depicted in the act of supplication. The Ara Pacis shows Aeneas with his
toga drawn over his head in an act of sacrifice accompanied by his father and
son, which demonstrated both religious and filial piety. In addition, Aeneas is
shown with his household gods, who he brought with him from Troy, who were
also Augustus's household gods, and who found their way into public worship
through the cult of the Lares. Augustus, like Aeneas, is depicted on the Ara Pacis
with his toga drawn over his head in an act of supplication along with the head
priests of the four official state colleges (see figs. 2 and 4). Augustus served as an
exemplar for the people of Rome by demonstrating his piety and then repeating
images of him doing so for the emulation of the people. In each instance where
the supplicants of the cult of the Lares are depicted, they are depicted as priests
in the same manner as the emperor himself, taking up his role in the political
myth.

The *vicomagistri* are shown on the altar now in the Vatican Museums receiving the Lares from Augustus. This scene may reference Augustus's act of founding the cult of the Lares, making the adherents of the cult and by extension, likely,
portions of the Roman populace at least partially responsible for the security of
the state and the Julian line (see fig. 39). The altar from the *vicus Aesculeti* shows
the *vicomagistri* in a similar manner, and careful attention is paid to show all
four *vicomagistri* by putting two on each side of the altar (see fig. 42). On each of

these altars depicting self-representation the *vicomagistri* are shown in an act of piety, with their togas drawn over their heads just as both Aeneas and Augustus were often depicted in state art, as on the Ara Pacis. Like the altar now in the Vatican and that from the *vicus Aesculeti,* the other three altars show the adherents of the cult at the crossroad altars in the act of sacrifice or just prior to it, sometimes showing animal victims.[40] Though these offerings served to put the emperor's household gods in the same league as the major deities of Rome, these offerings also elevated the status of the priests to those of the major priests of Rome. Perhaps even more significant than a priest imitating the chief priest of the city are the unofficial altars of the wards such as the altar of the Lares dedicated by women. Here two women are shown, similarly to Aeneas and Augustus and the *vicomagistri* in the act of sacrifice, with their togas drawn over their heads (see fig. 43 and 44). These nonelite women who, though adherents of the cult, were not officially affiliated with cult have taken up the practice of imitation.

Augustus's Rhetorical Strategy of Imitation

These scenes depicting the adherents of the cult of the Lares as Augustus is depicted in state art are easily read in the tradition of imitation, that is, the practice of imitating great speeches or speakers in rhetorical education as well as the broader practice of imitation that underlies the practice of modeling behavior in the epideictic genre in order to develop virtue, judgment, and ultimately citizenship. While Augustus's frequent use of this strategy is attested to across sources,

42. Altar of the Lares from the vicus Aesculeti. *Vicomagistri* with sacrificial victims, lictor, and flute player. Musei Capitolini, Centrale Montemartini, Rome. Inv. MC 855/S.
Photograph, K Angler, Neg. D-DAI-Rom 2001.2178.

43. Altar of the Lares Augusti
    dedicated by women. Woman
    sacrificing. Museo Nazionale
    delle Terme, Rome. Inv. 4481.
    Photograph, Rossa, Neg. D-DAI-Rom
    76.1785, su concessione del Ministero
    per beni e le Attività Culturali—
    Soprintendenza Speciale per i Beni
    Archeologici di Roma.

44. Altar of the Lares Augusti
    dedicated by women. Another
    woman sacrificing. Museo Nazio-
    nale delle Terme, Rome. Inv. 4481.
    Rossa, Neg. D-DAI-Rom 76.1784, su
    concessione del Ministero per beni e le
    Attività Culturali—Soprintendenza
    Speciale per i Beni Archeologici di
    Roma.

Dio highlights Augustus's strategy in a speech made by his character Maecenas, where he advises Augustus of the importance of being a model for "emulation" and living as if "on a stage."[41]

Perhaps nowhere is Augustus's strategy of serving as an exemplar for the actions of the Roman people more clear than when he models his *pietas*. Augustus, in addition to becoming *pontifex maximus* in 12 B.C.E., was also a member of all four of the priestly colleges in the city of Rome, which Galinsky notes allowed him to mediate the relationship between the Roman people and the gods.[42] While Augustus's holding of religious offices was obviously self-serving in that he could project his vision of the future as mandated by the gods, it also offered him a chance to model the behavior he wished the people to emulate. If the strife of the last hundred years had been caused by neglect of the gods, it was up to every Roman, regardless of social class or even gender, to do his or her part to make sure the gods were not neglected again. For wealthy Romans, that meant rebuilding temples; for urban freedmen, albeit of the highest standing, that meant serving as *vicomagistri*; and for urban plebs, nonelite women, and slaves living in the city, it meant demonstrating piety, in part by participating in the cult of the *lares Augusti*.

Taken together, the iconography of the restoration of the republic and the depiction of the adherents of the cult suggests that the Augustan political myth, as promulgated in state art, found salience with wealthy freedmen and the nonelite masses and ultimately shaped their collective identity. It is curious that images of the emperor and his family are not present on most altars of the Lares; as scholars have noted over time, the iconography of the altars tended toward representations of the adherents of the cult.[43] As the cult became firmly established and grew in popularity, it may have become unnecessary or even redundant to repeat images of the emperor when both the Lares and Genius were known to be those of Augustus or could be identified with inscriptions as on the altar of the Lares from the *vicus Aesculeti*. This reading suggests that as the iconography of the Cult of the Lares developed the duties of the priests made explicit references to the Julian line unnecessary, as the whole cult was dedicated the worship of the Lares and Genius of the *princeps* (and by extension the Julian line).

Moreover, it is not necessary to take the absence of the emperor and his family as an incongruity. In his discussion of official and vernacular discourse in relation to American memorials and public memory, historian John Bodnar characterizes vernacular discourses as "represent[ing] an array of specialized interests that are grounded in parts of the whole."[44] He goes on to say that whereas official culture "presents the past on an abstract basis of timelessness and sacredness . . . vernacular expressions convey what society really feels like rather than what it should be like."[45] In addition, Bodnar characterizes vernacular expressions as based in "firsthand experience."[46] If these characteristics of American vernacular discourse are applicable to Roman culture, then the absence of the emperor and his family is perhaps not all that surprising. Instead the adherents of the cult have depicted their first-hand experience with the cult—the act of sacrifice—which they themselves perform. Zanker supports this reading when he observes that, "since ritual and sacrifice played such a central role in everyday life, it is not surprising that this type of imagery came to dominate the new pictorial vocabulary."[47] The emphasis on lived experience in vernacular rhetorics, then, easily explains the absence of the emperor and his family in the iconography of the altars.

In addition, the iconography of the altars suggests that the cult shaped the collective identity of the adherents and the cult was rhetorically successful in targeting the myth of the Julian line to the plebs. In other words, the altars depict a political myth taking hold, which ultimately functions as a process that McGee calls "collectivization." The net effect of such collectivization is the emergence of what McGee calls "a third kind of rhetoric." This kind of rhetoric—distinct from the first two "dormant arguments" representing "general ideologies," and political myths that target "specific problems in specific situations"—in McGee's words "emerges when masses of persons begin to *respond* to a myth, not only by exhibiting collective behavior, but also by publicly ratifying the transaction wherein they give up control over their individual destinies for the sake of a dream." McGee goes on to say that "each political myth presupposes a 'people' who can legislate reality with their collective belief."[48]

The altars of the Lares represent the point at which some nonelite residents of urban Rome took up the political myth of Augustus, a political myth disseminated in the official rhetoric of state art. The altars then mark McGee's third stage of rhetoric when the Roman adherents of the cult became "a people" whose collective behavior, the act of sacrificing to the Lares and Genius Augusti, could continue the material prosperity and peace Rome experienced under Augustus— a specific solution to preventing a return to the chaos and impiety of the past. McGee's theory, then, helps point to the construction of the cult itself as a moment when Augustus's political myth caught on with some nonelites of urban Rome, including freeborn plebs, freedmen, and slaves. McGee's theory of the political myth also gives an explanation for the similarity in iconography across the altars: state art depicting the political myth formed "the inventional source for arguments of ratification among those seduced by it."[49] The plebeians taking on the dress of the emperor as a priest is also accounted for in McGee's explanation of the political myth as he claims that "the people" focus on the leader to establish a group identity."[50] The adherents of the cult of the Lares took up the role delegated to them by Augustus, who intentionally modeled this role as an exemplum. Therefore, the altars reflect not only how Augustus served as an exemplum for the adherents of the cult who imitated his piety, or how state art may have limited the inventional choices of the people, but how imitation served as a source of invention for the Roman people.

While the selection of the symbols of the restoration of the republic on the altars of the Lares shows that the adherents of the cult both bought into Augustus's restoration of the republic and the role assigned to them by the Augustan political myth, the selection of certain motifs over others (the laurels, *corona civica,* and *clipeus virtutis* versus the imperial family) suggests, as Galinsky argues, that the altars are examples of individual expression created by the adherents.[51] I would suggest that one reason the altars appear at first so similar to state art is that the state art such as the Ara Pacis and coins functioned intentionally for the adherents of the cult, and the altars form a kind of pastiche of the dominant iconography. Though the resemblance to state art does not suggest the adherents had no freedom or that they were not a rhetorical audience, it does obscure the agency of the plebs and ultimately reify the Augustan political myth.

The notion of "vernacular discourse" becomes significant in discussing the altars as pastiche. Ono and Sloop define "vernacular discourse" as "speech that resonates within local communities." Such discourse, according to Ono and Sloop, has two main characteristics—"*cultural syncretism* and its function as a pastiche."[52] In describing the pastiche function, Ono and Sloop note that a "vernacular discourse is constructed out of fragments of popular culture"; however, "vernacular discourse may borrow from, without mimicking popular culture."[53] Ono and Sloop's definition of a vernacular discourse, then, highlights the fact that the iconography of the altars of the Lares does not mean the adherents of the cult had no free expression or that they completely adopted the Augustan political myth. While the altars look like poor imitations of state art, they simply function as a pastiche of popular culture, in this case state-sanctioned art, but do have independent meaning.

Though the dominant iconography may have constrained the adherents of the cult of the Lares in selecting the motifs for the altars and obscured their agency, particularly to modern viewers, the depiction of the adherents of the cult suggests they were aware of their agency as citizens of the principate. This agency hinges on Ono and Sloop's description of vernacular discourses, the concept of "cultural syncretism." Ono and Sloop, building on the work of Todd Boyd, argue that it is possible for vernacular discourses to "affirm . . . various cultural expressions while at the same time protest[ing] against the dominant cultural ideology"; however, Ono and Sloop are quick to point out that vernacular discourses need not be "counter-hegemonic . . . but [can] also [function] as affirmative [discourses], articulating a sense of community that does not function solely as oppositional to dominant ideologies."[54] In other words, the iconography of the altars of the Lares need not contain counter-hegemonic themes to be considered a vernacular discourse. In the case of the altars of the Lares, because the iconography of state art used to form the pastiche had such strong associations with Augustus and the principate, the altars' function as a pastiche obscures the agency of the plebs who were important as a political base for Augustus and could be highly influential at the time of succession.

In the case of the cult of the Lares, nonelites, particularly freedmen, had much to gain and, it would seem, little to lose by accepting the role posited by Augustus. No doubt the cult of the Lares held great benefits for the *vicomagistri* in terms of increasing their social standing. Holding religious office in Rome was traditionally a sign of great social prestige, yet freedmen were excluded from holding major religious offices in Rome.[55] The cult of the *lares Augusti* offered freedmen an opportunity to gain social standing and display that standing in an officially sanctioned way. Still, there is no reason to assume that because the freedmen and other nonelite urban residents of Rome took up the cult of the Lares and aspects of the political myth of Augustus that they did so without knowing their own role in creating and sustaining the principate.

The iconography of the altars need not be read explicitly as complacency on the part of the Roman masses but instead may indicate how the adherents of the cult who commissioned the altars thought of themselves as citizens in Augustus's principate. If the altars of the Lares are taken as a vernacular discourse, which responds to the political myth of Augustus as put forth in state art, they merely indicate the role of some nonelites. The fact that the iconography of the altars tends towards representation of the adherents of the cult could be read simply as an espousal of the subject position of the adherents in Augustus's principate. On the altars that show the adherents of the cult in the act of sacrifice (the altar from the *vicus Aesculeti,* the altar from the *vicus Soriano,* the Altar in the Vatican, and the Altar Dedicated by Women) the adherents not only replicate Augustus's role in the political myth, but replace Augustus's role. Whereas in the political myth of Augustus, he has restored the gods' favor through his piety, bringing prosperity to the people of Rome, now it is the adherents of the cult of the Lares who are, through their piety, bringing prosperity to the people of Rome and sustaining the gods' favor. Though because of the nature of the cult it is impossible to take Augustus out of the myth entirely, the iconography of the altars stresses the adherents of the cult as agents rather than mere subjects in the Augustan political myth. While Augustus used the cult of the Lares to target the nonelite urban residents of Rome precisely because their political support would be of great importance at the time of succession, the adherents, in replacing Augustus's image with their own in the iconography of the altars, were also aware of their own political import in the principate, and the iconography of the altars of the Lares displays that importance.

THE ALTARS OF the *lares Augusti* are examples of vernacular rhetorics in the principate. The iconography of the altars can be read as accepting and reifying the restoration of the republic and the political myth of the Julian line. The altars represent the moment Augustus's political myth was taken up by the adherents of the cult. Though the adherents of the cult of the Lares adopted the role assigned to them in state rhetoric, the iconography of the altars stresses the agency of the adherents. Because the altars are characterized by the traits of vernacular discourse, at least some nonelite urban residents must have had a great deal of agency and formed a rhetorical audience. The iconography of the altars stresses this rhetorical agency both by showing the adherents of the cult as enacting piety and taking on responsibility for maintaining the gods' favor and by supporting the process of succession by tending to the gods of the Julian line. This agency, however, is masked by the influence of state iconography on the altars, which may have limited invention in the formation of a pastiche. At the same time, Augustus used the cult of the Lares to direct his political myth at some nonelite urban residents, particularly freedmen, who, regardless of the reasons, participated in it and repeated the motifs of state iconography, thereby reiterating the political myth as well as the legitimacy of the principate itself.

The altars of the Lares played two crucial roles in the formation and maintenance of the principate: they affirmed official rhetoric by repeating (aspects of) the Augustan political myth, and they reiterated the official rhetoric as only vernacular rhetoric could. Bodnar argues that "public memory emerges from the intersection of official and vernacular cultural expression."[56] Architectural historian Diane Favro has convincingly argued that Augustus's urban image utilized aspects of the rhetorical concept of memory in an attempt to shape public memory.[57] However, Favro also comments that, despite the careful organization of official rhetoric in the form of an urban image, Augustus "assiduously maintained the myth that other patrons helped shape the city's urban image. After restoring a temple, he frequently preserved the inscription of the original donor and at times claimed, not quite truthfully, that he encouraged others to undertake urban projects."[58] Favro claims that the attribution of various building projects and renovations to others was meant to avoid seeming too autocratic, which would not be accepted by the Roman people. Though no doubt this is true, I would suggest it became important for others to build and restore temples, monuments, theaters, and the like because, without these contributions to the city, there was no appearance of dialogue between the *princeps* and the people, nothing to stand in conversation with official rhetoric, to legitimate the official in the formation of public memory.

Augustus, by misrepresenting the patrons of building projects, recognized the importance of incorporating popular and official building projects. This suggests that the altars of the Lares were important not only for their value in monumentalizing the cult of the *lares Augusti*, a cult that came as close to the worship of a living person as the Romans could allow, or for serving as a record of how Augustus targeted nonelite urban dwellers with his political myth and how they responded, but also because the altars, as vernacular discourse, functioned to create a dialogue with official discourse to shape public memory. Both Galinsky and Zanker suggest that religion itself in the principate formed a kind of dialogue between the *princeps* and the people: "The religious exchange made possible direct communication between ruler and *plebs,* one in which aspiring members of the lower classes and even slaves could participate."[59]

In addition to functioning as vernacular discourse, the altars as visual rhetoric played an important role in public memory. Art historian Michael Ann Holly has begun to explore the relationship between art, memory, and history in Renaissance painting, arguing not only that objects of art shape subsequent accounts of their creation, but also that the act of remembering is inherently visual.[60] The altars, though not the largest or most impressive structures from the principate, were likely among the most numerous, and given the similarity of their iconography, this meant they were also among the most repetitive.[61] Indeed, the altars were dispersed throughout the city, making their way into literally every neighborhood.[62] The altars of the Lares, then, are rhetorically significant as individual expressions of the subject position of the nonelites in the principate. Their iconography suggests that the plebs were a rhetorical audience and that both Augustus and the adherents of the cult of the Lares were aware of the importance of their role in the principate. However, the altars also show how the prevalence of state iconography, even when functioning as a vernacular rhetoric, masks the subject position of the adherents of the cult. Ultimately, it is the relationship between official and vernacular rhetoric that creates public memory and systematizes later accounts of the principate.

7

(FREED)MEN AND MONKEYS

The fictional Trimalchio from Petronius's *Satyricon* is likely the best known *Augustalis,* a magistrate position usually filled by freed slaves in the western Roman empire, because he is the only one known to us from a literary source. It is hard to think of Trimalchio, who behaves in such a manner that he must be reminded "that such low fooling . . . [is] beneath his dignity" by his wife, Fortunata, of whom one of their dinner guests comments is herself so impure that "you would not have taken a piece of bread from her hand," as an ideal incarnation of citizenship.[1] After all, it would seem that Petronius wants his reader to find Trimalchio the absolute epitome of vulgarity.

Trimalchio, though, is not necessarily typical of what we know of the *Augustales,* predominantly through epigraphic evidence, with the exception that all *Augustales* seem to have been "enormously rich."[2] We know of the wealth of the *Augustales* not as demonstrated by elaborate dinner parties but instead from what they gave to their cities. Based on inscriptions from various towns located on the Bay of Naples, Steven E. Ostrow details "the donation of ubiquitous statues, distributions of food, a set of awnings for shade in an open-air theater, gladiatorial games, highway repairs . . . a public bath building, a basilica . . . an altar, and three temples."[3]

This munificence on the part of the *Augustales,* I argue, is a clear manifestation of "ideal citizenship" as instructed, in part, by Augustus's administration through visual and material rhetoric, including the *summi viri,* great men chosen from Roman history whose statues were displayed in the Forum of Augustus as models for emulation. While the *summi viri* were chosen for demonstrating a variety of virtues, all of which Augustus could claim to embody himself, chief among these were liberality, munificence, and beneficence, that is, "contribution[s] to the fabric of the city itself."[4] This munificence, perhaps, is the most significant addendum to Roman panegyric as marked by the *Res Gestae*, making a person's contribution to the city a mark of not only a good ruler but a good citizen.

I will take up two popular displays of citizenship in the early Roman empire, though outside the city of Rome. First, the *Augustales* was a college filled predominately, though not entirely, by freedmen whose duties included attending to the imperial cult in the West though outside of Rome. The second example revisits the flight of Aeneas, a popular scene in Augustan art that figured prominently in the Forum Augustum as parodied in the Bay of Naples. This wall painting is a clear rejection (of at least one theme) of the Augustan political myth, possibly arriving at a conclusion not all that different from Petronius.

These two examples are perhaps not representative of the reception of the Augustan political myth in any broad sense. Still, the *Augustales* offer evidence that, like the *vicomagistri*, certain segments of the population embraced the model of citizenship offered by Augustus, and in doing so they provided social stability and significant improvements to their Italian cities. At the same time, the *Augustales* demonstrated their munificence and social position, often through funerary monuments, creating images of prosperity that reaffirmed the model of citizenship created by Augustus, again reifying the Augustan political myth. The parody of the flight of Aeneas, quite to the contrary, suggests there were those who rejected, if not wholesale at least aspects of, the Augustan political myth and felt comfortable criticizing it in a vulgar but humorous way.

THE *AUGUSTALES*

Unlike the cult of the *Lares,* there is no clear evidence to suggest how the *Augustales* began, and scholars disagree on the origins. Steven Ostrow argues there is enough variation of incarnations of the college that it likely is not the product of top-down organization from Rome, whereas Lauren Hackworth Peterson argues, "Augustus conceived the Augustales as constituting an *ordo* in its own right."[5] The *Augustales* functioned as magistrates in the western cities they lived in and in social position ranked just below the *ordo decurion,* those with over 100,000 sestertii who filled magistrate positions and the assembly *decuriones* (sometimes translated as "town council") that functioned analogously to the senatorial class in Rome.[6] The newfound position of the *Augustales* was no small opportunity for freedmen (*libertini*) given that traditionally they were forbidden from holding religious or civic office.[7] While it is unclear what the exact qualifications were to become a member of the *Augustales,* without question enormous wealth ranked high with many having gained their fortunes as "craftsmen and merchants." Their duties included the care of the imperial cult, a *summa honoraria,* the price paid by magistrates when assuming office, as well as obligations that seem to have included giving liberally to the city.[8]

The motivation for this munificence has been debated. Scholars, perhaps mistakenly, have attributed it to the desire to climb socially that was channeled in productive ways (perhaps by Augustus's administration) by the creation of the *Augustales.* The focus on "social climbing" reflects what Lauren Hackworth Peterson has referred to as "Trimalchio vision," that is, scholars' readings of the *Augustales* through Petronius's social-climbing fictional character. Such readings "risk perpetuating ancient elite, pejorative attitudes about ex-slaves."[9] However, it would seem that munificence carried out for questionable motivations was not unique to freedmen. Cicero in his *De Officiis* cautions against munificence done for the sake of gaining a "reputation of generosity" that is merely "ostentatious," suggesting that the motives behind such acts were frequently questioned even among the elite.[10]

While the motivation for the *Augustales* to give liberally to a town opens the door to questioning their intentions, the invention of the magistrate position raises similar questions about Roman cities. Wealthy freedman in the Roman empire were not unlike their urban counterparts in Rome from which the *vico-magistri* were selected, inasmuch as they represented a population that posed a potential source of civil unrest, but also an untapped source of political support and civic potential. Ostrow suggests that the relationship between the Italian cities, particularly those on the Bay of Naples and the *Augustales,* was mutually beneficial.[11] Ostrow argues based on the account of Cassius Dio that freedmen, at least at Rome, had reacted violently to heavy taxes implemented by Octavian in 31 B.C.E. and thus were a potentially volatile segment of the population.[12] He also argues that it must have been psychologically distressing for wealthy freedmen to be only partially enfranchised; though they were Roman citizens, freedmen did not have the opportunity to advance socially through political or religious office.[13] The *Augustales,* then, offered a chance, like the cult of the *Lares,* for freedmen to gain social prominence. Many Augustan laws were designed to distinguish each social class from one another, both for stability but possibly also to encourage a certain level of social mobility that rewarded "good behavior."

Whereas social mobility was exceptionally rare in the republic, the Augustan social structure did offer very real social advancement.[14] For example, Ostrow argues that, though the Augustan manumission laws limited the number of slaves that could be freed, they also provided a way to stabilize the social order by letting slaves know what to expect. At the same time the manumission laws promoted competition to demonstrate the behavior of the best potential citizens: "all criminal behavior must be avoided and . . . at least some of the values of Roman morality and some sense of the patterns of Roman civic life could be inculcated to prepare the slave for his potential future role in free society."[15] The attempt to engineer citizenship through legislation was typically Augustan, though there were also less formal means of social advancement: scribes (*apparitore*) of the plebian class or the equestrians could move up to the next social class with the help of the *princeps* if appropriate civic character was observed.[16]

In the case of the *Augustales,* they were chosen by the decurions, and based on the prominence and position of the funerary monuments of the *Augustales* at Pompeii they were fully "assimilated" with the political elites.[17] Though often the *Augustales* have been viewed as social climbers, shouldering their freeborn sons with their political aspirations, inscriptions from Pompeii show that sons of the *Augustales* did stand for magistrate positions, suggesting the incorporation of the family of the *Augustales* into political life.[18] In addition to social mobility, *Augustales* were also granted special honors such as public funerals and special seats in the theater for their munificence. Still, Peterson cautions against reading these "rewards" as mere "social climbing," but instead to see the "very real" need of towns for the kinds of beneficence offered by the *Augustales.* As Ann Woods stresses, "In order for most municipalities to function properly, sufficient numbers of prosperous citizens had to be available to undertake . . . expenses."[19] For taking up these expenses, *Augustales* were fully assimilated into the political elite and honored by the decurions and the people.[20]

The arguments made by Ostrow that the *Augustales* were a socially stabilizing institution that rewarded good behavior with social advancement, and by Peterson, who, reacting to Petronius, argues that the *Augustales* met a need and greatly benefited their communities while fully assimilating into the political elite, are very convincing. Both views fit much more broadly with the Augustan political myth, particularly as the myth evolved with the *summi viri,* modeling ideal citizenship for emulation.

Munificence and Liberality

While one could argue that giving to one's community was always a form of civic participation in the republic, it had generally fallen to the wealthy families or triumphant generals to take on building projects. Aside from stressing piety, there was perhaps no greater behavior modeled for both future rulers and the Roman people than the importance of giving generously to the community in the form of civic improvements. Particularly the importance of building programs is stressed in Augustan rhetoric as eventually reflected in the *Res Gestae* dating to 14 C.E. Here, Augustus, relying on the epideictic genre to model ideal behavior, stresses his own contribution to the city:

I built the curia and the Chalcidium adjoining it, the temple of Apollo on the Palatine with its porticoes, the temple of the deified Julius, the Lupercal, the portico at the Circus Flaminius, which I allowed to be called Octavia after the name of him who constructed an earlier one on the same site, the state box at the Circus Maximus, the temples on the capitol of Jupiter Feretrius and Jupiter Tonans, the temple of Quirinus, the temples of Minerva, of Juno the Queen, and of Jupiter Libertas, on the Aventine, the temple of the Lares at the highest point of the Sacra Via, the temple of the Di Penates on Velia, the temple of Youth, and the temple of the Great Mother on the Palatine.

The Capitolium and the theater of Pompey, both works involving great expense, I rebuilt without any inscription of my own name. I restored the channels of the aqueducts which in several places were falling into disrepair through age, and doubled the capacity of the aqueduct called the Marcia by turning a new spring into its channel.[21]

And this is just the beginning of Augustus's recollection of the munificence he has shown to the Roman people, which includes many more public buildings, temples, streets, bridges, gladiatorial shows, games, and athletic competitions.[22] These lines of the *Res Gestae* demonstrate Augustus's liberality by displaying how much he has given to the Roman people both by creating lasting civic improvements and, more broadly, by creating spectacles for the entertainment of the people. Though the *Res Gestae* was not distributed until after his death, the acts described within the inscription changed the face of Rome and offered examples of the behavior of a good ruler.

Munificence was also stressed in Augustan rhetoric as a key virtue among the *summi viri* featured in Augustus's Forum. Each great man from Roman history was selected for displaying a number of virtues, including munificence demonstrated by well-known civic improvements. Just as Augustus was known for the transformation of the city of Rome from one of brick to one of marble, so too were the *summi viri,* who had augmented the landscape of Rome. Augustus himself "restored" or "imitated" temples, monuments, and other visual and material artifacts originally created by the *summi viri.*[23] For example, A. Postumius Regillensis was responsible for the Temple of Castor, L. Papirius Cursor for the Temple of Quirinus, C. Duilius for Janus Geminus, and M. Furius Camillus the Temple of Concordia, all of which were restored by Augustus.[24]

Gaius Duilius provides a clear example of both Augustan restoration and imitation. The construction of the Temple of Janus by Duilius is emphasized by the *elogium* that stood beneath his statue, reading in part: *Aedem apud forum holitorum ex spoliis Iano fecit* (From the spoils [from his Carthaginian victory] he built a temple to Janus near the vegetable market).[25] Tacitus later recounts the restoration of the temple, which was begun by Augustus and completed by Tiberius.[26] In addition to building the Temple of Janus, Duilius had received a "columna rostrata in the Roman Forum for his victory over the Carthaginians at Mylae in 260 B.C.; likewise Octavian had received a gilded columna rostrata in the Forum Romanum, also for a victory at Mylae."[27] Barbara Kellum makes the argument that, in choosing men for the *summi viri* whom Augustus's restorations or imitations would be associated with, Augustus "reinforced parallels" with their deeds.[28] This comparison serves as a form of visual/material amplification not unlike those found in epideictic texts to make Augustus's accomplishments seem more significant.

These *summi viri*, as well as Augustus himself, demonstrate that one mark of a good Roman citizen is munificence and that a sign of this virtue is funding material improvements to the city, which a Roman might be reminded of both upon seeing the statues of the *summi viri*, but also on seeing the restoration of the original projects. That is, the cityscape becomes as much a reminder of the importance of beneficence as the *summi viri* in the Forum of Augustus or later the *Res Gestae*. Often the Augustan restorations, as Augustus himself points out, left inscriptions in place to credit the original sponsor of a building.[29] Though often this is seen as a means of avoiding seeming too authoritative, it also aided in modeling a behavior for Roman citizens Augustus wished to have emulated. Significantly, while both the Aeneas group and the Romulus statues from the Forum of Augustus were replicated in Pompeii at the House of Eumachia, there may also have been statues of *summi viri* erected here as well, and as Joseph Geiger argues, the statues show a very early familiarity with the Forum of Augustus on the part of residents of Pompeii.[30] In other words, the *Augustales* of Pompeii would have been familiar with Augustan rhetoric modeling munificence as a virtue.

The munificence of the *Augustales*, then, despite whatever other incentives may have motivated it, is an expression of one of the ideals of Augustan citizenship as modeled in state-sponsored rhetoric such as the *Res Gestae* and the *summi viri*, which drew attention to and defined the Roman cityscape. Given the importance of narratives concerning the neglect of the built city, particularly of temples, by the Romans as one cause for the civil wars and the reminder of this neglect in Augustan rhetoric, munificence then takes on an added importance in maintaining the prosperity of the Augustan age.[31] At the same time, the munificence of the *Augustales* created material improvements to Italian cities, as did Augustus's transformation of Rome, while also offering a fulfillment and reification of the Augustan political myth.

The Munificence of the Augustales

The material contributions of the *Augustales* are well attested. The *Augustales*, in addition to their acts of munificence, often recorded precisely what it was they gave. Some of these records, such as that C. Minatius Bithus, are brief dedicatory inscriptions: "C. MINATIVS/ BITHVS · AVG/ EX · D· D/ AD · STRATAM/ REFIC HS ∞ ∞" (C. Minatius Bithus, *Augustales* by order of the decurions, [gave] 2,000 sestertii to street repairs).[32] This simple inscription, recorded as originating in Puteoli, recounts only Bithus's name, his status as an *Augustales,* which was conferred on him by a decree of the decurions, and his act of repairing the street. The acts of munificence by *Augustales* vary quite widely and include the constructions of temples to Victory Augustus, Pomona, Genius Stabiarum, a basilica, a public bath, theater awnings, and food distributions of bread and wine as well as cash donations to the grain supply and games.[33]

Often, particularly large acts of munificence were rewarded by the decurions and people with honors in addition to the magistrate position. N. Plaetorius Onirus, who gave theater awnings and money to the grain supply, was honored with both a *bisellium,* a special seat in the theater, and the *ornamentis decuriona-lia,* the dress entitled to be worn by the members of the town council.[34] Onirus was not alone in receiving honors for his munificence. Ann Woods describes the honors typically bestowed on holders of civic and religious office as including special dress, theater seats, symbols, attendants, titles, public funerals, public statues, and tomb sites.[35] The *Augustales* were honored in much the same manner as other Roman officials for their munificence. In addition to dedicatory inscriptions, the *Augustales* sometimes also recorded their munificence and honors on funerary monuments. Woods, who analyzes the motifs of the *Augustales'* funeral monuments, reports that honorary chairs including the *bisellium* account for roughly 7 percent of funeral decoration on the tombs of the *Augustales,* suggesting it was a fairly popular honor, and one significant enough for the *Augustales* to emphasize.[36]

The tomb of C. Calventius Quietus, located outside the *Porta Ercolano* on the road from Pompeii to Herculaneum, records that Quietus received the *bisellium,* which is depicted on the funerary monument, from the decurions and the people for his munificence, though what specifically that might have been is unknown (see fig. 45). The funeral monument occupies a highly visible piece of prime real estate that also housed funerary monuments for, as Ann Woods notes, the "city's most powerful citizens. Some tomb sites were awarded by the city to illustrious local benefactors."[37] Thus, the placement of the funerary monument, like the theater seat depicted on it, is an honor bestowed on Quietus. The placement of this and other tombs has led Peterson to argue that, far from being social-climbing outsiders, the *Augustales* were "assimilated" into the local elite. Thus, the *Augustales* offered legitimate social mobility for wealthy freedmen.

The inscription on the tomb of Quietus stresses that the decurions as well as the people, in this case of Pompeii, awarded the honors to Quietus; Quietus has not seized status symbols which did not rightly belong to him; rather, his

45. Tomb of C. Calventius Quietus,
Porta Ercolano, Pompeii, first
century.
*Photograph, Stephen Peterson, su
concessione del Ministero per i Beni
e le Attività Culturali—Soprintendenza Speciale per i Beni Archeologici di Napoli e Pompei.*

honors were earned (see fig. 46).[38] The inscription on the funeral monument
reads: "C[aio] Calventio Quieto/ Augustali/ Huic ob munificent[iam] decurio-
num/ Decreto et populi conse[n]su bisellii/ Honor datus est" ("To Caius Calventius Quietus, Augustalis. On account of his munificence he is honored with
a *bisellium* by decree of the decurions and with the consensus of the people").[39]
Additionally, the inscription is reminiscent of the lines that so often accompanied Augustus's honors, *"Senatus populusque romanus"* or *"senatus consulto,"*
and serves a similar purpose inasmuch as Augustus was constantly reminding
the Roman populace that he was not taking power or honors; rather, they were
bestowed on him for his deeds.[40]

Other Cities of Marble

The munificence of the *Augustales* reveals the Augustan political myth and the
administration of Augustus's use of imitation in instructing citizenship. There
is a line between imitation as an educational technique found in rhetorical treatises and "aping" or "mimicking." This difference is stressed by Quintilian, who
argues it is important for students to understand why certain models are considered exemplars and what aspects of those models are worthy of imitation.[41]
The education happens not in an act of emulation alone, but in the comprehen-
sion of the best characteristics of the exemplar that then allows the student not

46. Tomb of C. Calventius Quietus. Detail of inscription.
Photograph, Stephen Peterson, su concessione del Ministero per i Beni e le Attività Culturali— Soprintendenza Speciale per i Beni Archeologici di Napoli e Pompei.

just to imitate the exemplar, but to learn judgment and virtue. According to Quintilian, "Imitation . . . should not be restricted to words. What we must fix our minds on is the propriety with which great men handle circumstances and persons, their strategy, their arrangement, the way at which everything is aimed at victory."[42] Nor is it merely enough to imitate, but one must also add to the best models.[43] To merely imitate is to be "satisfied with producing an image of excellence, a mere outer skin, as it were, or rather a 'shape' like those which Epicurus says are given off by the surfaces of bodies."[44] This was, of course, the fear expressed by Isocrates that statues did not provide enough substance to imitate, but could produce only superficial copies. Quintilian cautions those who only imitate "superficial impressions" without full understanding will "commonly degenerate into something worse, and pick up those faults which are closest to the virtues they seek."[45] As Cicero points out, ostentation and munificence could quite easily be confused. This is an important distinction both in understanding how imitation was involved in instructing practices of citizenship, and also understanding the *Augustales* as incarnations of Augustan citizenship.

Often the *Augustales* have been read as "aping" Roman elites.[46] Certainly, this is the way that Petronius portrays Trimalchio, as a poor imitation of a Roman elite who mixes symbols of class he is not entitled to while remaining ignorant, vulgar, and ostentatious. The work of Woods, Peterson, and Laird has recouped the reputation of the *Augustales* from "Trimalchio vision," showing that these magistrates provided much needed services to their towns and were, for all purposes, fully assimilated into the local elites. It is important then to differentiate "imitation," which was intended to model citizenship, as it had been since the fifth-century Greece in epideictic texts and was in rhetorical education as clearly demonstrated by Quintilian from mere "aping."

The end result of the citizenship of the *Augustales,* expressed through their munificence, particularly in the Bay of Naples, was, in some ways, parallel to Augustus's transformation of the city of Rome, contributing to the "cultural achievement" that made Campania a getaway for successful Romans.[47] Though scholars have focused on how cities needed the *Augustales* as a source of financing for civic improvements, the Augustan political myth depended, too, on the *Augustales.* While the material improvements to their cities served to improve living conditions—thus fulfilling one aspect of the political myth that Augustus's reign brought peace and prosperity—the *Augustales,* in their eagerness to display their civic virtue and to do so in conspicuous ways, affirmed that social mobility was possible if one contributed to the community. In doing so, the *Augustales* not only reified the Augustan political myth, but offered an incarnation of an ideal of Augustan citizenship, yet another model for emulation.

THE FLIGHT OF AENEAS IN PRIVATE ART

While the *Augustales* offered a positive example of imitation, certainly there were those who rejected the model of Augustan citizenship set forth in the political myth and in state art. No doubt, Petronius's *Satyricon* is one such example, where class is separated from wealth as a criterion of "elite" status and ideal citizenship. The *Satyricon,* which begins with an indictment of rhetoric and continues to call attention to faulty imitations throughout, is a critique of both imitation and the results it produces. Petronius was not alone in this critique, nor in using satire, itself a form of imitation.

Replication

Augustus's use of Aeneas as an exemplar was, if not effective in promoting piety, at least popular. The statue group of Aeneas was widely replicated in fora throughout the provinces, including at Pompeii.[48] The replication of the statue group from the Forum of Augustus in a variety of media, including "tombstones, integrated into domestic painting, and reproduced on coins, gems, and lamps," easily overcame Isocrates's concern about circulation—that statues were

47. Shop on the *Via dell' Abbondanza* in Pompeii, first century.

Illustration, Tara Carleton Weaver following Spinazzola, Pompei, Fig. 182, su concessione del Ministero per i Beni e le Attività Culturali—Soprintendenza Speciale per i Beni Archeologici di Napoli e Pompei.

poor models of imitation because they were static and could not be widely cir-culated.[49] The so-called "flight of Aeneas" became a frequent image both in state and private art.[50] One such example from private art comes from the *Via dell' Abbondanza* in Pompeii where a "shopkeeper . . . decorated both sides of his shop and the entrance to his house with paintings . . . depicting Aeneas' family along with Romulus as victor" (see fig. 47).[51]

Art historians have speculated over the meaning of the replication of the images of state art in private settings. While in certain situations such as statuary in private villas, the end was likely moral improvement; that is, the homeowner sought to be more like the person depicted by the statue by emulating that per-son's virtues. In some cases, such as with the replication of the Aeneas group, art was meant, Zanker argues, to "express approval of the new regime," Augustus and the principate. In the case of the shop on the *Via dell' Abbondanza*, Zanker speculates on both the meaning to the shop owner and his motives, suggesting that the images serve "as symbols of *virtus* and as tokens of Roman pride and self-confidence within the community. [And] at the same time, they must have been popular with the customers, a way of promoting the little shop. As modern advertising need not have anything to do with the product being sold."[52] While Zanker's view is a bit cynical, the implication of his reading is certainly that Augustus's administration was popular, enough so as to appeal to potential customers in this case. Art historian Peter Stewart takes an even more jaded view, arguing that imitation of the Aeneas group came to be a kind of unceremonious flag-waving, so engrained in the common visual vocabulary that it failed to mean much at all.[53]

The Parody of Aeneas

Certainly not all appearances of the Aeneas group showed support for the reign of Augustus, however routine. Stewart's reaction to the Aeneas group featured outside the shop on the *Via dell' Abbondanza* is tied to his reading of another example of imitation of the statue group in the Forum of Augustus. One he refers to as "a very rare example of subversive imagery in the private sphere."[54] Stewart is referring to a wall painting from a villa near Stabiae, a city on the Bay of Naples south of Pompeii. Here Aeneas, Anchises, and Ascanius are shown "as apes each with [a] dog's head and oversized phallus" (see figs. 48 and 49).[55] Zanker reads this image as one "document[ing] the reaction of a homeowner fed up with the surfeit of ponderous imagery of Imperial art."[56] Stewart in contrast claims, "the irony is that 'subversion' of this sort was only possible when the imagery it mocked had become utterly familiar and inextricable from the

48. Parody of Aeneas from a villa near Stabiae. Museo Archeologico Nazionale di Naples, Gabinetto Segreto, inv. n. 9089. *Photograph, Kathleen Lamp, su concessione del Ministero per i Beni e le Attività Culturali— Soprintendenza Speciale per I Beni Archeologici di Napoli e Pompei.*

49. Parody of Aeneas.
    Re-creation.

    Illustration, Tara Carleton Weaver,
    su concessione del Ministero per
    i Beni e le Attività Culturali—
    Soprintendenza Speciale per I Beni
    Archeologici di Napoli e Pompei.

visual environment of everyday life. When this happens, questions about the effectiveness of propaganda, about its reception, and even about the likelihood of subversive responses, cease to be very meaningful."[57] While art historians have puzzled over the meaning and significance of this painting, it is quite clearly a parody on the "flight of Aeneas." At least from a rhetorical perspective, Stewart is perhaps too dismissive here.

At the very least, the existence of the image suggests that Augustus's reign was not so tyrannical that people did not feel comfortable mocking it.[58] The rather amusing play on the flight of Aeneas highlights the relatedness of imitation and parody, the appropriateness of humor to critique the powerful and highly emotional lines of argument contained in the Augustan political myth embodied in the Aeneas group. And finally, the image underscores the significance of the role of imitation in cementing the public memory of Augustus in the Roman principate. Whereas the reign of Augustus is seen as all-dominating because of the replication of state art such as the Aeneas and Romulus paintings on the *Via dell' Abbondanza,* his reign would be conceived of very differently if instead wall paintings, like the one from the villa near Stabiae, dominated.

Parody in Classical Rhetorical Theory

It is perhaps not surprising that a scene so heavily imitated would fall prey to such a parody; after all, Quintilian notes the closeness of imitation and parody when he defines the latter as "a name drawn from songs in imitation of others, but employed by an abuse of language to designate imitation in verse or prose."[59] Similarly, Cicero, though he does not use the term "parody," describes a type of "jest taken from things which is derived from a depraved sort of imitation, or mimicry."[60] Parody (or "mimicry") as a rhetorical figure is dependent on imitation. Whereas Stewart dismisses the significance of the image from Stabiae because of the frequency of the reproduction of the flight of Aeneas, the parody of the scene would not have been possible otherwise. Moreover, such a parody might have been the most appropriate response to critique the Augustan political myth as it was abbreviated in the flight of Aeneas.

Quintilian describes laughter as appropriate to drive out emotions created by the use of language meant to bring a scene before the audience's eyes or visualization techniques used by an opponent to convey emotion.[61] While humor functions very similarly to types of argument (for example using similarity, dissimilarity, partition), Quintilian recommends turning to humor to combat highly emotional cases. His rationale is relatively simple; in addition to laughter's capability to "dispel . . . these gloomy emotions, [it] frequently diverts attention from the facts, and sometimes also refreshes the bored or tired."[62] Cicero, too, described laughter as effective in "giv[ing] pleasure to an audience" but also because "it mitigates and relaxes gravity and severity and often . . . brakes the force of offensive remarks, which cannot easily be overthrown by arguments."[63] A populace lulled into complacency by Augustus's political myth might find a scene such as the parody of Aeneas remarkably refreshing; moreover, parody, and perhaps only parody, allowed a chance to snicker at the argument rooted in the founding myths, no doubt a type of patriotism generally hard to argue with by rational means.

Parody, according to Robert Hariman, is always subversive, inasmuch as it inherently, though briefly, creates an inversion of power.[64] Significantly, this subversive power is subtly conspiratorial in that laughter "often breaks out against our will, and not only forces the face and the voice to confess it, but convulses the whole body with its very violence," revealing one's true feelings and like-minded individuals.[65] At the same time, humor, in this case parody, is also a safe means of critiquing those in power. Because humor can "dispel hatred and anger," it is difficult for a person, especially a person in power who wishes to be seen as magnanimous, to be angry at the use of it. Quintilian recounts an instance of several young men at a party who were disparaging of King Pyrrhus. When the king asked for an explanation, one of the young men remarked "'To tell you the truth, if there had been any more in the bottle, we should have killed you' and this witticism made all the animosity of the charge evaporate."[66] While their disparaging comments were likely based in their true feelings for the king, when made a laughing matter the drunken transgressions were quickly dismissed.

While the parody of the flight of Aeneas was far from treasonous, it was a particularly appropriate way to combat the emotional nature of the Augustan political myth because of the closeness of imitation and parody, the subversive nature of parody, and the safeness of critique through humor. And yet, at least by Quintilian and Cicero's standards, the parody of Aeneas would have been rather inappropriate, both because of the vulgarity of the subject matter (though the image is not particularly risqué by Roman standards) and also, for Quintilian, because of the visual medium. Quintilian notes there is always something vaguely vulgar about humor: "There is an ambivalence about it: laughter is not far from derision. As Cicero says, it has a basis in a certain deformity and ugliness."[67] Quintilian constantly stressed, like Cicero, that the orator must use laughter tastefully, avoiding the "risqué jokes [that] will suit the lower ranks of society."[68] While there is a class component to which Quintilian not so subtly alludes, the closeness of parody with the mimicry of comedy actors or "buffoons," as both Quintilian and Cicero put it, causes them to separate this type of parody from that appropriate to the orator.[69] The "obscenity" of the parody of Aeneas, then, would not befit the orator.

The image of the parody of Aeneas is inappropriate to the orator, at least as outlined by Quintilian, for another reason as well. Though humor relies heavily on bodily imitation, as described by Cicero and Quintilian, it leaves room for "humorous actions or words" as well as "ocular demonstration"—that is, the orator gesturing to a referent to create a joking comparison—and Quintilian vehemently objects to visual representations that elide the need for an orator.[70] In discussing the use of visual appeals to pity, Quintilian dismisses the use of "a picture painted on a board or canvas" both because in judicial oratory they bring the crime to the present (rather than leaving it as a matter of past fact) but also because such visual displays reveal the orator's "depths of incompetence" because he thinks "a dumb image will speak for him better than his own words."[71] Here, Quintilian, like Isocrates, is very uncomfortable with leaving the interpretation of images, be it assignation of the "right" memory of a ruler to a statue, or feeling the correct emotion in association with images of a crime, up to an audience.

The parody of Aeneas from Stabiae would have been inappropriate to Quintilian and Cicero, crossing the line into vulgarity and eliding the need for an orator in the traditional sense. Still, it is clear that the practice of imitation as a means of instruction about citizenship, once largely the domain of epideictic rhetoric as described by Isocrates, though apparently always in competition with visual media, increasingly became a multimedia undertaking in the principate and was responded to in kind.

The intent in producing the parody of Aeneas, as with all authorial intent, is unknowable, and there are many possible readings. For example, Galinsky argues that the pious Aeneas was at odds with the warrior Aeneas who was already established prior to the *Aeneid*, particularly in Sicily, and the parody could be no more than a commentary on the Augustan revision of the Aeneas myth.[72] Still, it is tempting to read the parody as a larger commentary on the practice of using imitation to instruct citizenship. Isocrates expresses anxiety over visual exemplars; Quintilian cautions against the corruption that comes from merely imitating without understanding models or developing judgment; and Petronius's Trimalchio is (from the elite perspective) the result of such "aping" without the development of virtue or judgment. It is tempting, then, to read the parody of Aeneas in this vein. That is, the parody may serve as a commentary on the use of imitation in the Augustan political myth to instruct practices of citizenship by the Roman people and, perhaps like Petronius, those who embraced them; Trimalchio "apes" the political elite. In the villa near Stabiae, it is the exemplar of the Aeneas group that it is called into question, perhaps for producing such "apes."[73] Thus, it is tempting to read the parody as a commentary on Augustan exemplars and the citizens they produced, even if such a consideration assumes an elite perspective. Certainly, the resident of the villa near Stabiae knew precisely what was expected of him based on the exemplum of Aeneas (and Augustus) and responded as he saw fit, raising, no doubt, a few chuckles, ancient and modern.

THOUGH THE *AUGUSTALES* and the parody of the flight of Aeneas from Stabiae at first seem unrelated, both are examples of responses to Augustan rhetoric that depended largely on the practice of imitation of models of ideal citizenship. In the case of the *Augustales*, the resulting emulation, by most accounts, worked out quite well. The *Augustales* enjoyed prestigious social positions and were virtually assimilated into the elite ranks while meeting the needs their cities and fellow citizens. In turn, the *Augustales* recorded their acts and honors, usually in the form of dedicatory inscriptions and funeral monuments confirming the peace and prosperity promised by the Augustan political myth, in turn becoming exemplars of ideal citizenship.

The parody of Aeneas, on the other hand, suggests that both the rhetorical strategies and the ideals communicated by the Augustan political myth were recognizable and assailable. The two examples taken together reiterate the importance of popular support and vernacular rhetorical expressions. How different Augustus's reign would be remembered if the majority of popular rhetorics looked not like the Altars of the Lares or the funeral monuments of the *Augustales* but the wall painting from Stabiae. It is, ironically, the parody that calls to attention the significance of the emulation of the Augustan political myth, highlighting the widespread popularity of Augustus, stressing the reification of the myth in popular rhetorics, and demonstrating the melding of state and popular rhetorics into public memory. It is the creation of this public memory, the amalgamation of individual statues, coins, monuments, and altars that continued to shape the inventional process of later rhetorical acts and to systematize responses to the principate.

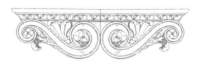

CONCLUSION

A New Narrative

Though Ronald Syme labeled Augustus's reign a "revolution," there was not anything inherently revolutionary about the principate. Nor was there much that was, strictly speaking, new. More often than not, Augustus turned back to the things that had worked well in the republic, making changes to fit the needs of the principate. The scale of his reforms and the blend of innovation and tradition were, however, unprecedented.[1] Augustan rhetoric is no exception. Recognizing the significance of Augustus in the history of rhetoric is, of course, dependent on understanding the significance of Augustan rhetoric. To characterize this significance is no easy task because it depends on first understanding the rhetorical practices of the Roman republic, which are still largely under-theorized.

While the techniques of Augustan rhetoric were not "new," Augustus did face new challenges, new rhetorical situations. He had to argue the legitimacy of his rule, and certainly Augustan rhetoric does this. Augustus also had to negotiate with the Roman people, through rhetorical media that were widely accessible, regarding what it meant to be a ruler, an administrator, and a citizen of the principate. If the principate "broke the power of the old aristocracy," as Syme claims, on a very fundamental level, the principate was in need of people to run the new system of government.[2] While certainly there was some continuity in the senate, Augustus's transformation of the Roman republic depended on the creation of a bureaucracy and administrators to staff that bureaucracy. Those who filled these new positions, which Suetonius notes Augustus created "to enable more men to take part in the administration of the State," oversaw "new offices: the charge of public buildings, of the roads, of the aqueducts, of the channel of the Tiber, of the distribution of grain to the people." Like all Roman citizens and the *princeps* himself, they needed to understand their role and what was expected of them in the principate.[3]

A new system of government, one that broke the power of the ruling class and created a new administrative system that relied on those who had not formerly participated in the Roman government, depended on epideictic rhetoric to reinvent and reiterate a shared culture. The education of the (future) ruler, the administrators, and the citizens fell, as it had for centuries, largely to the epideictic genre, which not only flourished but expanded greatly in the principate. The expanse of rhetoric across genres in the principate far exceeded the bounds of the spoken or written word and extended into the very fabric of the city itself.

In Quintilian's terms, Augustan rhetoric is a shift from a practical to a productive art that saw rhetorical training funneled into a variety of nontraditional media that used rhetorical techniques predominantly from, though not limited to, the epideictic genre. Though Quintilian argues against the inclusion of visual and material media, his argument, like that of Isocrates, recognizes that such media function in a way that if not identical was similar enough to rival traditional oratorical practice. Isocrates and Quintilian, then, in excluding visual and material rhetorics, are arguing for the supremacy of oratory and promoting their own careers as rhetoricians. Whereas Isocrates draws out epideictic speeches and sculpture as two competing arts for memorializing, Quintilian clearly recognizes that many in his own time equated rhetoric with persuasion broadly and that orators often incorporated visual media into their oratorical practices. Quintilian rejects such practices. Augustus, it would seem, did not. In fact, the wide-reaching implementation of visual and material rhetorics typifies Augustan rhetoric and marks its innovation.

Dionysius of Halicarnassus describes a renaissance of rhetoric in the early empire, a return to the Isocratean model that unifies rhetoric and philosophy. The Greek Atticism of which Dionysius is representative depended on imitation of exemplars to produce not only style but also judgment and civic virtue. Though Augustan rhetorical practices went well beyond simple imitation, exemplars are featured prominently in Augustan rhetoric. Traditional Roman rhetorical practices—be they the enshrining of a memory in a building or wax funeral mask, using enshrined memory as a locus for invention for a speech, turning systems of memory outwards to help an audience recall the main points of a speech, or using a painting to literally bring a scene before the eyes of an audience—were already highly visually and materially oriented by the end of the Roman republic. Augustan rhetoric, then, joined traditional Roman practices with those of Greek Atticism popular in the principate to produce an innovative rhetorical practice made up of monuments, altars, coins, city planning, and the like to produce an Augustan culture both rooted in and productive of the old (and new) philosophical art of rhetoric. It is this Augustan culture, which forms a philosophy of a good ruler, a good citizen, and a good man, that Dionysius credits with a renaissance of rhetoric.

The claim that Augustan culture created a renaissance of rhetoric is, of course, controversial. While the decline theory of rhetoric in the principate has largely been dismissed among contemporary scholars, a lingering concern for the quality of Augustan rhetoric remains.[4] That is, was Augustan rhetoric a true renaissance of rhetoric that relied on a new shared concept of civil life in Rome (and in the provinces) or was Augustan culture oppressive?

Objections vary, but perhaps the most frequent begins with a dismissal of all communication from the *princeps,* regardless of media, by classifying it as "propaganda." Art historian Peter Stewart cautions that "propaganda" is a modern concept: monuments "are certainly 'propagandistic' inasmuch as they foster a supremely favorable conception of the ruling power, publicizing it in the most conspicuous manner.... [Still,] the Roman world, as far as we can tell, had nothing like a modern propaganda machine; no organs of systematic publicity; no ministry of information; certainly no spin-doctors.... No one forced the population to make these things; there was no methodical propagation of the imperial image as, arguably dictators' images are deliberately propagated in many modern states. It would be unacceptably cynical and anachronistic to dismiss the spontaneous, voluntary impetus behind a lot of Roman 'propagandistic' art."[5] Though one can debate the point at which "propaganda" developed, Stewart's point remains that Augustus's administration lacked the kind of "systematic plan" necessary to meet accepted definitions of propaganda.[6] Stewart also points to a more significant problem in ignoring the agency of those who produced popular art.

In its most extreme forms, the objection to Augustan culture takes on a totalitarian historical perspective that equates Augustus with Fascist rulers like Hitler, Stalin, or Mussolini and challenges the "voluntary" nature of popular art, suggesting the people were acting under coercion based in terror or sycophancy. Methodological and historical problems aside, such a reading of the period falsely applies a uniform position to the Roman populace, denying them much, if any, agency.[7] Often questions about the "quality" of Augustan rhetoric hinge on this idea that the people had no agency (particularly to speak against Augustus) and therefore could not be a rhetorical audience. These concerns stem from either from a totalitarian perspective ("the loss of freedom") or, similarly, from a position concerned about culture as oppressive.

While certainly Mussolini's portrayal of himself as a new Augustus does not benefit Augustus's legacy, no doubt the overwhelming sameness in appearance of everything Augustan is largely responsible for such conclusions. Augustan culture was meant to shape ideal civic participation, particularly when it took the form of epideictic rhetoric. What is perceived as "sameness" is the result of the intersection of state and popular rhetorics, with the dominance of state iconography influencing motifs in popular rhetoric, thus masking the subject position of those responsible for the creation of popular rhetorical artifacts. This does not mean that those who created popular rhetorics were without agency, just that their agency is obscured from contemporary eyes.

To the degree that state-sponsored rhetoric bestowed meaning to the cityscape and shaped public memory, it could potentially limit the means of invention and therefore become oppressive. However, the creation of public memory, embodied in visual and material media in the principate, requires state and popular rhetoric to merge. Failing to recognize the significance of popular rhetorics denies the agency of the Roman people. It is unfortunate that in reifying the Augustan political myth, all too often the nonelites on whom Augustus's reign depended, disappear, their voices dismissed as mere "propaganda." The "sameness" of everything Augustan is not the only source of the elision of much of the Roman populace. As those with the original social knowledge to "read" the Augustan cityscape died out, its meaning was reassigned, as Isocrates feared could happen without a rhetorician to assign unambiguous meaning through language. For those without the social knowledge to "read" Augustan culture, the literary record becomes a very tempting place to turn. However, quips from various first-century commentators—Pliny, Juvenal, Petronius—reveal a vested interest in delineating new parameters of elite standing based predominantly on taste. These objections are not substantially different from the initial banning of rhetoric by the censors out of fear that it might promote some type of social mobility, and it is at those who have gained social (or financial) mobility by participating in models of citizenship rooted in Augustan culture that these quips are aimed. I do not suggest that the principate was genuinely democratic, only that to read Augustan rhetorical practices predominantly through the literary record, just as to use a totalitarian lens, or focus on the "sameness" of Augustan culture, leaves out a great deal.

A question raised by a student in a recent graduate seminar cut to the heart of the problems with how rhetoric in the principate is often considered: why did the Roman emperors have to justify themselves? Never mind that the question fails to recognize the precarious position of Augustus, that "the first *princeps* was more or less constantly threatened by the ever-present forces of opposition"; the question clearly frames Augustus's power as absolute and presumably militarily based, without the need of the people's consent, let alone favor, and therefore without a need for rhetoric.[8]

At the time of the completion of this manuscript, the Arab Spring had turned to summer with fall fast approaching. While I am hesitant to draw significant comparisons between Augustus and the current developments in the Middle East for reasons too numerous to count, I hope I will be permitted one comparison. On an episode of National Public Radio's *This American Life,* producer Nancy Updike and Marc Lynch, associate professor of political science and international affairs at George Washington University, humorously discussed what appears to be a pattern in steps taken by many Middle Eastern dictators to avoid resigning from office. While the list probably warrants further inquiry by scholars of rhetoric, Lynch made a comment that emphasized the importance not just of justifying a reign to the people but of the significance of communication between rulers and the ruled: "Arab leaders have grown accustomed over decades to not having to respond to their people. And they're not used to having to really take seriously what their people say. And I think that decades of that really breeds this tin ear. When they're finally forced to listen, they're unable to hear."[9] Though Lynch was speaking about the underlying causes of the popular uprisings in Tunisia, Egypt, Libya, and Syria, his comment gets at the heart of the significance of rhetoric in many societies, including Augustan Rome.

It is this same relationship between ruler and ruled that Isocrates is focused on in *To Nicocles* when he takes on the voice of the king to praise "those discourses which advise me on my conduct in general and on political matters, and among these, those which teach dynasts how they should treat their people, and the citizens how they should regard their leaders."[10] Suetonius, too, claiming to quote Augustus's position on the *summi viri* in the Forum of Augustus, stresses the importance of this relationship: "'I have contrived this to lead the citizens to require me, while I live, and the rulers of later times as well to attain the standard set by those worthies of old.'"[11] Both of these accounts stress not only the importance of instructing citizens on their role but the importance of instructing rulers of their responsibilities. Certainly Suetonius suggests that Augustus was well aware that all involved in the emerging Roman empire had to meet expectations. It is rhetoric that provides instruction of these expectations, and that allows for a bilateral discourse between ruler and ruled that revises this tacit contract of expectations. With this in mind, rhetoric is not merely the way a ruler communicates with the people or even the way the people communicate with a government, though it can be both.

Augustan rhetoric is both the bilateral communication of expected roles and how that communication (re)frames the government, citizenship, and the expectations each has of the other. This (re)framing is not unilateral. That is, such expectations were not "top down." Augustus and the people negotiated the role of the new Roman government and *princeps.* The evolution of Augustan rhetoric suggests the principate was presented and then accepted or rejected by the people, and the process was subsequently revised, enacted, and repeated. In the principate, this type of rhetoric, broadly defined, took place across media, requiring one to step beyond oratory and the literary record, and it was largely dependent on epideictic rhetoric and thus on imitation of exemplars. Recognizing Augustan rhetoric, then, requires looking not only at rhetorical treatises or even the poetry and history of the age as "productive" manifestations of a once largely "practical" art, to use Quintilian's language, for that would limit scholars to the literary record and exclude the vast majority of citizens of the principate, including Augustus's largest political base. To recognize Augustan rhetoric requires looking at visual and material artifacts.

This reading of nontraditional rhetorical artifacts has at times been questioned as "anachronistic," the imposition of the rhetorical turn on a period of history when only oratory would have been accepted as rhetoric. This objection is often phrased as "would an ancient Roman have thought of these 'things' as rhetoric" or "art and architecture are parallel arts that rival oratorical practice." I have countered these objections on several levels: first, by showing that the visual and material are ever present in Roman rhetorical theory and practice; then, by examining how techniques popular in the epideictic genre as described in the handbook tradition manifest on the Ara Pacis; and finally, by suggesting that republican rhetorical practices always had a visual and material component not easily parsed from verbal communication in the relationship between wax funeral masks kept in the family atrium and funeral orations. Together, these traditions merge with the old philosophical rhetoric of Isocrates that stresses imitation and was taken up by those such as Dionysius of Halicarnassus to form the visually and materially based Augustan rhetoric.

The epideictic genre in particular as well as Isocrates and Dionysius (and Greek Atticism) have all enjoyed a recent recouping in the field of rhetorical studies. Still, I fear it is too easy to dismiss the significance of panegyric, and to think of Augustan rhetoric only as epideictic is to frame it too narrowly. Such a classification risks too much of a focus on form, as does Kennedy's appraisal of the Ara Pacis: "A more exquisite and better preserved example of Augustan rhetoric at its best is the Ara Pacis Augustae in the Campus Martius, the altar of Augustan peace, which blends the human pageantry and achievements of contemporary Rome with the world of nature and the legends of Rome's foundations. This is not oratory, but a manifestation of epideictic rhetoric, an eloquent encomium of Rome and Augustus with its own invention, arrangement, style, and delivery."[12] While Kennedy alludes to the beauty of the altar, this beauty had a very specific purpose, one that too often conceals the proposition of a model of civic virtue and Roman ideals just below the surface.

The focus on form over content is not the only danger in applying the label of "epideictic" to Augustan rhetoric. According to Richard Leo Enos, "Because of Rome's revolution from Republic to Empire, rhetoric lost the environment that made it a source of political power. While its force in law continued throughout the Empire, it is clear that rhetoric's educational mission shifted, and the pragmatic orientation of Republican schools of declamation correspondingly shifted in emphasis to the appreciation of rhetoric for aesthetic features of eloquence."[13] In focusing, again, on aesthetics, the purpose of the emphasis on style found in many rhetorical treatises including Dionysius of Halicarnassus's *Ancient Orators*—namely to develop taste, civic judgment, and wisdom—is easily glossed over. Couching the epideictic genre in the model of the Greek *paideia* no doubt helps, but this is only part of the innovation of Augustan rhetoric and serves only to give Augustan rhetoric a theoretical and educational underpinning. What the Augustan cultural campaigns did was offer exemplars once available to only a few elite Roman families to the populace. Isocrates's concern with using statues to memorialize was not only that they were poor models of imitation, but that they would not circulate broadly, or they might not reach the right people—"gatherings of men of good sense . . . whose respect is worth more than that of all others." While certainly not every person in the principate had the primary education, skills, or desire to advance socially, financially, or politically in the principate, Augustan culture and rhetoric allowed access to models of civic virtue to more than just the literate elite.

There is the last line of resistance in accepting Augustus as a significant figure in the history of rhetoric: people do not seem to like him much. Of course, scholars only rarely admit to this. For whatever reason, the end of the Roman republic has perpetually fascinated historians and history buffs alike and is continually portrayed in popular culture. This fascination has led most to formulate opinions of Cicero, Cleopatra, Julius Caesar, Marcus Antonius, and Octavian, even if those opinions often rely on the portrayal of largely fictionalized characters, which in turn rely on ancient gossip and/or pure supposition. The distaste for Octavian/Augustus is blatantly evident in Tacitus, though relatively easily explained, but often this distaste seeps into modern conceptions.

A much-admired classics professor referred to Augustus as a "cold fish" because he was uninterested in Cleopatra, sexually anyhow. A similar statement comes at the beginning of Stacy Schiff's popular history on Cleopatra. When clarifying her terminology, Schiff comments, "We know him today as Augustus, a title he assumed only three years after Cleopatra's death. He appears here as Octavian, two Caesars, as ever, one too many."[14] The quips of my professor and of Schiff reflect a little-admitted truth—some affections are mutually exclusive—and for whatever reasons, many people hold strong affections and animosities towards those on the scene at the end of the republic.

As scholars of rhetoric, we are predisposed to sympathize with Cicero and to identify with what was, according to him, a free state where any man could rise to power and glory based purely on oratorical prowess. Cicero's legacy has given us the decline theory regarding the practice of rhetoric in the principate. As appealing as Cicero's legacy is, it has stood as a barrier to approaching a significant period in the history of rhetoric quite long enough. George Kennedy once referred to Augustus as the "the greatest rhetorician of antiquity."[15] I believe scholars should discard the qualifiers often attached to Augustus's rhetorical practice.

NOTES

Introduction

1. Cassius Dio, *Roman History*, 56.30. Ian Scott-Kilvert translates γηίνην, literally "of earth," as "clay." The reference in Dio is to a kind of mud-brick. I have altered his translation to "brick" for clarity's sake for contemporary readers. While this quote is most likely fabricated, Augustus does discuss his building program at length in the *Res Gestae*, 19ff. Portions of the introduction originally appeared in article form; see Kathleen Lamp, "'A City of Brick': Visual Rhetoric in Roman Rhetorical Theory and Practice," *Philosophy and Rhetoric* 44.2 (2011): 171–93; rpt. by permission of the publisher, Penn State University Press.

2. Suetonius, *Lives, The Deified Augustus*, 28.

3. Cassius Dio, *Roman History*, 56.30.

4. Cassius Dio, *Roman History*, 52.30.

5. Quintilian, *De Institutione*, 2.15.6–9.

6. Kennedy, *Art of Rhetoric*, 378.

7. Kennedy, *Art of Rhetoric*, 382–84.

8. Kennedy, *Art of Rhetoric*, 378.

9. Zanker, *Power of Image*, 3.

10. See Favro, *Urban Image*; Holscher, *Language of Images*.

11. Kennedy, *Art of Rhetoric*, 382.

12. Mommsen, *History of Rome*, 125. Kennedy addresses the "decline narrative" as generated in classical sources explicitly and rejects it (*New History*, 186–91).

13. Pernot, *Rhetoric in Antiquity*, 129–30.

14. Pernot, *Rhetoric in Antiquity*, 129.

15. Dionysius of Halicarnasus, "Ancient Orators," 1–3. See Pernot, *Rhetoric in Antiquity*, 130.

16. Pernot, *Rhetoric in Antiquity*, 131. Pernot cites "Longinus," *On the Sublime*, 44.1; Tacitus, *Dialogus*, 36.2, to support the idea that classical rhetoricians viewed rhetoric as continuing in their own time.

17. Pernot, *Rhetoric in Antiquity*, 132.

18. Pernot, *Rhetoric in Antiquity*, 134.

19. Walker, *Rhetoric and Poetics*, 88.

20. Pernot makes a similar point in *Rhetoric in Antiquity*, 132–35, 145.

21. Pernot, *Rhetoric in Antiquity*, x.

22. Pernot, *Rhetoric in Antiquity*, 178, 181.

23. Pernot, *Rhetoric in Antiquity*, 200.

24. Walker, *Rhetoric and Poetics*, 71.

25. Pernot, *Rhetoric in Antiquity*, 180.

26. Pernot, "Epideictic Rhetoric."

27. Jowett and O'Donnell, *Propaganda and Persuasion*, 33, 42. Jowett and O'Donnell trace the origin of the term "propaganda" back to the early Catholic Church, though they (problematically) argue for the idea as older, identifying the concept in Aristotle's concern of ends/means (*Propaganda and Persuasion*, 15, 31, 38).

28. Jowett and O'Donnell, *Propaganda and Persuasion*, 16.

29. Dionysius (ca. 60–7 B.C.E.) likely came to Rome just prior to Augustus's sole reign and remained in the city; see Usher's Introduction to Dionysius of Halicarnasus, *Critical Essays,* vii. Dionysius's theoretical work *On Imitation* is very fragmentary, though his critical works, including *The Ancient Orators,* make his position on rhetorical education clear. His surviving works on rhetoric and literary criticism are collected in the Loeb edition of *Critical Essays.* The dating of "Longinus" is another problematic matter. Kennedy assumes a first-century date, but others argue for the third century (*Art of Rhetoric,* 370).

30. Kennedy, *Art of Rhetoric,* 301–427. Livy wrote during the principate, but only the chapter summaries of his history of the principate have survived.

31. Though Velleius experienced the period, he is not particularly accurate in reporting events he did not experience firsthand (Wells, *Roman Empire,* 33–35).

32. Wells, *Roman Empire,* 36.

33. Tacitus, *Annals,* 4.34.

34. The most influential work on Augustan visual culture remains Zanker's *The Power of Image in the Age of Augustus.* See also Galinsky, *Augustan Culture.*

Chapter 1: Augustus's Rhetorical Situation

1. The start date of the principate varies depending on which historic event one considers definitive in marking Augustus's sole rule: the battle of Actium of 31 B.C.E., 29 B.C.E. when Augustus received *imperium* for 10 years, 27 B.C.E. when Octavian received the title "Augustus" and "restored the republic," or 23 B.C.E. when Augustus took tribunician power (Syme, *Roman Revolution* 1; Wells, *Roman Empire,* 55–7; Cassius Dio, *Roman History,* 52.1; Augustus, *Res Gestae* 34).

2. I say "pseudo" because, as Anthony Corbeill notes, the difference was that the *populares* claimed to represent the people's interest, though there was little difference between those in the *optimates* and *populares* in terms of class standing (*Nature Embodied,* 111–12).

3. Syme, *Roman Revolution,* 7.

4. Syme, *Roman Revolution,* 8. There was not anything inherently revolutionary about Octavian's rise. Galinsky terms Octavian's rise an "evolution" (*Augustan Culture,* 8–9).

5. The work of Fergus Miller offers the most neutral and in-depth discussion of the role of oratory in relation to class ("Political Character," 2).

6. Walker, *Rhetoric and Poetics,* 78–79.

7. See Rostovtzeff, *Rome,* 97–103.

8. See Rostovtzeff, *Rome,* 104, 110.

9. See Rostovtzeff, *Rome,* 121–25.

10. See Rostovtzeff, *Rome,* 126–31.

11. See Rostovtzeff, *Rome,* 132, 137–38.

12. There were other powerful players on the scene, including Lepidus and Dollabella. Octavian was slow to gain recognition as Caesar's rightful (political) heir. Marching on Rome, he demanded political recognition. Eventually he found it, in large part, through the aid of Cicero. See Rostovtzeff, *Rome,* 138–39, 140.

13. See Rostovtzeff, *Rome,* 140–41; Wells, *Roman Empire,* 13.

14. Wells, *Roman Empire,* 14; see also Rostovtzeff, *Rome,* 142–44.

15. Wells, *Roman Empire*, 15; Rostovtzeff, *Rome*, 154–55.

16. Tacitus, "The Annals," 1.2.

17. Vasaly argues that Cicero hyperbolized the prospective bloodshed of the Catilinarian Conspiracy to draw a comparison with the civil wars in the minds of his audience (*Representations*, 78–79).

18. Cassius Dio, *Roman History*, 53.17. Despite the Roman distrust of monarchy, Dio is clear that Augustus's reign was a monarchy. Of the classical historians, only Velleius seems to have felt differently, though Dio had the benefit of hindsight (see Velleius Paterculus, *Compendium*, 2.28).

19. Galinsky, *Augustan Culture*, 159.

20. Galinsky, *Augustan Culture*, 6–7.

21. Eder, "Augustus and the Power of Tradition," 118–19.

22. Galinsky, *Augustan Culture*, 8.

23. Quintilian, *De Institutione*, 2.4.2.

24. Quintilian, *The Orator's Education*, 2.4.2.

25. Quintilian does describe myth as falling within the realm of history and both myth and history as within the realm of rhetoric, which is not to say he literally believed myths. In fact, he recommended debating the credibility of myths (*De Institutione*, 2.4.18–19). Cicero, also a skeptic on many Roman religious practices, draws a sharper distinction between myth and history, suggesting myths are primarily about the pleasure of the audience (*De legibus*, 1.1.4). See Fox, *Roman Historical Myths*, 6. Bremmer and Horsfall, in their work on myth, caution contemporary readers from making a sharp distinction between myth and history based on Livy (whose position is nearer to Quintilian's than Cicero's). Bremmer and Horsfall suggest several myths are based on historical characters, but they shy away from claims that suggest Virgil thought Aeneas was "real" (*Roman Myth*, 5).

26. For dating, origins, and various accounts, see Harrison, "Aeneas," 22–23; Bremmer and Horsfall, *Roman Myth*, 12–24.

27. For more on the Lavinium/Alba debate, see Bremmer and Horsfall, *Roman Myth*, 15–20.

28. Bremmer and Horsfall, *Roman Myth*, 24; Stahl, "Death of Turnus," 175.

29. Stahl, "Death of Turnus," 174–75.

30. Galinsky, *Aeneas*, 4, 10.

31. Stahl, "Death of Turnus," 174–75.

32. The Julian line had traced its lineage back to Venus and Aeneas for some time. For example, the moneyer Sextus Julius Caesar minted a coin in 127 B.C.E. that featured a helmeted Roma with an anchor on the obverse and Venus and Cupid on the reverse. It was common for moneyers to put their family name, ancestors, or other symbols associated with their lineage on coins (see Crawford, *Roman Republican Coinage*, 284). Julius Caesar exploited this lineage particularly well, claiming his maternal line went back to the kings of Rome while his paternal line could be traced to Venus herself (see Bremmer and Horsfall, *Roman Myth*, 22; Suetonius, *Lives, The Deified Julius*, 6).

33. Virgil, *Aeneid*, 1.259ff.

34. Bremmer and Horsfall, *Roman Myth*, 24; Harrison, "Aeneas," 23.

35. Bremmer and Horsfall, *Roman Myth*, 22, 27.

36. Rose and Scheid, "Romulus and Remus," 1335.

37. This is an extremely abbreviated version of the Romulus and Remus myth. For a more complete account, see Rose and Scheid, "Romulus and Remus," 1335; Bremmer and Horsfall, *Roman Myth*, 25–48.

38. Vasaly, *Representations*, 80.

39. Vasaly, *Representations*, 81.

40. Cassius Dio, *Roman History*, 53.16.

41. There is some evidence to suggest this part of the mythic history of Rome is perhaps more history than myth (Cornell, "Tarquinius Superbus, Lucius," 1475).

42. Livy, 1.58.

43. Livy, 1.59.

44. Tacitus, *Annals*, 1.1.

45. Cassius Dio, *Roman History*, 52.1.

46. Cassius Dio, *Roman History*, 53.17.

47. Drummond, "Tullius, Servius," 1558.

48. Suetonius, *On Rhetoricians*, 2.

49. Suetonius, *On Rhetoricians*, 1.

50. This is not to say that the introduction of Greek rhetoric made the republic more democratic (see Kennedy, *A New History*, 115; Pernot, *Rhetoric in Antiquity*, 101).

51. For more on oratory supporting democratic practice in Rome, see Millar, *Political Character*. As Pernot eloquently puts it, "The Latin authors of the 1st Century AD never stop wearing widow's weed for Cicero" (*Rhetoric in Antiquity*, 132).

52. Enos, *Roman Rhetoric*, 47; Syme, *Roman Revolution*, 15.

53. Tacitus, "The Annals," 1.2; Wells, *Roman Empire*, 14.

54. Cassius Dio, *Roman History*, 54.26, 52.20.

55. Tacitus, *Dialogus*, 38–39.

56. Tacitus, *Dialogus*, 19.5, 20.3.

57. Tacitus, *Dialogus*, 10.8.

58. Tacitus, *Dialogus*, 5.4.

59. For example, in *For Quinctius*, Cicero had to be careful not to offend Sulla (see Kennedy, *A New History*, 129–31).

60. Tacitus, *Dialogus*, 27.3; Suetonius, *Lives, The Deified Augustus*, 51. Bauman gives a detailed discussion of the limits of free speech and those tried for defamation (*Crimen Maiestatis*, 251–65).

61. I have not discussed the *maiestas*, treason trials, or the *delators* who eventually made their livelihood from such accusations. Though these trials existed in the republic, they took on new meaning and frequency in the empire and certainly represented a significant change in forensic oratory. These trials occured under Augustus, and the laws pertaining to them may have been extended under Augustus, but they did not gain prominence until Tiberius (see Balsdon and Lintott, "Maiestas," 913–14). For conspiracy trials under Augustus, see Bauman, *Crimen Maiestatis*, 171–97. For the trial of Julia, see Bauman, *Crimen Maiestatis*, 198–205. For the dates of laws used for *maiestas* trials and the argument for an Augustan date, see Bauman, *Crimen Maiestatis*, 266–92.

62. Tacitus, "The Annals," 1.2.

63. Cassius Dio, *Roman History*, 54.30.

64. Cassius Dio, *Roman History*, 54.26.

65. Cassius Dio, *Roman History*, 53.17.

66. Cassius Dio, *Roman History*, 52.31.

67. Cassius Dio, *Roman History*, 53.21. The Senate continued to meet through the third century c.e. The Popular Assembly was stripped of much of its power under Tiberius.

68. Cassius Dio, *Roman History*, 54.13.

69. Cassius Dio, *Roman History*, 54.14; Suetonius, *Lives, The Deified Augustus*, 32.

70. Cassius Dio, *Roman History*, 54.14.

71. Cassius Dio, *Roman History*, 55.3–4.

72. Cassius Dio, *Roman History*, 52.14.

73. Suetonius, *Lives, The Deified Augustus*, 37.

74. Pernot, *Rhetoric in Antiquity*, 132.

75. Lauer, "Ritual and Power," 430; Walker, *Rhetoric and Poetics*, 84.

76. Pernot, *Rhetoric in Antiquity*, 131.

77. Pernot, *Rhetoric in Antiquity*, 200.

78. Walker, *Rhetoric and Poetics*, 71.

79. Quintilian, *De Institutione*, 3.7.1–2.

80. Kennedy, *New History*, 195.

81. Pernot, *Rhetoric in Antiquity*, 179.

82. Walker, *Rhetoric and Poetics*, 88–89; see also Pernot, *Rhetoric in Antiquity*, 132–33.

83. Pernot, *Rhetoric in Antiquity*, 133–34.

Chapter 2: Seeing Rhetorical Theory

1. Portions of this chapter originally appeared in article form; see Kathleen Lamp, "'A City of Brick': Visual Rhetoric in Roman Rhetorical Theory and Practice," *Philosophy and Rhetoric* 44.2 (2011): 171–93; rpt. by permission of the publisher, Penn State University Press.

2. Pernot, *Rhetoric in Antiquity*, x, 196–97. For Pernot, "speech" is the limiting term in the definition.

3. Pernot, *Rhetoric in Antiquity*, 197.

4. Obviously these examples easily qualify as rhetoric under contemporary definitions. For example, Blair, Jepperson, and Pucci argue, "Public commemorative monuments are rhetorical products of some significance. They select from history those events, individuals, places and ideas that will be sacralized by a culture or polity" ("Public Memorializing in Postmodernity," 263).

5. Aristotle, *On Rhetoric*, 1355a. For examples of scholars using Aristotle's definition, see O'Gorman, "Aristotle's Phantasia," 16–40; Newman, "Aristotle's Notion," 7, 23.

6. Quintilian, *De Institutione*, 2.14.3.

7. Quintilian, *De Institutione*, 2.15.4–6.

8. Butler, the translator, suggests the definition Quintilian references by Isocrates is in a lost treatise or possibly is the work of the younger Isocrates (note to Quintilian, *De Institutione*, 302). Butler traces the other definitions as well; see Plato, *Gorg.* 453 A; Cicero, *De Inventione*, 1.5.6, and *On Oratory*, 1.31.138.

9. Quintilian, *De Institutione*, 2.15.6–9. The Latin corresponding to "He relied no longer on the power of speech, but appealed directly to the eyes of the Roman people" reads "non orationis habuit fiduciam sed oculis populi Romani vim attulit." Butler translates *orationis* as "eloquence." The more literal "speech" is perhaps more accurate. Butler also translates *actione* as "eloquence," but it could also be translated as "performance" or "delivery."

10. Quintilian, *De Institutione*, 2.15.6.

11. Quintilian, *De Institutione*, 2.15.11.

12. Quintilian, *De Institutione*, 2.17.1–5.

13. Tacitus, *Dialogus*, 3. See Walker, *Rhetoric and Poetics*, 102–4.

14. Tacitus, *Dialogus*, 13. See Walker, *Rhetoric and Poetics*, 102.

15. See Bradley's introduction to Suetonius's *Lives*.

16. Suetonius, *Lives, The Deified Augustus*, 86, 89.

17. Cassius Dio, *Roman History*, 53.30, 54.28, 54.34.

18. Cassius Dio, *Roman History*, 55.34, 55.4.

19. Pernot, *Rhetoric in Antiquity,* 136.

20. Pernot, *Rhetoric in Antiquity* 199. Pernot is referencing poetry specifically here.

21. O'Gorman, "Aristotle's Phantasia," 17, 20, 21, 34–35; Newman, "Aristotle's Notion," 21–22.

22. O'Gorman, "Aristotle's Phantasia," 25.

23. O'Gorman, "Aristotle's Phantasia," 21.

24. O'Gorman, "Aristotle's Phantasia," 34.

25. Vasaly, *Representations,* 90.

26. Quintilian, *De Institutione,* 8.3.61–63. Butler translates *verbis depingitur* as "word-picture." "Verbal depiction" would work as well.

27. Quintilian, *De Institutione,* 8.3.67.

28. Quintilian, *De Institutione,* 8.3.8. It is worth noting that Quintilian uses this word for a type of actual painting as well, suggesting the concept is not limited by medium (see 7.10.6).

29. Quintilian, *De Institutione,* 6.2.26.

30. Quintilian, *De Institutione,* 6.2.29–30. Cicero and "Longinus" give similar summaries of *phantasia* (see Cicero, *On Oratory,* 3.100.65; "Longinus," *On the Sublime,* 15.1–2).

31. "Longinus," *On the Sublime,* 15.11.

32. Vasaly, *Representations,* 24.

33. Vasaly, *Representations,* 94.

34. Cicero, *On Oratory,* 2.88.

35. Cicero, *On Oratory,* 2.86. Quintilian uses practically the same language and examples in discussing techniques of memory (*De Institutione,* 11.2.9–10, 19).

36. Quintilian, *De Institutione,* 11.2.21.

37. Cicero, *On Oratory,* 2.87.

38. Quintilian, *De Institutione,* 11.2.32.

39. Quintilian, *De Institutione,* 11.2.34.

40. Favro, *Urban Image,* 7.

41. Quintilian, *De Institutione,* 2.15.6.

42. Polybius *Histories,* 6.15.8, qtd. in Favro, *Urban Image,* 53, 55.

43. Favro, *Urban Image,* 53.

44. Cicero, *Ad att.,* 4.17, qtd. in Favro, *Urban Image,* 63.

45. Cicero, *Ad att.,* 12.19, qtd. in Favro, *Urban Image,* 22.

46. Favro, *Urban Image,* 49; see Vitruvius, *On Architecture,* 6.5.2.

47. Suetonius, *Lives, The Deified Augustus,* 1.

48. Suetonius, *Lives, The Deified Augustus,* 29.

49. Aldrete, *Gestures and Acclamations,* 18–19.

50. Aldrete, *Gestures and Acclamations,* 21.

51. Vasaly, *Representations,* 42, 46, 59, 81–84.

52. Vasaly, *Representations,* 19, 26. Pernot makes a similar argument (*Rhetoric in Antiquity,* 102).

53. Vasaly, *Representations,* 101. Cicero did not deliver the Second Action against Verres (Kennedy, New History, 131–32).

54. Tacitus, *Dialogus,* 19–20.

55. Vasaly, *Representations,* 99.

56. Favro, *Urban Image,* 7.

57. Favro, *Urban Image,* 153.

58. Favro, *Urban Image,* 7, 86, 153.

59. Enos, "Rhetorical Archaeology," 39.

60. Tacitus, *Dialogus,* 19–20.

61. Zanker, *Power of Image,* 101.

Chapter 3: The Augustan Political Myth

1. Suetonius, *Lives, The Deified Augustus,* 28. Portions of this chapter originally appeared as an article: Kathleen Lamp, "The Ara Pacis Augustae: Visual Rhetoric in Augustus' Principate," *Rhetoric Society Quarterly* 39.1 (2009): 1–24; rpt. by permission of the publisher (Taylor and Francis LTD, www.tandf.co.uk/joutrnals).

2. Suetonius, *Lives, The Deified Augustus,* 8, 84; Quintilian, *De Institutione,* 12.6.1.

3. Kennedy, *Art of Rhetoric,* 378, 383.

4. I am sensitive to the question of who "authored" the Ara Pacis. While the "Senate and Roman People" are attributed as commissioning the altar, it seems likely Agrippa, Augustus's general and right-hand man, was responsible for gathering the sculptors of the Ara Pacis, who were probably not from Rome. While it is impossible to say how much influence Augustus had over the altar, it is likely that he had a hand in all state-sponsored building projects, particularly those in the area of the Ara Pacis, including the sundial, mausoleum, and *ustrinum* which related directly to his family line. (See Strong, *Roman Art,* 83.)

5. Augustus, *Res Gestae* 12.

6. Fullerton discusses the Augustan political myth specifically in reference to the coin production of 13–12 B.C.E. ("Domus Augusti," 483). "Political myth" is McGee's term ("In Search of 'The People,'" 344–46).

7. I agree with Kleiner that the goddess's identity is of secondary importance. Her imagery obviously is meant to denote abundance, and her exact identity may be intentionally vague (*Roman Sculpture,* 96).

8. Kleiner, *Roman Sculpture,* 90; Strong, *Roman Art,* 80–83.

9. Holscher, *Language of Images,* 121–22, 111.

10. Strong, *Roman Art,* 83.

11. Kleiner, *Roman Sculpture,* 90; Strong, *Roman Imperial,* 19.

12. Zanker, *Power of Image,* 101; Favro, *Urban Image,* 19.

13. Stahl, "Death of Turnus," 75.

14. "Cicero," *Rhetorica ad Herennium,* 3.7.13. I am using the Loeb edition of the *Ad Herennium,* which includes the work in the volumes of Cicero's writings. Because of this compilation, I have listed the work of the unknown author of the *Ad Herennium* under "Cicero" on my bibliography.

15. Quintilian, *De Institutione,* 3.7.10.

16. Castriota, "Introduction," 8.

17. Eder, "Augustus and the Power of Tradition," 87.

18. Ogilvie, *The Romans and Their Gods,* 1.

19. Ogilvie, *The Romans and Their Gods,* 5.

20. Ogilvie, *The Romans and Their Gods,* 5, 21.

21. Holscher, *Language of Images,* 81.

22. Holscher, *Language of Images,* 33, 46.

23. Cicero, *De Inventione,* 1.15.20; Quintilian, *De Institutione,* 4.1.5.

24. Cicero, *De Inventione,* 1.15.20–21.

25. Kleiner, *Roman Sculpture,* 93; Hannestad, *Roman Art and Imperial Policy,* 73–74.

26. Virgil, *Aeneid,* 3.389–95. Verbatim English translations from Virgil are reprinted by permission of the publishers and the Trustees of the Loeb Classical Library from *Virgil: Volume 1,* Loeb Classical Library Volume 63, translated by H. R. Fairclough, pp. 399, 589, 593, 441.

Cambridge, Mass.: Harvard University Press, © 1999, by the Presidents and Fellows of Harvard College. Loeb Classical Library ® is a registered trademark of the Presidents and Fellows of Harvard College.

27. Hannestad, *Roman Art and Imperial Policy,* 73–74; Kleiner, *Roman Sculpture,* 93.

28. Aristotle, *On Rhetoric,* 1368a.38.

29. Quintilian, *De Institutione,* 8.4.20.

30. Kleiner, *Roman Sculpture,* 93; Hannestad, *Roman Art and Imperial Policy,* 73–74.

31. Strong, *Roman Art,* 84.

32. Kleiner, *Roman Sculpture,* 93.

33. Stahl, "Death of Turnus," 175.

34. Virgil, *Aeneid,* 6.788–6.797.

35. Romulus and Remus were the product of Mars's rape of Rhea Silvia, Vestal Virgin and daughter of Numitor, the usurped king of Alba Longa. See Harris and Platzner, *Classical Mythology Images,* 783–84.

36. Hannestad, *Roman Art and Imperial Policy,* 68.

37. Kellum, "Display," 290.

38. Harris and Platzner, *Classical Mythology Images,* 784.

39. Bremmer and Horsfall, *Roman Myth,* 37.

40. Ovid, *Metamorphoses,* 15.819–31; rpt. by permission of the publishers and the Trustees of the Loeb Classical Library from Ovid: Volume 4, Loeb Classical Library Volume 43, translated by Frank J. Miller, pp. 423, Cambridge, Mass.: Harvard University Press, © 1964, by the Presidents and Fellows of Harvard College. Loeb Classical Library ® is a registered trademark of the Presidents and Fellows of Harvard College.

41. Tacitus, *Ann.* 1.10.

42. Ogilvie, *The Romans and Their Gods,* 6.

43. Ogilvie, *The Romans and Their Gods,* 7.

44. Horace, *Carmina,* 3.6.1–8; rpt. by permission of the publishers and the Trustees of the Loeb Classical Library from Horace: Volume 1, Loeb Classical Library Volume 33, translated by Niall Rudd, pp. 163, Cambridge, Mass.: Harvard University Press, © 2004, by the Presidents and Fellows of Harvard College. Loeb Classical Library ® is a registered trademark of the Presidents and Fellows of Harvard College.

45. Ogilvie, *The Romans and Their Gods,* 109.

46. Quintilian, *De Institutione,* 1.6.5; 1.11.1–2, 2.4.15, 2.4.20, 3.4.15.

47. Suetonius, *Lives, The Deified Augustus,* 40.

48. Suetonius, *Lives, The Deified Augustus,* 34; Cassius Dio, *Roman History,* 56.2.

49. Zanker, *Power of Image,* 159.

50. Hannestad suggests the processional is idealized because not everyone could have been present who is depicted (*Roman Art and Imperial Policy,* 68).

51. Ogilvie, *The Romans and Their Gods,* 21.

52. Castriota, "Introduction," 2.

53. Castriota, "Introduction," 6.

54. Meier, "C. Caesar Divi Filius," 69–70.

55. Cassius Dio, *Roman History,* 54.14; Suetonius, *Lives, The Deified Augustus,* 32.

56. Eder, "Augustus and the Power of Tradition," 115.

57. Wells, *Roman Empire,* 63.

58. Eder, "Augustus and the Power of Tradition," 120.

59. Kleiner, *Roman Sculpture,* 92–93.

60. Cassius Dio, *Roman History,* 56.5.

61. Kleiner, *Roman Sculpture,* 60; Favro, *Urban Image,* 120.

62. Hannestad, *Roman Art and Imperial Policy,* 64.

63. Kleiner, *Roman Sculpture,* 98

64. Kleiner, *Roman Sculpture,* 92.

65. Eder, "Augustus and the Power of Tradition," 121.

66. Eder, "Augustus and the Power of Tradition," 121.

67. Claridge, *Rome,* 187.

68. Kleiner, *Roman Sculpture,* 96–97; Hannestad, *Roman Art and Imperial Policy,* 73.

69. Stahl, "Death of Turnus," 174–75; Eder, "Augustus and the Power of Tradition," 87.

70. Virgil, *Aeneid,* 6.851–53.

71. Virgil, *Aeneid,* 4.272–76.

72. Hannestad uses Ovid's *Fasti* to support a reading of the goddess as either *Tellus or Italia* (*Roman Art and Imperial Policy,* 62); see Ovid, *Fasti,* 1.712 ff.

73. Kleiner, *Roman Sculpture,* 96.

74. Horace, *Carmina,* 29ff, qtd. in Hannestad, *Roman Art and Imperial Policy,* 72.

75. Tacitus, *Annals,* 2.1.

76. Velleius Paterculus, *Compendium,* 2.89.

77. Tacitus, *Annals,* 1.3.

78. Meier, "C. Caesar Divi Filius," 63.

79. On consensus, see Pernot, *Rhetoric in Antiquity,* 180.

80. Quintilian, *De Institutione,* 3.7.1–2; 3.8.1–2.

81. Quintilian, *De Institutione,* 2.10.11.

82. Sarah Newman makes a similar argument about agency and the rhetorical techniques of *enargeia,* "bringing-before-the-eyes," in Aristotle, *On Rhetoric* (1).

83. Bodnar, *Remaking America,* 13.

84. Bodnar, *Remaking America,* 13–14.

85. Tacitus, *Annals,* 1.7.

Chapter 4: Let Us Now Praise Great Men

1. Isocrates, *Isocrates I,* 2.38; 3.57.

2. Isocrates, *Isocrates I,* 2.36.

3. Isocrates, *Isocrates I,* 9.73–75.

4. For a discussion of the fees charged by Isocrates, see Mirhady and Too's introduction to *Isocrates I.*

5. Walker reads Isocrates less cynically, arguing that he did not favor oligarchy over democracy but rather was a "political pragmatist" (*Rhetoric and Poetics,* 132).

6. The issue of bending the truth in panegyric to render a more favorable characterization of the person praised is discussed in Aristotle as well (*On Rhetoric,* 1367a–67b).

7. Galinsky makes the argument that Aeneas was generally not renowned for his piety prior to Vergil's *Aeneid* (*Aeneas,* 4).

8. On imitation in Augustan art, see Zanker, *Power of Image,* 159; Kennedy, *Art of Rhetoric,* 382; Galinsky, *Augustan Culture,* 204.

9. Kellum ties the Forum of Augustus to imitation in literature ("Sculptural Programs," 126). Luce regards both the forum and Livy's history as stemming from a view of history as a progression of great men ("Livy, Augustus, and the Forum Augustum," 129). Walker would, of course, identify both literature and history as genres of epideictic, making it the common denominator here.

10. Cassius Dio, *Roman History,* 55.10. There are numerous descriptions of the Forum of Augustus and Temple of Mars Ultor that are dependent on the archeological evidence. See Zanker, *Forum Augustum*; Zanker, *Power of Images,* 193–210. For inscriptions from the *summi*

viri, see Geiger, *First Hall of Fame*, 129–57; Anderson, *Historical Topography*, 65–100. For a detailed reading of the symbolism of the forum, see Galinsky, *Augustan Culture*, 197–211.

11. Velleius Paterculus, *Compendium*, 2.100.2; Suetonius, *Lives, The Deified Augustus*, 29; Augustus, *Res Gestae* 2; Ovid, *Fasti*, 5.569.

12. Suetonius, *Lives, The Deified Augustus*, 21.3; Cassius Dio, *Roman History*, 54.8; Ovid, *Fasti*, 5.579; Anderson, *Historical Topography*, 67.

13. Galinsky, *Augustan Culture*, 199; Anderson, *Historical Topography*, 70; 72–73.

14. Galinsky, *Augustan Culture*, 198; Anderson, *Historical Topography*, 73; Zanker, *Power of Image*, 196.

15. Zanker, *Forum Augustum*, 21–22; Ovid, *Fasti* 5.567.

16. Zanker, *Power of Image*, 196–201; Zanker, *Forum Augustum*, 19.

17. Zanker, *Power of Image*, 195.

18. Galinsky, *Augustan Culture*, 200; Kellum, "Sculptural Programs," 217–18.

19. Augustus, *Res Gestae* 35; Kellum, "Sculptural Programs," 128.

20. Pliny, *Natural History*, 35.93–94, 35.27; 34.48; Zanker, *Forum Augustum*, 23–24; Galinsky, *Augustan Culture*, 199, 208; Kellum, "Sculptural Programs," 130. For more on Alexander in the forum, see Pliny, *Natural History*, 34.48.

21. Ovid, *Fasti*, 5.563–66. Rowell suggests that the Julian line had to be included because there were not enough distinguished Octavii to make much of a presence ("Forum," 138–39).

22. Suetonius, *Lives, The Deified Augustus*, 31.

23. Galinsky, *Augustan Culture*, 206.

24. The statues are contrastingly described in classically sources. See Suetonius, *Lives, The Deified Augustus*, 31; Cassius Dio, *Roman History*, 55.10. On the marble vs. bronze discussion, see Rowell, "Forum," 140; Rowell, "Vergil," 267; Anderson, *Historical Topography*, 82. On placement of bronze statues, see Zanker, *Power of Image*, 215.

25. Kellum describes these as "shields with the Zeus Ammon heads," a "god . . . closely identified with the great Greek Alexander" ("Sculptural Programs," 129).

26. Velleius Paterculus, *Compendium*, 2.39.3; Galinsky, *Augustan Culture*, 207–8.

27. Galinsky, *Augustan Culture*, 203.

28. On the architectural precedents, see Galinsky, *Augustan Culture*, 200.

29. Galinsky, *Augustan Culture*, 202–3.

30. Cassius Dio, *Roman History*, 55.10.

31. Rowell, "Forum," 141. Some aspects of Dio's account have been called into question. See Anderson, *Historical Topography*, 93.

32. Rowell hints at this significance, though it is not his main interest ("Forum," 141).

33. Suetonius, *Lives, The Deified Augustus*, 29.

34. Anderson, *Historical Topography*, 89–91; Walker, *Rhetoric and Poetics*, 84–88.

35. Kennedy, *New History*, 106

36. Walker, *Rhetoric and Poetics*, 71. Pernot recounts the expansion of types of epideictic rhetoric in the empire based on Menander (*Rhetoric in Antiquity*, 132–33, 179–80). The idea that epideictic underlies all rhetorical practice is found in Cicero, *On Oratory*, 2.82.

37. Walker, *Rhetoric and Poetics*, 120. Walker is following Dionysius's view here. Pernot offers a view similar to Walker's in that he feels the "practical" genres persisted in the provinces and that rhetoric continued, though changed at Rome (*Rhetoric in Antiquity*, 131–33).

38. See Pernot, *Rhetoric in Antiquity*, 180.

39. Isocrates, *Isocrates I*, 3.10–11. Isocrates expresses similar sentiments in *Nicocles* and *To Nicocles* (*Isocrates I*, 3.51, 3.57, 3.60–61, 2.11).

40. Cicero, *On Oratory*, 2.85.

41. Bonner, *Education in Ancient Rome,* 18; see Horace, *Sermones,* 1.4.109–26.

42. Pernot, *Rhetoric in Antiquity,* 101. It is worth noting that ethos in Greek and Roman rhetoric are two very different ideas, with the former having to do with credibility and the latter with emotion.

43. One could rightly argue that in the republic *auctoritas* was inherited, though how one embodied *auctoritas* was, to a degree, a construction and therefore a product of education and socialization.

44. Pernot, *Rhetoric in Antiquity,* 101.

45. Bonner, *Education in Ancient Rome,* 33–34.

46. Pernot, *Rhetoric in Antiquity,* 145.

47. Cicero, *On Oratory,* 2.22, 1.34.

48. Cicero, *On Oratory,* 2.21, 1.28.

49. Cicero, *On Oratory,* 3.36.

50. Cicero, *On Oratory,* 1.9.

51. One could argue that Quintilian is representative of the more technically focused handbook tradition in Rome.

52. Cicero, *On Oratory,* 2.22.

53. Quintilian, *De Institutione,*10.2.132; 1.7.65; 2.3.97; 10.2.35.

54. Pernot, *Rhetoric in Antiquity,* 143–44.

55. Dionysius of Halicarnasus, "Ancient Orators," 4.

56. See Usher's introduction to Dionysius of Halicarnasus, *Critical Essays,* xxi–xxii, and his introduction to "Ancient Orators," 1–3.

57. Pernot, *Rhetoric in Antiquity,* 137. See Dionysius of Halicarnasus, "Ancient Orators," 4.2. Bonner makes a point similar to Pernot's: "There was also a genuine earnestness about his moral outlook . . . as may be seen, for instance, in his recommendation of the study of Isocrates' speeches for their inculcation of the most desirable virtues" (*Education in Ancient Rome,* 31). See Dionysius of Halicarnasus, "Ancient Orators, Isocrates," 5–8.

58. Pernot, *Rhetoric in Antiquity,* 144.

59. There are a number of secondary sources that detail the practice based primarily on the following primary sources: Polybius, *Histories,* 6.53; Pliny, *Natural History,* 35.6; Cicero, *Letters,* 9.21; Cicero, *On Oratory,* 2.55; Seneca, *De Beneficiis,* 3.28. For a summary, see Rowell, "Forum," 131–43; Anderson, *Historical Topography,* 86. There was likely a point when the wax masks were replaced with busts that were carried, possibly on shields, *imagines clipeatae.* See Pliny, *Natural History,* 35.2; Rowell, "Forum," 136; Zadocks-Josephus Jitta, *Ancestral Portraiture in Rome,* 42–46, 37–38; Anderson, *Historical Topography,* 86; Galinsky, *Augustan Culture,* 207.

60. Polybius, *Histories,* 6.53.9–54.3.

61. Cicero, *Letters,* 9.21.3.

62. Cicero, *Letters,* 9.21.3, paraphrase by the author.

63. Rowell, "Forum," 136.

64. Pliny says that in addition to *imagines* families had "archive-rooms" where "books of records" and "written memorials of official careers" were kept (*Natural History,* 35.2.7). Pernot suggests that at least some families also kept copies of the eulogy (*Rhetoric in Antiquity,* 92).

65. Polybius, *Histories,* 6.55.4

66. Cicero, *On Oratory,* 2.55.

67. Rowell, "Forum," 137.

68. Pernot, *Rhetoric in Antiquity,* 92.

69. Pliny, *Natural History,* 35.2.7. Pliny suggests war spoils kept in the house continually functioned as "triumphs" pushing the current residents to military greatness.

70. Polybius, *Histories*, 6.53.3.

71. Rowell, "Forum," 137. Seneca pokes a bit of fun at families who seriously invest in the notion of a pedigree. Seneca, *De Beneficiis*, 3.28.

72. Pliny, *Natural History*, 35.6.

73. Pliny, *Natural History*, 35.4–5.

74. Pliny, *Natural History*, 35.5.

75. Stewart, *Social History of Roman Art*, 42–43.

76. Statius, *Silvae*, 2.2.69–72, qtd. in Stewart, *Social History of Roman Art*, 43.

77. Stewart, *Social History of Roman Art*, 43.

78. Badian, "Calpurnius Piso Caesoninus," 281. Piso was a relative of Julius Caesar and friend of the Epicurean philosopher Philodemus.

79. Too, *Idea of the Library*, 196, 200.

80. Too, *Idea of the Library*, 196, 203.

81. Quintilian, *De Institutione*, 10.2.16; see Epicurus, *Epistula ad Herodotum*, 46–48.

82. Given Epicurus's view on (political) oratory, this is somewhat fitting; see Kennedy, *New History*, 93–94; Quintilian, *De Institutione*, 12.2.24.

83. Zanker, *Mask*, 203.

84. Zanker, *Mask*, 205–6.

85. Zanker, *Mask*, 205.

86. See Juvenal, 2.1–7, and similarly Petronius, *Satyricon*, 48.8.

87. Zanker, *Mask*, 208. Again this is the emphasis on "encyclopedias" as foundational to Atticism and the Second Sophistic as mentioned by Pernot (*Rhetoric in Antiquity*, 142–44).

88. Suetonius, *Lives, The Deified Augustus*, 31.

89. Pliny, *Natural History*, 35.2.7.

90. For literary influences of and comparisons to the *elogia*, including Livy, see Luce, "Livy, Augustus, and the Forum Augustum," 137; Anderson, *Historical Topography*, 87. Luce suggests Verrius Flaccus, the author of the *annals maximi*, is likely the author; Zanker argues for C. Julius Hyginus (Luce, "Livy, Augustus, and the Forum Augustum," 135; Zanker, *Power of Image*, 212).

91. Pliny, *Natural History*, 22.6.13; Zanker, *Power of Image*, 195.

92. Virgil, *Aeneid*, 6.756–853.

93. Norden, *P. Vergilius Maro Aeneis Buch VI*, 305–9; Rowell, "Virgil," 272.

94. Rowell, "Forum," 143.

95. Kellum, "Sculptural Programs," 126.

96. Kellum, "Sculptural Programs," 115–16; Anderson, *Historical Topography*, 83. The number of "known" *summi viri* differs depending on whether they are known through archaeological evidence or literary evidence. The latter are less trustworthy, but provide several additional names.

97. Kellum, "Sculptural Programs," 116–18.

98. Luce, "Livy, Augustus, and the Forum Augustum," 128. The *summi viri* from the forum and Augustus's instructions for his own funeral were closely linked. See Rowell, "Forum."

99. Rowell, "Vergil," 274–75.

100. Kellum, "Sculptural Programs," 118; Anderson, *Historical Topography*, 83.

101. The "consideration of war" in the Forum of Augustus is a little tricky, given that such matters had to be considered outside the boundary of the city.

102. Walker, *Rhetoric and Poetics*, 133–34.

103. Walker, *Rhetoric and Poetics*, 134.

104. Rowell has argued as much of the book 6 of the *Aeneid*, to which the Forum Augustum forms a visual parallel ("Vergil," 274).

105. Rowell, "Vergil," 276.

106. Pliny, *Natural History,* 36.102. Kellum, following Einoholz, claims Pliny favored the forum because of its use of colored marble, something the classical historian particularly liked; see Kellum, "Sculptural Programs," 109, note 4.

107. Walker doubts the *Apologia* was ever delivered (*Rhetoric and Poetics,* 121).

108. Walker, *Rhetoric and Poetics,* 123.

109. It is clear that the Forum of Augustus was not maintained as likely intended by later emperors. See Zanker, *Power of Image,* 215.

Chapter 5: Coins, Material Rhetoric, and Circulation

1. There is some evidence to suggest that the statue groups from the forum were replicated elsewhere. For example, the Aeneas group was found in several colonies in Spain as well as at Pompeii. At Pompeii it is also possible there was a local "hall of fame."

2. Mattingly, *Roman Coins,* 140.

3. Mattingly, *Roman Coins,* 143–44.

4. Mattingly *Roman Coins,* 140.

5. The *tresviri monetales* was an early office on the *cursus honorum,* the ladder of offices that culminated in the consulship.

6. Sydenham, *Coinages of Augustus,* 7; Mattingly, *Coins of the Roman Empire,* xiv, xcv.

7. Mattingly, *Coins of the Roman Empire,* xiii.

8. Mattingly, *Roman Coins,* 101. There was a short period of activity by the triumvirs in 43 B.C.E.; see Sutherland, *Roman Coins,* 102; Sydenham, *Coinages of Augustus,* 32; Mattingly, *Coins of the Roman Empire,* xiv.

9. Mattingly, *Roman Coins,* 101; Mattingly, *Coins of the Roman Empire,* xiii.

10. Sutherland, *Roman Coins,* 137–39; Mattingly, *Roman Coins,* 122.

11. Mattingly, *Roman Coins,* 130.

12. Mattingly, *Coins of the Roman Empire,* xvii. There were several phases prior to the implementation of the system of mints described by Mattingly. Around 82 B.C.E., the senatorial mint at Rome became inactive. See Mattingly, *Coins of the Roman Empire,* xii. Early after Augustus's rise to sole power, he had imperial mints in the provinces in places like Asia Minor. In 23 B.C.E., he reopened the senatorial mint in Rome for the minting of bronze coins, which continued until 4 B.C.E. and then resumed again late in Augustus's reign. In 19 B.C.E., Augustus added the right to mint silver and gold coins to the senatorial mint in Rome but discontinued this practice, or more accurately allowed it to become superfluous, in 12 B.C.E. It is likely this addition was "for the prestige of the mint" at Rome (Sutherland, *Roman Coins,* 145). Around 15 or 14 B.C.E., Augustus established an imperial mint at Lugdunum for the minting of gold and silver coins and closed all other imperial mints (Mattingly, *Roman Coins,* 101–22; Sydenham, *Coinages of Augustus,* 4–34).

13. Mattingly, *Coins of the Roman Empire,* xvii; Sutherland, *Roman Coins,* 9.

14. Mattingly, *Roman Coins,* 139, 141, 164; Sutherland, *Roman Coins,* 9; Carson, *Romans* vol. no. 1: 67. Mattingly suggests six broad classifications for coin types in the empire: (1) the emperor and the imperial family; (2) the senate and the Roman people; (3) Rome, Italy, and the provinces; (4) Religious types; (5) historical types; and (6) animate and inanimate objects. For Mattingly, the first three are major categories with some overlap with the latter three minor categories (*Roman Coins,* 144–72).

15. Numismatists have not settled on the full name for the moneyer whose name is abbreviated "C. F. TRO." Presuming the coin was minted in 13 B.C.E., it is unlikely this depiction of Augustus is related to his election as *pontifex maximus* in the following year (Fullerton, "Domus Augusti," 476).

16. Fullerton, "Domus Augusti," 476.

17. On the idea of the circulation of the themes form the Ara Pacis, see Fullerton, "Domus Augusti," 476. Geiger argues that the "national epic" written by Virgil was in the works around 27 B.C.E. and book 6, which most clearly recounts the Augustan political myth, was recited before Marcellus's death in 23 B.C.E. (*Aeneid*, 49, 51).

18. Fullerton makes the argument that the coins of 13–12 B.C.E. should be read serially ("Domus Augusti," 483).

19. Mattingly, *Roman Coins*, 143.

20. Hannestad, *Roman Art and Imperial Policy*, 68.

21. Hannestad, *Roman Art and Imperial Policy*, 68.

22. Mattingly, *Coins of the Roman Empire*, 21.

23. Virgil, *Aeneid*, 8.678–84; rpt. by permission of the publishers and the Trustees of the Loeb Classical Library from *Virgil: Volume 2*, Loeb Classical Library Volume 64, translated by H. R. Fairclough, pp. 107–9, Cambridge, Mass.: Harvard University Press, © 1999, by the Presidents and Fellows of Harvard College. Loeb Classical Library ® is a registered trademark of the Presidents and Fellows of Harvard College.

24. Fullerton, "Domus Augusti," 480–81; Mattingly, *Coins of the Roman Empire*, cvii; Cassius Dio, *Roman History*, 54.12; Livy, 28; Velleius Paterculus, *Compendium*, 2.81.

25. The divine Julius was often represented by a comet because, several months after the death of Caesar in 44 B.C.E. while Octavian was holding games in his adopted father's honor, a comet was seen and interpreted as a sign of Caesar's deification (Galinsky, *Augustan Culture*, 17; Cassius Dio, *Roman History*, 45.7.1).

26. Fullerton, "Domus Augusti," 24.

27. Fullerton, "Domus Augusti," 474. Fullerton's argument is strengthened by the fact that Reginus's types are essentially copies of his relative C. Antistius Vetus's types in 18 B.C.E. In addition, Fullerton argues that the selection of republican types here "testif[ies] to the control still exercised by moneyers over type selection [and] that the other selected types designed to glorify the emperor can thus be seen to some degree as a matter of choice rather than strictly of compulsion" ("Domus Augusti," 474).

28. For example, a sestertius issued by Agrippa in 38 B.C.E. shows the portrait heads of Octavian on the obverse and Julius Caesar on the reverse. The legend on the obverse reads CAESAR.DIVI.F., and the reverse reads DIVOS.IVLIVS, identifying Octavian as "son of the divine" and Julius Caesar as "the deified Julius" (see Carson, *Principal Coins of the Romans*, vol. 1: 78). A denarius of similar subject matter from 19–16 B.C.E. minted in Spain shows a portrait head of Augustus laureate on the obverse with the legend CAESAR AVGVSTVS. The reverse depicts the *sidus Julium*, the comet that appeared after the death of Caesar, with the inscription DIVVS IVLIVS (Carson, *Principal Coins of the Romans*, vol. 2: 9).

29. Sutherland, *Roman Coins*, 119.

30. The last event has led scholars to argue that Agrippa was an intermediary heir, meant to rule only until his children Gaius and Lucius came of age (see Fullerton, "Domus Augusti," 476–77; Sutherland, *Coinage*, 57–58).

31. Fullerton, "Domus Augusti," 480.

32. Fullerton, "Domus Augusti," 480.

33. The inscription reads CAESAR AVGVSTVS DIVI F PATER PATRIAE. The coin in the image is off-struck, obscuring "patriae."

34. Mattingly, *Coins of the Roman Empire*, cxvi. The inscription reads C. L. CAESARES AVGVSTI F. COS DESIG PRINC IVVENT.

35. Mattingly, *Coins of the Roman Empire*, cxvi.

36. Wells, *Roman Empire*, 66–72.

37. So for example, the As from the senatorial mint at Rome dating from 10–14 C.E., which no longer bears the name of the moneyers, features Tiberius on the obverse with the inscription TI.CAESAR.AVGVSTVS.F. IMPERAT and the reverse the standard SC, but rather than the name and the title of the moneyers, the coin is inscribed PONTIFEX.TRIBVN.POTESTATE.XII (see Mattingly, *Coins of the Roman Empire*, plate 20.16).

38. Mattingly, *Coins of the Roman Empire*, cxvii–cxviii; Carson, *Principal Coins of the Romans*, vol. 2: 13.

39. The inscription reads TI.CAESAR.AVGVSTI.F.IMPERAT.V.

40. The inscription reads CAESAR.AUGUSTVS.DIVI.F.PATER. PATRIAE.

41. Carson, *Principal Coins of the Romans*, vol. 2: 13.

42. Tacitus, *Annals*, 1.3; Wells, *Roman Empire*, 71; Mattingly, *Coins of the Roman Empire*, cxvi.

43. Cassius Dio, *Roman History*, 55.9; Suetonius, *Lives, Tiberius*, 10; Wells, *Roman Empire*, 70. For more on the issues of Tiberius's succession see Syme, "History."

44. An Aureus from a triumviral issue dating to 42 B.C.E. shows the portrait head of Octavian on the reverse and the flight of Aeneas on the reverse (see Carson, *Principal Coins of the Romans*, vol. no. 1, plate 262). A denarius from an Italian mint dating to 31–29 B.C.E. shows Venus on obverse and Octavian with a spear on the reverse (see Sutherland, *Roman Coins*, plates 206, 207).

45. For example, a Denarius dating from between 31 and 29 B.C.E. from an Italian mint features Pax with an olive branch and cornucopia (see Sutherland, *Roman Coins*, plate 209). A denarius from the same mint and date features Victory on a globe with a wreath and palm (see Sutherland, *Roman Coins*, plate 213). Both issues specifically reference Actium.

46. A good example of exceedingly complex and condensed iconography is the denarius from an eastern mint dating from 29–27 B.C.E., an early example of the development of the themes of the political myth. Augustus is shown seated in the curule chair, which Mattingly argues could reference his first granting of *tribunicia potestas* or, I would suggest, the three curule triumphs of 29 B.C.E., holding victory with the inscription IMP CAESAR in reference to his imperial power granted in 29 B.C.E. and a direct reference to Actium (Mattingly, *Roman Coins*, cxx, cxxiv; Augustus, *Res Gestae* 4). The winged thunderbolt on the obverse is a reference to Jupiter and suggests Jupiter provided the victory to Octavian (Fears, "Cult of Virtues," 57).

47. See Augustus, *Res Gestae*, 34.

48. Augustus, *Res Gestae*, 10.

49. See Ovid, *Fasti*, 3.423–26.

50. Fullerton, "Domus Augusti," 479–80.

51. "SC" stands for *senatus consultm*.

52. Mattingly, *Coins of the Roman Empire*, xcix. A typical sestertius, like the sestertius of C. Gallius Lupercus, moneyer in 22 B.C.E., shows the normal obverse of the sestertius and the SC reverse with the inscription around the edge reading C. GALLIVS.C.F.LVPERCVS. (the moneyer's name), III.VIR.A.A.A.F.F. (the abbreviation for the full title of the moneyer, *tresvir aere argento auro flando feriundo*); see Carson, *Principal Coins of the Romans*, vol. 2: 10. There are some variations. For example, the As of the moneyer Calpurnius Piso features a portrait head of an ancestor for the reverse, which is a frequent feature of republican coinage.

53. Pliny, *Natural History*, 16.5.

54. Augustus, *Res Gestae* 34.

55. CAESAR.AVGVSTVS. TRIBVNIC.POTEST or AVGVSTVS TRIBVNIC POTEST.

56. Augustus, *Res Gestae* 10.

57. Wells, *Roman Empire*, 7.

58. Eder, "Augustus and the Power of Tradition," 110.

59. See Sutherland, *Roman Coins*, 129–32.

60. Sutherland, *Roman Coins*, 139; see also Grant, *Roman History*, 79–80; Mattingly, *Roman History*, 102, 105.

61. Mattingly, *Coins of the Roman Empire*, c.

62. Augustus, *Res Gestae* 34.

63. Carson, *Principal Coins of the Romans*, vol. 2: 11; Mattingly, *Coins of the Roman Empire*, 42.

64. Carson, *Principal Coins of the Romans*, vol. 2: 11; Cassius Dio, *Roman History*, 55.6.

65. Cassius Dio, *Roman History*, 55.6.

66. Wells, *Roman Empire*, 7.

Chapter 6: The Augustan Political Myth in Vernacular Art

1. Zanker, *Power of Images*, 278.

2. Tacitus, *Dialogus*, 10.13.

3. Bizzell and Herzberg, *Rhetorical Tradition*, 31.

4. Enos, *Roman Rhetoric*, 60.

5. Enos, *Roman Rhetoric*, 221.

6. Tacitus, *Dialogus*, 10.13.

7. For an example, see Enos, *Rhetorical Tradition*, 61.

8. Raaflaub and Samons, "Opposition to Augustus," 445–46. Classicists have argued about the reasons for Ovid's banishment, which range from his violation of Augustus's moral reforms to plotting to influence succession against Augustus's wishes (see Raaflaub and Samons, "Opposition to Augustus," 445–46; Nugent, "Tristia 2"; 239-257; Bauman, *Crimen Maiestatis*, 243–45).

9. Five of the seven altars are shown. Additionally I consider a second altar from the Vatican and the "Soriano Altar" which is now in the Capitoline Museum. It is clear that there is consistency in the iconography of the altars, suggesting that, though only a very few of the original altars remain, these are fairly representative. I am generalizing my findings, but hesitantly given the sample size. Also, though some freedmen (who were plebs), freeborn plebs, slaves, and nonelite women belonging to these classes did participate in the cult, not all did, and the experience of the participants is not transferable to all nonelite Romans.

10. Upon being freed, freedmen would have joined the ranks of the plebeians. Altars such as the Altar of the Lares Dedicated by Women and the Altar of the Lares Dedicated by Slaves were not the official altars of the wards; however, slaves and women did participate in the cult. Galinsky suggests such altars were extremely simple so as not to outdo the official altars (*Augustan Culture*, 308).

11. There are various explanations of the state of the cult of the *lares Compitales* before Augustus's reforms. According to classicist John Fine, the standard understanding is that in 64 B.C.E. the senate did away with the cult and its priests only for it to be restored in 56 B.C.E. by the Lex Clodia before it was limited again by Caesar. Fine questions this last part, instead claiming the cult simply fell into disuse based on his reading of Suetonius ("A Note on the Compitalia," 268).

12. Both "political myth" and "collective identity" are McGee's terms ("In Search of 'The People,'" 346).

13. Galinsky, *Augustan Culture*, 288.

14. The political importance of the cult was tied to the political importance of the plebs. For more on the role of the plebs in the principate; see Syme, *Roman Revolution*, 119; Yavetz, *Plebs*, 58–102. To say simply that Octavian inherited the support of the plebs from Caesar,

though in some ways essentially true, is a bit of an oversimplification. For a more nuanced account; see Yavetz, *Plebs*. The religious duties of the cult were overseen by the priests of each district. Each *vicus* had eight priests, four *magistri,* and four *ministri,* comprised of urban plebs, most often freedmen, who were in charge of the construction of the altar of their ward. They were responsible for two large religious festivals each year, which included making sacrifices at the neighborhood altars, as well as some public safety duties such as firefighting and policing. In return, the *vicomagistri,* as the priests were known, had their names recorded each year next to those of the consuls and were allowed attendants at games and wore a special toga. Therefore serving as a priest of the cult, though religious in nature, as was often the case in Rome, also served as a symbol of social standing; see Galinsky, *Augustan Culture,* 300–302; Zanker, *Power of Image* 121–31; Taylor, *Divinity of the Roman Emperor,* 185–86.

15. Fullerton, "Domus Augusti," 473–74, 483.

16. Galinsky, *Augustan Culture,* 302, 306; Ryberg, *Rites of the State Religion,* 55–61. Though Galinsky does not give his criteria for judging the quality of the altars, it likely involves the building materials of the altars, which he describes as "inferior" in comparison to the single altar made of Luna marble, as well as the quality of the sculpture; Galinsky, *Augustan Culture,* 302, 306. Ryberg, who is quick to point out the altars "differ widely in quality and detail," comments on the simplicity of the iconography, the "crudity" of details and sculpture, and also on the scale of the figures (*Rites of the State Religion,* 55–61).

17. Galinsky, *Augustan Culture,* 302.

18. Ryberg, *Rites of the State Religion,* 53.

19. Galinsky, *Augustan Culture,* 302.

20. A number of scholars including Ono and Sloop, Bodnar, and Hauser have used the official/vernacular distinction, and each defines these terms slightly differently. I rely predominantly on the work of Ono and Sloop and Bodnar. Ono and Sloop define vernacular discourse as "discourse that resonates within and from historically oppressed communities," in opposition to the "discourse of the empowered, discourse of those who control design, and create public space" ("Critique of Vernacular Discourse," 19, 20). Bodnar also defines vernacular in opposition to official discourse. He says official discourse comes from leaders who "share a common interest in social unity, the continuity of existing institutions, and loyalty to the status quo. They attempt to advance these concerns by promoting interpretations of past and present reality that reduce the power of competing interests that threaten the attainment of their goals. Official culture relies on 'dogmatic formalism' and the restatement of reality in ideal rather than complex or ambiguous terms. It presents the past on an abstract basis of timelessness and sacredness." In opposition, "vernacular culture . . . represents an array of specialized interests that are grounded in parts of the whole." In addition, according to Bodnar, vernaculars are based in "values" and views of reality derived from "firsthand experience. . . . Normally vernacular expressions convey what social reality feels like rather than what it should be like. Its very existence threatens the sacred and timeless nature of official expressions" (*Remaking America,* 13–14).

Hauser is more interested in what vernacular discourse can tell scholars about public opinion and the public sphere as well as individuals' historicity, that is, "the actors' awareness of history and society as human constructs." Hauser describes vernacular expressions as informal expressions "of who we are, what we need and hope for, what we are willing to accept, and our commitment to reciprocity." Yet in terms of public discussions he says, they "are our continuous means to form shared meaning; discover new cultural, political and social possibilities; and shape an understanding of our common interests." In addition, Hauser describes vernacular expressions in Bakhtinian terms as between authoritative and internally persuasive dialogue (*Vernacular Voices,* 8, 11, 116).

21. The role of the plebs in Rome inevitably comes down to one question—how democratic was the Roman republic? There have been various answers to this question. Some credited the patron/client relationship (a view that's largely discounted now) with supplying democracy to the plebs via a patron who functioned as a representative. Others cite the plebs' ability to shut down the city by rioting as one means of political expression. While these two means of democracy suggest the republic was less democratic, Fergus Millar suggests the republic was more democratic because politicians, regardless of party, were from the upper classes, but elections and the power of oratory to sway elections required the participation of plebs as audiences and voters. Millar offers a good summary of perspectives as well as his own, even if, in my opinion, he makes oratory and elections a bit more significant than they might have been ("Political Character," 2–3; "Popular Politics," 93–97).

22. Millar, "Popular Politics," 107.

23. Augustus, *Res Gestae* 34.

24. Cassius Dio, *Roman History*, 53.16.

25. Sutherland, *Roman Coins*, 137.

26. For more on the history of the *corona civica*, see Pliny, *Natural History,* 22.4. See also Augustus, *Res Gestae,* 399, note by translator.

27. Galinsky, *Augustan Culture*, 37.

28. Ryberg, *Rites of the State Religion*, 55.

29. Galinsky, *Augustan Culture*, 80–90.

30. Velleius Paterculus, *Compendium,* 2.89.

31. Yavetz suggests that the plebs really didn't care all that much about politics or tradition provided they had corn (*Plebs*, 93). Others such as Millar argue that the plebs were better citizens than this and did participate through voting ("Political Character," 2).

32. The altar is often called the "Vatican Altar" of the Lares to avoid calling it the "Belvedere Altar" or the "Altar formerly known as the Belvedere Altar." Unfortuantely there is a second Altar of the Lares in the Vatican (not shown) that is also sometimes called the "Vatican Altar." I refer to the "Belvedere Altar" as "the altar now in the Vatican."

33. Galinsky, *Augustan Culture*, 302. Galinsky suggests the desire for "self-representation" was simply a reflection that the *vicomagistri* were in charge of determining the iconography of the altars; Galinsky, *Augustan Culture*, 302. Zanker does not address the theme of self-representation specifically, but he does make a broad comment, "The most ambitious from all classes begin actively to pursue religious offices. In the new or revised cult activities there were ample opportunities for self-promotion and, at the same time, for showing solidarity with the new state" (*Power of Image*, 129). Zanker's comment may be applicable to the theme of self-representation on the altar of the Lares. That is, the cult of the Lares provided a safe venue for self-advancement without rivaling the power of the *princeps.*

34. Taylor, *Divinity of the Roman Emperor,* 186.

35. Ryberg, *Rites of the State Religion,* 56.

36. Ryberg, *Rites of the State Religion,* 56.

37. Which figure is Lucius and which is Augustus is somewhat debated. Ryberg thinks the center figure is Lucius, who was made an augur in 2 b.c.e. Both Galinsky and Zanker seem to think the center figure is Augustus depicted as *pontifex maximus.* The identity of the female figure is heavily debated also and may be Livia, Julia, Iuventas, or Cybele. Ryberg argues for Livia, Galinsky for Cybele. For a good summary of the debate, see Galinsky. Like the identity of the other figures, the significance of the chicken is debated. It may be a reference to the position of augur that Lucius received in 2 b.c.e. whose job it would have been to take the auspices, and/or the chicken eating may be a good omen and a reference to Gaius, who is not shown in this

scene and was on campaign. See Galinsky, *Augustan Culture*, 306; Zanker, *Power of Image*, 121; Ryberg, *Rites of the State Religion*, 60.

38. Ryberg, *Rites of the State Religion*, 60–61.

39. Galinsky, *Augustan Culture*, 309. For Suetonius's account, see his *Lives, The Deified Augustus*, 57.

40. These are the altar dedicated by women, the second Vatican altar, and the altar "Soriano" that is now in the Capitoline. The latter two are not pictured.

41. Cassius Dio, *Roman History*, 52.34.

42. Perhaps this is most obvious in that, as Zanker notes, Augustus himself took all the auspices, which were, of course, always favorable, but also that he had most books of prophecy destroyed, in what was an effort not only to control the past but also the future (Galinsky, *Augustan Culture*, 313; Zanker, *Power of Image*, 121).

43. Galinsky, *Augustan Culture*, 302.

44. Bodnar, *Remaking America*, 14.

45. Bodnar, *Remaking America*, 14.

46. Bodnar, *Remaking America*, 13–14.

47. Zanker, *Power of Image*, 116.

48. McGee, "In Search of 'The People,'" 346–67.

49. McGee, "In Search of 'The People,'" 346.

50. McGee, "In Search of 'The People,'" 345.

51. Galinsky, *Augustan Culture*, 302.

52. Ono and Sloop, "Critique of Vernacular Discourse," 20–21.

53. Ono and Sloop, "Critique of Vernacular Discourse," 23.

54. Ono and Sloop, "Critique of Vernacular Discourse," 21.

55. Zanker, *Power of Image*, 129; Galinsky, *Augustan Culture*, 310.

56. Bodnar, *Remaking America*, 13.

57. Favro, *Urban Image*, 7, 153.

58. Favro, *Urban Image*, 232. Favro, *Urban Image* is basing her criticism on Augustus's claims in the *Res Gestae*. See Augustus, *Res Gestae* 19–20.

59. Zanker, *Power of Image*, 116. See also Galinsky, *Augustan Culture*, 310.

60. Holly, *Past Looking*, 79.

61. Coins were no doubt the most frequently viewed iconography. Still, the presence of the altars of the Lares at intersections throughout the city would have had a substantial impact on the appearance of the cityscape.

62. Ovid, *Fasti*, 5.145; Favro, *Urban Image*, 124.

Chapter 7: (Freed)men and Monkeys

1. Petronius, *Satyricon*, 52, 37.

2. Petronius, *Satyricon*, 37.

3. Ostrow, "Augustales Along the Bay of Naples," 69.

4. Kellum, "Sculptural Programs," 118.

5. Ostrow, "Augustales Along the Bay of Naples," 68; Peterson, *Freedman in Roman Art*, 58.

6. Laird, "Evidence in Context," 22.

7. Ostrow, "Augustales Along the Bay of Naples," 71. Generally there were two magistrate positions, the *duumvir* and *aedile*, and two assemblies, the *ordo decuriones* and a popular assembly.

8. Ostrow, "Augustales Along the Bay of Naples," 69–70.

9. Peterson, *Freedman in Roman Art*, 10.

10. Cicero, "De Officiis," 1.44.

11. Ostrow, "Augustales Along the Bay of Naples," 72.

12. Ostrow, "Augustales in the Augustan Scheme," 376; Woods, "Funerary Monuments," 34. See Cassius Dio, *Roman History*, 50.10; Syme, *Roman Revolution*, 284.

13. Ostrow, "Augustales Along the Bay of Naples," 71.

14. Woods makes the argument that the chaos of the end of the late republic led to a great deal of social mobility, inasmuch as it was hard to keep track of people to enforce the laws associated with social class. In this respect, the Augustan laws were as much about keeping track of people as promoting social mobility; see "Funerary Monuments," 35.

15. Ostrow, "Augustales Along the Bay of Naples," 8–9.

16. Ostrow, "Augustales Along the Bay of Naples," 364–73.

17. Peterson, *Freedman in Roman Art*, 70; Woods, "Funerary Monuments," 95.

18. Peterson, *Freedman in Roman Art*, 72. Interestingly, in two instances at Pompeii it seems to have been a family member, in one case an *Augustalis's* son standing for office, who built large funerary monuments for an *Augustalis*, suggesting it was not always the freedman who held political aspirations for the family. See Woods, "Funerary Monuments," 71–72.

19. Woods, "Funerary Monuments," 49.

20. Peterson, *Freedman in Roman Art*, 71–72. There is plenty of evidence to suggest that at least some elites (Peterson would say "ultra-elites") were not pleased with these honors; see Woods, "Funerary Monuments," 46. See also Horace, *Carmina*, 4.15–16; Suetonius, *Lives, Gaius Caligula*, 26; Suetonius, *Lives, Domitianus*, 8; Martial, 5.8, 5.14, 5.23.

21. Augustus, *Res Gestae* 19–20.

22. Augustus, *Res Gestae* 21–23.

23. Suetonius, *Lives, The Deified Augustus*, 28.3; Kellum, "Sculptural Programs," 118–19.

24. Anderson, *Historical Topography*, 83–85.

25. Translation by the author following Geiger's restoration of the inscription: "navis oc[toginta et Macellum |[oppidum c[epit]. Pri[m]us d[e Poenis n]avalem trium]- | [phum egit. H] uic per missum est, u[t ab e]pulis domum | [cum tibici] ne e[t f]unali rediret, [ei s[tatua c[um] | [columna] pr[ope a]ream Vulc[ani p]os[i]ta est. | Aedem apud foru]m ho[litorum ex spoliis Iano fecit]" (*First Hall of Fame*, 144).

26. Tacitus, *Annals*, 2.49.

27. Kellum, "Sculptural Programs," 119.

28. Kellum, "Sculptural Programs," 119.

29. Favro points out that, in fact, Augustus often took credit for building structures he merely renovated or doing the same under the names of his family members (*Urban Image*, 120, 232).

30. Geiger, *First Hall of Fame*, 194–95.

31. Horace, *Carmina*, 3.6.1–8.

32. As in *CIL* (*Corpus Inscriptionum* Latinarum) vol. no. 10:1885; Mommsen, *Inscriptiones*, 231; translation by the author.

33. See *CIL* vol. no. 10:1887, 10:531, 10:772, 10:1838, 10:4792, 10:1217, 10:1887, 10:1217, 10:1574; Mommsen *Inscriptiones*, 231, 64, 88, 228, 473, 141, 231, 141, 195). See also Ostrow, "Augustales Along the Bay of Naples," 69.

34. The full inscription reads: "N · PLAETORIO · ONIRO / AVGVSTALI / BISELLIARO / HONORATO · ORNAMENTIS /DECVRIONALIBVS / POPVLVS · ABELLANVS/ AERE · CONLATO · QVOD / AVXERIT EX · SVO · AD / ANNONARIAM · PECVNIM / HS · X · N · ET VELA IN THAEATRO / CVM · OMNI · ORNATV / SVMPTV · SVO · DEDERIT / L · D · D · D," as in *CIL* vol. no. 10:1217; see Mommsen, *Inscriptiones*, 141.

35. Woods, "Funerary Monuments," 48–49.

36. Woods, "Funerary Monuments," 113.

37. Woods, "Funerary Monuments," 72. Woods makes the case that the funerary monument was possibly built by Quietus's son to raise to visibility of the family name when he was running for office ("Funerary Monuments," 71).

38. Peterson, *Freedman in Roman Art,* 63.

39. CIL vol. no. .10:1026; Mommsen, *Inscriptiones*, 119. Translation by Petersen, *Freedman in Roman Art,* 62.

40. For example, see Augustus, *Res Gestae* 34–35.

41. Quintilian, *The Orator's Education,*10.2.14–15. Dionysius of Halicarnasus makes a similar point ("Ancient Orators," 4).

42. Quintilian, *The Orator's Education,* 10.2.27.

43. Quintilian, *The Orator's Education,* 10.2.8–9.

44. Quintilian, *The Orator's Education,* 10.2.15–16.

45. Quintilian, *The Orator's Education,* 10.2.16.

46. This idea of aping seems to have originated in secondary scholarship with Duthoy. See Woods, "Funerary Monuments," 13; Duthoy, "La Fonction," 153.

47. Ostrow, "Augustales Along the Bay of Naples," 89–91.

48. Galinsky, *Augustan Culture*, 204; Maiuri, "Parodia Di Enea," 109; Geiger, *First Hall of Fame,* 194–95.

49. Stewart, *Social History of Roman Art,* 126.

50. Stewart, *Social History of Roman Art,* 126.

51. Zanker, *Bilderwang*, 2. Though the paintings were displayed publicly, I am using "private" to signify private sponsorship as opposed to state sponsorship.

52. Zanker, *Bilderwang*, 1–2.

53. Stewart, *Social History of Roman Art,* 126–27.

54. Stewart, *Social History of Roman Art,* 126.

55. Zanker, *Bilderwang*, 1.

56. Zanker, *Bilderwang*, 1.

57. Stewart, *Social History of Roman Art,* 126–27. Stewart actually objects rather strenuously to the term "propaganda," arguing that it is a thoroughly modern concept and inappropriate to apply to the Roman period. Here he seems to apply the term to references to propaganda in work done by other art historians (*Social History of Roman Art*, 112).

58. For an example of this stance, see Bizzell and Herzberg, *Rhetorical Tradition,* 31.

59. Quintilian, *The Orator's Education,* 9.2.35; see also Quintilain, *De Institutione*, 6.3.97–98. The Latin reads "incipit esse quodam modo παρῳδή, quod nomen ductum a canticis ad aliorum similitudinem modulates abusive etiam in versificationis ac sermonum imitatione servatur." For a brief review of "parody" in classical rhetoric, see Hariman, "Political Parody," 250–53. For a summary on the use of parody in Roman literature, see Fowler and Fowler, "Parody, Latin," 1115.

60. Cicero, *On Oratory*, 2.59.242.

61. Quintilian, *The Orator's Education,* 6.3.1. Quintilian begins his discussion of laughter in book 6.3 after discussing the use of *phantasia* and *enargeia* (*De Institutione*, 6.2.29ff).

62. Quintilian, *The Orator's Education,* 6.3.1.

63. Cicero, *On Oratory*, 2.54.216, 2.58.236.

64. Hariman, "Political Parody," 249.

65. Quintilian, *The Orator's Education,* 6.3.9; see also Cicero, *On Oratory*, 2.58.235.

66. Quintilian, *The Orator's Education,* 6.3.10.

67. Quintilian, *The Orator's Education,* 6.3.8; see Cicero, *On Oratory*, 2.58.236.

68. Quintilian, *The Orator's Education,* 6.3.28.

69. Quintilian, *The Orator's Education,* 6.3.29; Cicero, *On Oratory,* 2.60.244.

70. Cicero, *On Oratory,* 2.59.242; Quintilian, *The Orator's Education,* 6.3.9.

71. Quintilian, *The Orator's Education,* 6.1.32–33.

72. Galinsky, *Aeneas,* 3–4.

73. The concept of "aping" did exist in classical Rome. Though the etymology of *simia* is questionable, it may be related to *similis* meaning "like, resembling, similar." Additionally, while *similis* can be used as an example or parallel case, it can also be used to denote a false impression, a simulation. The word *simius,* meaning monkey or ape, was often used as a derogatory term but could also take on the same connotations as "aping" in contemporary usage. Both Cicero and Quintilian caution against mimicry that is too obscene or vulgar; they generally use "*scurrilis,*" an adjective meaning literally "buffoon-like" from the noun *scurra,* originally meaning a "fashionable city idler" though the terms comes to refer to men who were "professional buffoons" and who used "offensive wit" (Glare, *Oxford Latin Dictionary,* 1763–64). Cicero and Quintilian also caution against the orator becoming like the "*mimus,*" actors in a farce or mimes (Cicero, *On Oratory,* 2.59.239, 2.60.244; Quintilian, *De Institutione,* 6.3.29).

Conclusion

1. Galinsky makes this point often, labeling the Augustan reforms as "an evolution" (*Augustan Culture,* 9, 299).

2. Syme, *Roman Revolution,* 8; Linderski, "Mommsen and Syme," 48.

3. Suetonius, *Lives, The Deified Augustus,* 37.

4. For example, Kennedy claims, "To win men's minds without opening the door to the dangers of public debate Augustus developed new techniques of verbal and visual persuasion which took over some of the functions and adapted some of the methods of traditional oratory," particularly the use of rhetorical proof and the use of imitation (*Art of Rhetoric,* 382).

5. Stewart, *Social History of Roman Art,* 112.

6. Jowett and O'Donnell, *Propaganda and Persuasion,* 15–16.

7. There are few known instances of censorship of any kind from the principate, and Ovid's case is often over-interpreted. Classicists feel there was "some measure of opposition, or at least some reservation [to the principate], among Augustan poets"; that is, even those under the patronage of the *princeps* felt free to express reservations (Raaflaub and Samons, "Opposition to Augustus," 445, 436). On the limits of free speech, see Bauman, *Crimen Maiestatis,* 251–65.

8. Raaflaub and Samons, "Opposition to Augustus," 417.

9. Updike, "Know When to Fold 'Em."

10. Isocrates, *To Nicocles,* 3.10–11.

11. Suetonius, *Lives, The Deified Augustus,* 31.5

12. Kennedy, *Art of Rhetoric,* 383–84.

13. Enos, *Roman Rhetoric,* 53.

14. Schiff, *Cleopatra,* 5.

15. Kennedy, *Art of Rhetoric,* 378.

BIBLIOGRAPHY

Aldrete, G. S. *Gestures and Acclamations in Ancient Rome.* Baltimore: Johns Hopkins University Press, 1999.

Anderson, J. C. *The Historical Topography of the Imperial Fora, 182.* Brussels: Latomus, 1999.

Aristotle. *On Rhetoric.* Trans. George Kennedy. New York: Oxford University Press, 1991.

Augustus. *Res Gestae Divi Augusti.* Trans. Frederick Shipley. Loeb Classical Library. Cambridge, Mass.: Harvard University Press, 2002.

Badian, E. "Calpurnius Piso Caesoninus, Lucius." In *The Oxford Classical Dictionary,* ed. Hornblower and Spawforth, 281.

Balsdon, John, and Andrew Lintott. "Maiestas." In *The Oxford Classical Dictionary,* ed. Hornblower and Spawforth, 913–14.

Bauman, Richard A. *The Crimen Maiestatis in the Roman Republic and Augustan Principate.* Johannesburg, South Africa: Witwatersrand Univeristy Press, 1967.

Bitzer, Lloyd. F. "The Rhetorical Situation." In *Contemporary Rhetorical Theory: A Reader,* ed. John L. Lucaites, Celeste M. Condit and Sally Caudill. 217–25. New York: Guilford Press 1999.

Bizzell, Patricia, and Bruce Herzberg. *The Rhetorical Tradition: Readings from Classical Times to the Present.* Boston: Bedford/St. Martin's, 2001.

Blair, Carole, Marsha S. Jepperson, and Enrico Pucci Jr. "Public Memorializing in Postmodernity: The Vietnam Veterans Memorial as Prototype." *Quarterly Journal of Speech* 77.3 (1991): 263–88.

Bodnar, John. *Remaking America: Public Memory, Commemoration and Patriotism in the Twentieth Century.* Princeton, N.J.: Princeton University Press, 1992.

Bonner, Stanley Frederick. *Education in Ancient Rome: From the Elder Cato to the Younger Pliny.* Berkeley: University of California Press, 1977.

Bremmer, J. N., and N. M. Horsfall. *Roman Myth and Mythography.* London: University of London, Institute of Classical Studies, 1987.

Carson, R. A. G. *Principal Coins of the Romans.* 3 vols. London: British Museum, 1980.

Cassius Dio. *The Roman History: The Reign of Augustus.* Trans. Ian Scott-Kilvert. London: Penguin, 1987.

Castriota, David. "Introduction: Political Art and the Rhetoric of Power in the Historical Continuum." *Artistic Strategy and the Rhetoric of Power: Political Uses of Art from Antiquity to the Present,* ed. David Castriota, 1–13. Carbondale: Southern Illinois University Press. 1986.

Cicero. *De Inventione.* Trans. H. M Hubbell. Loeb Classical Library. Cambridge, Mass.: Harvard University Press, 2000.

———. "De Officiis." In *The Ethical Writings of Cicero.* Trans. Andrew P. Peabody, 1–247. Boston: Little, Brown, and Co., 1887.

———. *The Letters to his Friends.* Trans. W. G. Williams. Loeb Classical Library. Cambridge, Mass.: Harvard University Press, 1959. Vol. 2.

———. *On Oratory and Orators.* Trans. J. S. Watson. Carbondale: Southern Illinois University Press, 1970.

"Cicero." *Rhetorica ad Herennium.* Trans. Harry Caplan. Loeb Classical Library. Cambridge, Mass.: Harvard University Press, 1968.

Claridge, Amanda. *Rome: An Oxford Archaeological Guide.* New York: Oxford University Press, 1998.

Corbeill, Anthony. *Nature Embodied: Gestures in Ancient Rome.* Princeton, N.J.: Princeton University Press, 2003.

Cornell, Tim J. "Tarquinius Superbus, Lucius." In *The Oxford Classical Dictionary,* ed. Hornblower and Spawforth, 1475.

Crawford, Michael. *Roman Republican Coinage.* London: Cambridge University Press, 1974. Vol. 1.

Dionysius of Halicarnassus. "The Ancient Orators." In *Critical Essays,* trans. Stephen Usher. Loeb Classical Library. Cambridge, Mass.: Harvard University Press, 1985. Vol. 1: 1–15.

Drummond, Andrew. "Tullius, Servius." In *The Oxford Classical Dictionary,* ed. Hornblower and Spawforth, 1558.

Duthoy, Robert. "La Fonction Sociale De L'augustalite." *Epigraphica* 36 (1974): 134–54.

Eder, W. "Augustus and the Power of Tradition: The Augustan Principate as Binding Link between Republic and Empire." In *Between Republic and Empire,* ed. Raaflaub and Toher, 71–122.

Enos, Richard Leo. "Rhetorical Archaeology: Established Resources, Methodological Tools, and Basic Research Methods." In *The Sage Handbook of Rhetorical Studies,* ed. Andrea Lunsford, 35–52. Los Angeles: Sage, 2009.

———. *Roman Rhetoric: Revolution and the Greek Influence.* West Lafayette, Ind.: Parlor Press, 2008.

Favro, Diane. *The Urban Image of Augustan Rome.* Cambridge, U.K.: Cambridge University Press, 1996.

Fears, Rufus J. "The Cult of Virtues in Roman Imperial Ideology." *Aufstieg und Niedergang der Romischen Welt* 17.3 (1981): 827–948.

Fine, John V. A. "A Note on the Compitalia." *Classical Philology* 27 (1932): 268–73.

Fowler, Peta G., and Don P. Fowler. "Parody, Latin." In *The Oxford Classical Dictionary,* ed. Hornblower and Spawforth, 1115.

Fox, Matthew. *Roman Historical Myths: The Regal Period in Augustan Literature.* Oxford, U.K.: Oxford University Press, 1996.

Fullerton, Mark D. "The Domus Augusti in Imperial Iconography." *American Journal of Archaeology* 89.3 (1985): 473–83.

Galinsky, Karl. *Aeneas, Sicily, and Rome.* Princeton, N.J.: Princeton University Press, 1969.

———. *Augustan Culture.* Princeton, N.J.: Princeton University Press, 1996.

Geiger, Joseph. *The First Hall of Fame: A Study in the Forum Augustum. Mnemosyne.* Leiden: Brill, 2008.

Glare, P. G. W. ed. *Oxford Latin Dictionary.* Oxford, U.K.: Clarendon Press, 1992.

Grant, Michael. *Roman History from Coins; Some Uses of the Imperial Coins to the Historian.* Cambridge, U.K.: Cambridge University Press, 1958.

Hannestad, Niels. *Roman Art and Imperial Policy.* Jutland Archaeological Society Publications, 19. Moesgard, Denmark: Aarhus University Press, 1986.

Hariman, Robert. "Political Parody and Public Culture." *Quarterly Journal of Speech* 94.3 (2008): 247–72.

Harris, Stephen L., and Gloria Platzner. *Classical Mythology Images and Insights.* 2nd ed. Mountain View, Calif.: Mayfield, 1998.

Harrison, Stephen J. "Aeneas." In *The Oxford Classical Dictionary,* ed. Hornblower and Spawforth, 22–23.

Hauser, Gerard. *Vernacular Voices: The Rhetoric of Publics and Public Sphere.* Columbia: University of South California Press, 1999.

Holly, Michael Ann. *Past Looking: Historical Imagination and the Rhetoric of the Image.* Ithaca, N.Y.: Cornell University Press, 1996.

Holscher, Tonio. *The Language of Images in Roman Art.* Trans. Anthony Snodgrass and Annemarie Kunzl-Snodgrass. Cambridge, U.K.: Cambridge University Press, 2004.

Horace. *Carmina.* In *Odes and Epodes.* Trans. Rudd Niall. Loeb Classical Library. Cambridge, Mass.: Harvard University Press, 2004.

Hornblower, Simon, and Antony Spawforth, eds. *The Oxford Classical Dictionary.* 3rd ed. Oxford, U.K.: Oxford University Press, 2003.

Isocrates. *Isocrates I.* Trans. David Mirhady and Yun Lee Too. Austin: University of Texas Press, 2000.

Jowett, Garth S., and Victoria O' Donnell. *Propaganda and Persuasion.* Beverly Hills, Calif.: Sage, 1986.

Kellum, Barbara Ann. "Display at the Aedes Concordiae Augustae." In *Between Republic and Empire,* ed. Raaflaub and Toher, 276–96.

———. "Sculptural Programs and Propaganda in Augustan Rome: The Temple of Apollo on the Palatine and the Forum Augustus." PhD diss., Harvard University, 1981.

Kennedy, George A. *The Art of Rhetoric in the Roman World.* Princeton, N.J.: Princeton University Press, 1972.

———. *A New History of Classical Rhetoric.* Princeton, N.J.: Princeton University Press, 1994.

Kleiner, D. E. E. *Roman Sculpture.* New Haven: Yale University Press, 1992.

Laird, Margaret. "Evidence in Context: The Public Funerary Monuments of the Seviri Augustales." PhD diss., Princeton University, 2002.

Lamp, Kathleen. "The Ara Pacis Augustae: Visual Rhetoric in Augustus' Principate." *Rhetoric Society Quarterly* 39.1 (2009): 1–24.

———. "'A City of Brick': Visual Rhetoric in Roman Rhetorical Theory and Practice." *Philosophy and Rhetoric* 44.2 (2011): 171–93.

Lauer, Ilon. "Ritual and Power in Imperial Roman Rhetoric." *Quarterly Journal of Speech* 90.4 (2004): 422–45.

Linderski, J. "Mommsen and Syme: Law and Power in the Principate of Augustus." In *Between Republic and Empire,* ed. Raaflaub and Toher, 42–53.

"Longinus." *On the Sublime.* Trans. Donald Russell. Loeb Classical Library. Cambridge, Mass.: Harvard University Press, 1995.

Luce, T. J. "Livy, Augustus, and the Forum Augustum." In *Between Republic and Principate,* ed. Raaflaub and Toher, 123–38.

Maiuri, Amedeo. "La Parodia Di Enea." *Bollettino d'arte* 35 (1950): 108–12.

Mattingly, Harold. *Coins of the Roman Empire in the British Museum: Augustus to Vitellius, vol. I.* London: Published for the Trustees of the British Museum by British Museum Publications, 1975.

———. *Roman Coins: From the Earliest Times to the Fall of the Western Empire.* London: Methuen and Co., 1967.

McGee, Michael Calvin. "In Search of "The People." In *Contemporary Rhetorical Theory,* ed. John Louis Lucaites, Celeste Michelle Condit, and Sally Caudill, 341–56. New York: Guilford, 1999.

Meier, C. "C. Caesar Divi Filius and the Formation of the Alternative in Rome." In *Between Republic and Empire,* ed. Raaflaub and Toher, 54–70.

Millar, Fergus. "The Political Character of the Classical Roman Republic, 200–151 B.C." *The Journal of Roman Studies* 74 (1984): 1–19.

———. "Popular Politics at Rome in the Late Republic." In *Leaders and Masses in the Roman World,* ed. I. Malkin and Z. W. Rubinsohn. Leiden: E. J. Brill, 1995. 91–114.

Mommsen, Theodor. *A History of Rome under the Emperors: Based on the Lecture Notes of Sebastian and Paul Hensel, 1882–86.* Trans. Clare Kroijzl. London: Routledge, 1992.

———, ed. *Inscriptiones Bruttiorum, Lucaniae, Campaniae, Siciliae, Sardiniae latinae.* Vol. 10. Inscriptiones Bruttiorum Lucaniae Campaniae. Berlin: Georgium Reimerum, 1883.

Newman, Sara. "Aristotle's Notion of 'Bringing-before-the-Eyes': Its Contributions to Aristotelian and Contemporary Conceptualizations of Metaphor, Style and Audience." *Rhetorica* 20.1 (2002): 1–23.

Norden, Eduard. *P. Vergilius Maro Aeneis Buch VI.* Sammlung Wissenschaftlicher Kommentare Zu Griechischen Und Romischen Schriftstellern. Leipzig: B. G. Teubner, 1903.

Nugent, S. G. "Tristia 2: Ovid and Augustus." In *Between Republic and Empire,* ed. Raaflaub and Toher, 239–57.

Ogilvie, R. M. *The Romans and Their Gods in the Age of Augustus.* London: Chatto & Windus, 1969.

O'Gorman, Ned. "Aristotle's Phantasia in the Rhetoric: Lexis, Appearance, and the Epideictic Function of Discourse." *Philosophy and Rhetoric* 38.1 (2005): 16–40.

Ono, Kent A., and John M. Sloop. "The Critique of Vernacular Discourse." *Communication Monographs* 62 (1995): 19–46.

Ostrow, S. E. "Augustales Along the Bay of Naples: A Case for Early Growth." *Historia* 34.1 (1985): 64–101.

———. "The Augustales in the Augustan Scheme." In *Between Republic and Empire,* ed. Raaflaub and Toher, 364–79.

Ovid. *Fasti.* Trans. J. G. Frazer. Loeb Classical Library. Cambridge, Mass.: Harvard University Press, 1931.

———. *Metamorphoses.* Trans. Frank Justus Miller. Loeb Classical Library. Vol. 2. Cambridge, Mass.: Harvard University Press, 1964.

Pernot, Laurent. *Rhetoric in Antiquity.* Trans. W. E. Higgins. Washington, D.C.: Catholic University Press of America, 2005.

———. "Epideictic Rhetoric in Antiquity: Issues and Interpretations." Paper presented at biannual conference for Rhetoric Society of America, Philadelphia. May 25–28, 2012.

Peterson, Lauren Hackworth. *The Freedman in Roman Art and Art History.* Cambridge, U.K.: Cambridge University Press, 2006.

Petronius. *Satyricon.* Trans. Michael Heseltine. Loeb Classical Library. Cambridge, Mass.: Harvard University Press, 2005.

Pliny. *Natural History.* Trans. D. E. Eichholz. Loeb Classical Library. 10 vols. Cambridge, Mass.: Harvard University Press, 1962.

Polybius. *The Histories.* Trans. W. R. Paton. Loeb Classical Library. 3 vols. Cambridge, Mass.: Harvard University Press, 1960.

Quintilian. *De Institutione Oratoria.* 4 vols. Trans. H. E. Butler. Loeb Classical Library. Cambridge, Mass.: Harvard University Press, 1970.

———. *The Orator's Education,* 5 vols. Trans. Donald A. Russell. Loeb Classical Library. Cambridge, Mass.: Harvard University Press, 2001.

Raaflaub, Kurt A., and L. J. Samons II. "Opposition to Augustus." In *Between Republic and Empire,* ed. Raaflaub and Toher, 417–54.

Raaflaub, Kurt A., and Mark Toher, eds. *Between Republic and Empire: Interpretations of Augustus and His Principate.* Berkeley: University of California Press, 1990.

Rose, Herbert Jennings, and John Scheid. "Romulus and Remus." In *The Oxford Classical Dictionary,* ed. Hornblower and Spawforth, 1335.

Rostovtzeff, M. *Rome.* Trans. J. D. Duff, ed. Elias J. Bickerman. London: Oxford University Press, 1960.

Rowell, Henry T. "The Forum and Funeral *Imagines* of Augustus." *Memoirs of the American Academy in Rome* 17 (1940): 131–43.

———. "Vergil and the Forum of Augustus." *American Journal of Philology* 62 (1941): 261–76.

Ryberg, Inez Scott. *Rites of the State Religion.* Memoirs of the American Academy in Rome, 22. 1955.

Schiff, Stacy. *Cleopatra: A Life.* New York: Little, Brown, and Co., 2010.

Spinazzola, Vittorio. *Pompei All Luce Degli Scavi Nuovi Di Via Dell' abbondonza (Anni 1910–1923).* Rome: Libreria dello Stato, 1953.

Stahl, H. P. "The Death of Turnus: Augustan Vergil and the Political Rival." In *Between Republic and Empire,* ed. Raaflaub and Toher, 174–211.

Stewart, Peter. *The Social History of Roman Art.* Cambridge, U.K.: Cambridge University Press, 2008.

Strong, Donald. *Roman Art.* New York: Penguin Books, 1982.

———. *Roman Imperial Sculpture.* London: Alec Tiranti, 1961.

Suetonius. *Lives of the Caesars.* 2 vols. Trans. J. C. Rolfe. Ed. G. P. Goold. Loeb Classical Library. Cambridge, Mass.: Harvard University Press, 1998.

———. *On Rhetoricians (The Lives of Illustrious Men).* Vol. 2. Trans. J. C. Rolfe. Loeb Classical Library. Cambridge, Mass.: Harvard University Press, 1965.

Sutherland, C. H. V. *Coinage in Roman Imperial Policy 31 B.C.–A.D. 68.* London: Methuen, 1951.

———. *Roman Coins.* New York: G. P. Putnam's Sons, 1974.

Sydenham, E. A. *The Coinages of Augustus.* Numismatic Chronicle Reprint Series. New York: Attic Books, 1977.

Syme, Ronald. "History or Biography: the Case of Tiberius Caesar." *Historia: Zeitschrift fur Alte Gerschichte* 23.4 (1974): 481–96.

———. *The Roman Revolution.* Oxford, U.K.: Oxford University Press, 1939.

Tacitus. "The Annals." Trans. Ronald Mellor. In *The Historians of Ancient Rome*, ed. Ronald Mellor. 2nd ed. New York: Routledge, 2004. 451–516.

———. *The Annals of Imperial Rome.* Trans. Michael Grant. London: Penguin, 1996.

———. *Dialogus.* Trans. William Peterson. Loeb Classical Library. London: William Heinemann, 2006.

Taylor, R. L. *The Divinity of the Roman Emperor.* Middletown, CT: American Philological Association, 1931.

Too, Yun Lee. *The Idea of the Library in the Ancient World.* Oxford, U.K.: Oxford University Press, 2010.

Updike, Nancy. "Know When to Fold 'Em: Act II: Kings Do Not Fold." *This American Life*, National Public Radio. Chicago: Chicago Public Media. April 8, 2011.

Vasaly, Ann. *Representations.* Berkeley: University of California Press, 1993.

Velleius Paterculus. *Compendium of Roman History.* Trans. Frederick Shipley. Loeb Classical Library. Cambridge, Mass.: Harvard University Press, 1924.

Veyne, Paul. *Bread and Circuses: Historical Sociology and Political Pluralism.* Trans. Brian Pearce. London: Penguin, 1992.

Virgil. *Aeneid.* Trans. H. R. Fairclough and G. P. Goold. Loeb Classical Library. 2 vols. Cambridge, Mass.: Harvard University Press, 1999.

Walker, Jeffrey. *Rhetoric and Poetics in Antiquity.* Oxford, U.K.: Oxford University Press, 2000.

Wells, Colin. *The Roman Empire.* Palo Alto, Calif.: Stanford University Press, 1984.

Woods, Ann. "The Funerary Monuments of the Augustales in Italy." PhD diss., University of California, 1991.

Yates, Frances A. *The Art of Memory.* Chicago: University of Chicago Press, 1966.

Yavetz, Z. "The Personality of Augustus: Reflections on Syme's *Roman Revolution.*" In *Between Republic and Empire,* ed. Raaflaub and Toher, 21–41.

———. *Plebs and Princeps.* Oxford, U.K.: Oxford University Press, 1969.

Zadocks-Josephus Jitta, A. N. *Ancestral Portraiture in Rome and the Art of the Last Century of the Republic.* Amsterdam: Noord Hollandsche, 1932.

Zanker, Paul. *Bilderzwang: Augustan Political Symbolism in the Private Sphere.* In *Image and Mystery in the Roman World: Three Papers Given in Memory of Jocelyn Toynbee.* Gloucester: A. Sutton, 1988.

———. *Forum Augustum: Das Blidprogramm.* Tubingen, 1968.

———. *The Mask of Socrates: The Image of the Intellectual in Antiquity.* Trans. Alan Shapiro. Berkeley: University of California Press, 1995.

———. *The Power of Image in the Age of Augustus.* Trans. Alan Shapiro. Jerome Lectures. Ann Arbor: University of Michigan Press, 2003.

INDEX

Acropolis (Athens), 65–66

Actium, Battle of (31 B.C.E.): altar iconography and, 114, 116–17; coin iconography and, 95, 171n45, 171n46; Octavian's victory at, 11, 12, 118; peace following, 13, 47; Principate starting date and, 158n1; restoration of the republic following, 114; Roman mythic history and, 46–47, 85

Aeneas, myth of, 14–15; in altar imagery, 118, 121–22; in Ara Pacis friezes, 40, 42–45, 44 (fig. 2), 48; in Augustan imagery, 59 (fig. 7), 60; Augustan political myth and, 15, 18; in coin imagery, 95, 171n44; in Forum Augustum statue group, 60, 63 (fig. 11), 64 (fig. 12), 65, 132; as history, 159n25; imitation and, 140–42, 141 (fig. 47); parodies of, 132, 142–43, 142 (fig. 48), 143 (fig. 49), 144, 145–47

Aeneid (Virgil), 14–15, 18; Ara Pacis and, 43, 44–45, 44 (fig. 2), 53; Augustan political myth established in, 45, 84, 85–86, 113; fate as described in, 45; Forum Augustum and, 76, 77; sow prophecy in, 43; writing of, 170n17

Agrippa: in Ara Pacis friezes, 40; artists located by, 41; Augustus's eulogy for, 27; coin images of, 85 (fig. 15), 90 (fig. 18), 92, 93; coins issued by, 170n28; death of, 51, 90; fictitious speeches attributed to, 27; as intended successor, 85–86, 89–90, 93, 170n30

Alba Longa, Kings of, 65

Aldrete, Gregory, 33, 35

Alexander the Great, 65

altars, 9, 87. *See also* Altars of the Lares; Ara Pacis Augustae (Altar of Augustan Peace)

Altars of the Lares: Ara Pacis as influence on, 118–19; artistic significance of, 173n16; Augustan political myth as depicted on, 117–23, 118 (fig. 36); construction of, 110, 111–13; dynastic scene depicted on, 120–21, 121 (fig. 40); iconography of, 110–11, 113–17, 114 (fig. 32), 115 (fig. 33), 119 (figs. 37–38), 126–29, 172n9; imitation as rhetorical strategy in, 123–29; locations of, 172n9, 175n61; as pastiche of dominant iconography, 127–29; public memory and, 129–30; sacrifices depicted on, 123, 123 (fig. 42), 124 (figs. 43–44), 126; self-representation on, 174n33; vernacular rhetoric of, 110–11, 129–30; as visual rhetoric, 130

amplification, 48; Ara Pacis use of, 56; in coinage, 107–8; definitions, 44; Forum Augustum use of, 65

Ancient Orators (Dionysius), 69, 154, 158n29

Anderson, James C., 76

Annals (Tacitus), 16–17

Antonius, 10, 11, 12, 17, 27, 38, 61, 114, 154

"aping," 138–40, 178n73

Apollo (Roman deity), 115

Apollodorus of Pergamum, 7, 27

Apollo Sandaliarius (Roman deity), 121

Apologia (Apuleius), 79

Apuleius, 79

Aquillius, Manius, 25

Arab Spring, 152

Ara Pacis Augustae (Altar of Augustan Peace), 40 (fig. 1); Aeneas scene on, 42–45, 44 (fig. 2); Altars of the Lares influenced by, 118–19; antecedents of, 41; artistic significance of, 41, 66; authorship of, 163n4; coinage influenced by, 83–84,

ABOUT THE AUTHOR

KATHLEEN S. LAMP is an assistant professor of English at Arizona State University. Lamp holds a B.A. in classical archaeology and communication from Randolph-Macon Woman's College and a M.A. and Ph.D. in speech communication from the University of Illinois at Urbana-Champaign. She has also participated in excavations at Carthage and is an alumna of Duke University's Intercollegiate Center for Classical Studies program in Rome. Her research focuses on the intersections of classical rhetorical theory and official and popular rhetorics in visual and material form and has appeared in *Rhetoric Society Quarterly* and *Philosophy and Rhetoric.*